F.V.

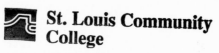

A SOCIAL HISTORY OF THE LABORING CLASSES

Problems in American History

Series editor: Jack P. Greene

Each volume focuses on a central theme in American history and provides greater analytical depth and historiographic coverage than standard textbook discussions normally allow. The intent of the series is to present in highly interpretive texts the unresolved questions of American history that are central to current debates and concerns. The texts will be concise enough to be supplemented with primary readings or core textbooks and are intended to provide brief syntheses to large subjects.

Forthcoming titles in this series:

A SOCIAL HISTORY OF THE LABORING CLASSES

From Colonial Times to the Present

JACQUELINE JONES

Brandeis University

First published 1999

2 4 6 8 10 9 7 5 3 1

Blackwell Publishers Inc.
350 Main Street
Malden, Massachusetts 02148
USA

Blackwell Publishers Ltd
108 Cowley Road
Oxford OX4 1JF
UK

Library of Congress Cataloging-in-Publication Data

Jones, Jacqueline, 1948–
    A social history of the labouring classes : from colonial times to the present / Jacqueline Jones.
        p.   cm. — (Problems in American History)
    Includes bibliographical references and index.
        ISBN 0–631–20769–4 (alk. paper). — ISBN 0–631–20770–8 (pbk. : alk. paper)
        1. Working class—United States—History.   2. United States—Social conditions.   3. United States—History.   I. Title.
    II. Series.
    HD8066.J66   1999
    305.5′62′0973—dc21   98–40544
                                                                                    CIP

British Library Cataloguing in Publication Data
A CIP catalogue record for this book is available from the British Library.

Typeset in 11 on 13 pt Sabon
by Ace Filmsetting Ltd, Frome, Somerset
Printed in Great Britain by T. J. International, Padstow, Cornwall

This book is printed on acid-free paper.

Contents

For Rose and Albert Abramson, with love

Introduction

Throughout American history, most men and women (and considerable numbers of children too) have spent most of their waking hours working. If we define work in the broadest sense, as any activity that leads to the production of goods and services, then the term covers a significant realm of human activity – not just wage-earning, but also caring for children and making a home, promoting neighborly cooperation, and contributing to the welfare of the community, whether local or national. This book employs just such a definition of work, and considers the interconnectedness of various groups of American workers, from the colonial period through the late twentieth century.

Over the last couple of decades, scholars have explored the social dimensions of labor history, and examined southern indentured servants in the seventeenth-century Chesapeake tobacco fields, "good wives" in the New England colonies, skilled tradesmen and Hudson-Valley farm tenants during the Revolutionary era, the seamstresses and domestic servants of early nineteenth-century New York City, slaves on antebellum rice and cotton plantations, Pittsburgh steel workers and Birmingham coal miners, Atlanta's African-American laundresses, chain gangs in the Jim-Crow South, and French Canadians at work in Rhode Island's textile factories during World War II, among others. Today, labor historians also focus on ways in which workers either accommodated themselves to or resisted the demands imposed upon them in the workplace; some men and women attempted to set their own pace of work in defiance of a boss or a driver, and some (those who were free) joined unions or quit their jobs and moved on in search of better prospects.

Though rich in detail, monographs in the field of labor history remain somewhat fragmented, reflecting the fact that scholars have attempted to refine their subjects according to a daunting number of social characteristics – the time and place in which a particular group labored, their gender, race, socio-economic condition, religious and ethnic background – the list goes on and on. This volume seeks to synthesize the recent work of historians in favor of a story that encompasses workers throughout the economy – waged and unwaged, men and women, black and white, native-born and immigrant, agricultural and industrial.

The complementary nature of labor patterns is a major focus of this study. For example, through the centuries, women have performed a considerable amount of labor at home without pay and – after the colonial period at least – without much in the way of social status. As people began to associate work with cash payment, the duties of the housewife, though accorded rhetorical glorification, assumed the character of a family responsibility, and not a form of "work." To cite another example: in the antebellum rural South, plantation owners relied on enslaved workers, but they also debated the trade-offs of using either poor whites, free Negroes, or slaves in various enterprises. In Southern cities, white tradesmen resented the competition posed by their enslaved counterparts. And too, the millions of Eastern-European immigrants who arrived in the United States between 1880 and 1920 provided the muscle power that helped to fuel an economic revolution, in the process allowing native-born white workers to pursue jobs in the expanding retail sales, clerical, and business sectors of the economy. Finally, during the first half of the twentieth century, white women and African-American men and women enjoyed their greatest employment opportunities during periods of worldwide military conflict, when large numbers of white men joined the army and employers were desperate for workers. These examples suggest that if we isolate specific groups of workers from other workers at the same time, we miss a crucial dimension of labor history.

Moreover, it is not always easy to categorize workers of any particular time or place as simply "women," "blacks," or "Southerners" (for instance). American labor history amounts to a kaleidescope of sorts, with workers continually shifting their forms of individual and collective self-identification; some workers have banded together during one period on the basis of the skills they had in common with one another, and during another period on the basis of the religion or the skin color they shared with co-workers. For this reason, this book focuses on American laboring classes, rather than on a single working class. On the Lower East Side of New York City in the early twentieth century, Jewish women garment workers acted upon a number of different social signifiers, depending on the context of the times – they were union activists and Jews, women and the daughters of Eastern-European immigrants, New Yorkers, political radicals, and young people. At different times, they had to contend with arrogant bosses and paternalistic male co-workers, with condescending middle-class allies, with anti-Semites and anti-union police officers and public officials. Like other kinds of workers, these women did not comprise so much a single, monolithic group as much as a group constantly reconfiguring itself in response to changes in technology and the political landscape.

This volume also seeks to integrate African-American workers into the larger story of labor history. Too often relegated to the margins of scholarship, or segregated into separate scholarly journals or monographs, black workers have shaped American history in dramatic ways. They not only constituted a significant part of the labor force, but they also kept alive the ideals of freedom and equality when those ideals existed primarily as rhetorical nation-building devices only. Furthermore, during certain periods of American history, white workers have perceived blacks as a negative reference group, scapegoating them and taking pride in the privileges that a white skin conferred, especially when times were hard.

Indeed, in certain instances, black workers have played a political role disproportionate to their numbers, as in the antebellum North, when white people, native-born and immigrant, perceived a small number of blacks as threatening to the social order.

Americans have always considered work to be a crucial component of civic identity. The Puritans devoted themselves to their "callings" so that their work would serve to glorify God. Thomas Jefferson proclaimed the sturdy yeoman farmer to be the pillar of the New Republic. In the 1850s the emerging Republican Party envisioned free labor as the future of the nation. During the Great Depression, New Dealers legislated their belief that the welfare of industrial workers was the key to the good society. This book chronicles the major transformations in the American political economy; but the story that unfolds on the following pages suggests that, despite technological and demographic changes over the centuries, work has remained central to our sense of power and justice, and central to our sense of who we are as a people.

I would like to acknowledge the assistance of Alex Lichtenstein, who read the entire manuscript of this book in draft form and offered a number of valuable comments and suggestions.

1

"Strangers" and Other Workers in the Seventeenth-Century Colonies

In October 1659, a young servant named Sarah Taylor appeared in court on the Isle of Kent (located between Maryland's Eastern and Western Shores in the Chesapeake Bay) to file a formal complaint alleging "divers wrongs and abuses given her by her Master and Mrs.[,] Capt Thomas Bradnox & Mary his wife." Sarah Taylor charged that both of the Bradnoxes had beaten her black and blue, and she maintained that other servants in the household could corroborate her story from first-hand observation. The court also heard testimony from Mrs Bradnox, who admitted that, "for the neglecte of her Mayd Sarah in severall things, she had given her correction & produceth the sticke in court wherewith shee had beate her." However, at the same hearing, Captain Bradnox countered with the claim that Sarah had run away from his household, and that at least two of his neighbors were guilty of "entertaining" her – that is, providing her with lodging while the Bradnox household was deprived of her labor. (Capt. Bradnox was himself a commissioner on the same court, though he recused himself from this particular case.) Rendering judgment, the commissioners in attendance decided that it was Sarah, and not her master and mistress, who deserved punishment; they suspended the sentence that she be whipped (taking note that she stood before them already bruised and battered), but ordered "that shee shall on her Knees aske her

Mr & Mrs Forgiveness, And promise amendment for the future." After complying with the order, Sarah Taylor was returned to her master's household.

Two years later Sarah and Mr and Mrs Bradnox were back in court. This time Sarah detailed a beating she had received from both of them; they claimed that she had spoiled a batch of bread through her carelessness. During the hearing that followed, Joseph Newman, a former boarder in the Bradnox household, testified that he had witnessed an occasion when the master came upon the young woman reading a book, and "took up a thre futted sto[o]le and stroke Sarah Tayler on the head with it for takeing a booke in hure hand to read." In response, the commissioners decided to release Sarah Taylor from her service with the couple, "in regard of the Eminent Danger likely to Insew by the Invetterat Mallice of hur Master & Mistress toward hure." The Bradnoxes were members of the island's elite, but perhaps by this time they had exhausted the good will of their friends on the court; between Sarah Taylor's first formal complaint and her second, the couple had been charged with and then acquitted for the crimes of torturing and murdering another indentured servant, Thomas Watson. And though a former sheriff himself, Capt. Bradnox had appeared in court periodically for other offenses, including drunkenness, profanity, embezzlement, and theft. Sarah Taylor escaped with her life and her freedom, but only because the Bradnoxes took to an extreme the imperative that inspired landowners throughout the colonies – to make do, and if possible to do well, with a chronic shortage of labor.[1]

In pressing her claim against an abusive master and mistress in court, and especially in winning that claim, Sarah Taylor was not typical of the servants who toiled in the British North American colonies during the seventeenth century. Still, her case is instructive on several levels. Like most workers at this time, she was young (probably about 20) and bound to a master – that is, forced to serve him and his wife for a certain number of years (probably seven) after her arrival in Maryland from England. The demands of the staple-crop economy meant that indentured servants in the Chesapeake region routinely suffered what was termed "hard usage" by masters and mistresses desperate to extract as much work as possible from them. Almost all labor took place within households, and those households were embedded within small communities characterized by various degrees of cohesion. As a member of the Bradnox household, Sarah Taylor toiled in the company of other servants, probably in the fields as well as in the house itself, but she also found some refuge with neighbors during her time of need.

Within colonial households, degrees of dependency bound child to parent, servant to master, wife to husband, hireling to employer. Indeed, it would be difficult to extricate household and community relationships from work relationships in mid-seventeenth century Kent County, Maryland – or for that matter, anywhere in the colonies. Nevertheless, while she was going about her work, Sarah Taylor discovered all too soon that neither her gender nor her Englishness protected her from the wrath of her master and mistress; but she did win her freedom from colonial magistrates who felt duty bound to protect her from the "Eminent Danger" posed by the captain and his wife.

In the Europeans' New World, labor was the key to wealth, and the accumulation of wealth was the ultimate aim of the colonial enterprise. New England and the Chesapeake, two regions distinct in both geographical and demographic terms, followed strikingly divergent paths of economic development – the former characterized by village-based networks of craft and crop exchange, with most labor provided by family members; the latter by scattered plantations devoted to staple-crop agriculture, with labor provided by young indentured servants (most of them English and male). However, despite dfferences in their respective regional economies, English settlers in the northern and southern British American colonies faced similar challenges in wringing a living and extracting a surplus – if not a profit – from the land.

Willingly or not, all of these settlers served as foot-soldiers in England's ongoing war for empire; for the beleaguered colonists, mere self-preservation amounted to a significant victory on behalf of the Crown. In the words of one British official, the colonies must aspire to become "one continued Fortress," a bastion "enclos'd by *Military Lines*, impregnable."[2] No matter where they lived, these transplanted English men and women were forced to set about creating labor systems calculated to deploy precious human resources in the most efficient way possible, and at the same time insure the safety of English settlements. Yet frequently the twin goals of economic development and military defense conflicted with each other, as when the colonists found themselves dependent on whole groups of workers who were the sworn enemies of, or at least resistant to, the colonial mission.

In the late twentieth century we think of paid work (outside the home) in terms of discrete tasks performed by a worker who receives a set amount of cash in return. However, in the seventeenth century, labor was a more expansive concept, and covered a wide range of human endeavors. For example, the English colonists who inhabited fragile outposts clinging to the eastern seaboard would have found it difficult to separate the work of tilling the soil from the work of defending their households or villages; the axe, hoe, and musket were all tools of the colonists' trade. New England Puritans planted their settlements in the rocky hills of Massachusetts with the intention of furthering the work of the Lord; they warred against not only Indian infidels and French marauders, but also against human sinfulness. Settlers throughout the colonies grew crops to keep themselves and their neighbors alive, and also contributed to regional economies located within a transatlantic trade system. Depending upon their religious convictions and their political aspirations, colonists also devoted time and effort to the work of creating well-ordered communities and monitoring the behavior of the people who lived in them; this kind of work revealed that privileged people possessed a most valued currency in the form of political power.

By the time of the American Revolution, it would be possible to isolate a number of dualities that shaped late colonial labor systems – the presumed rights of white people in contrast to the subordination of enslaved people of African descent; the work of men in contrast to the work of women; the dependence of servants and children in contrast to the self-determination of masters and employers. However, in exploring the issue of seventeenth-century labor, we should avoid positing stark contrasts between whites and blacks, males and females, young and old, and instead appreciate the myriad ways in which degrees of unfreedom shaped the lives of the majority of workers. Indeed, in assessing the status of various kinds of workers, it is best to locate them along a continuum of dependence, a continuum that seventeenth-century English people considered the natural order of things.

In contrast to the Spanish empire-builders to their south, the colonists of British North America lacked the military strength to exploit the labor of large numbers of indigenous peoples. New Englanders settled among scattered Indian groups, some of whom were decimated and weakened by diseases introduced by European explorers and fishermen several decades before. Virginians planted their colony in the midst of the Powhatan Confederacy consisting of 30 tribes and 14,000 people, about a quarter of whom were men armed and ready to do battle with the interlopers. All along the eastern seaboard, skirmishes among the French, Dutch, Swedes, and English were part and parcel of larger rivalries among the great European powers, rivalries carried out in Africa, the West Indies, and South America. In contrast, Indians represented a new and unknown enemy to the English colonists; after the disastrous Jamestown massacre, which claimed 347 lives in 1622 (one-quarter of the English population), and after the bloody Pequot War in southern New England in 1637, most settlers abandoned the idea that Indians were worth converting or even reducing to servitude or slavery. Simply put, the colonists decided they wanted Indian land more than Indian laborers.

The colonists readily appropriated from the Indians knowledge about fishing, hunting, gathering wild foods, and preparing fields for cultivation, and instituted trade relations with those groups they considered (not always accurately) reliable and harmless. For their part, Indian traders sought to consolidate their own power over neighboring groups by controlling the supply of English goods, objects that had both talismanic properties as well as practical purpose – the "white beades for their women, Hatchetts . . . Howes to pare their Corne ground, knyves and such like."[3]

The English brought with them certain standards that defined the realm of productive labor; when they judged Indians according to these standards, they found them lacking in both industry and morality. The colonists left behind a homeland wracked by political upheaval and civil war, a society becoming ever more aggressive in its pursuit of wealth, a place where overpopulation created patterns of underemployment among workers and potential workers. In contrast, indigenous groups in North America provided for themselves in ways marked by stability and continuity. According to the colonists, Indians might "work," but they failed to "toil" – that is, they did not labor steadily under the direction of another person, nor did they accumulate much in the way of material goods, or "improve their time" through education and new forms of technology. The English considered Indian women drudges because they cultivated the fields, gathered nuts in the forest and shellfish from the sea, and constructed houses – all while their husbands went off to hunt game (in English eyes a gentleman's sport and not a source of subsistence). In the annals of English empire, Indians were warriors, and artistic renderings showed them arrayed with a variety of weapons – bows and arrows, muskets, spears, and knives – but not farming tools like hoes.

Some colonists paid Indian men to hunt game or retrieve wandering cattle for them, though hiring them for jobs that necessitated the use of guns was problematic in the long run. Colonial militiamen might rely on Indian scouts to help them find their way through the wilderness; but again, this kind of work necessitated the use of firearms. To stay on the safe side, the colonists preferred to enslave only Indian women and children (usually those captured in battle). Male prisoners of war were often sold to West Indian planters.

A few Indians continued to live among the English. For

example, in New England certain communities were designated as towns of "Praying (ie., Christian) Indians," men and women who in most cases subsisted on the margins of local economies as day laborers or as peddlers of baskets and other traditional crafts. John Eliot, who preached among the Natick, Massachusetts, Indians, declared in 1652 that "they begin to grow industrious, and find something to sell at Market all year long."[4] Eliot thus considered Indians industrious to the extent that they remained sedentary and produced commodities to sell in the marketplace – either crops or crafts. In sum, regardless where they lived in the British North American colonies, few English settlers considered Indians to be a viable labor source.

The chronic shortage of labor that plagued the seventeenth-century colonists inspired them to create variations of the rural labor system they had known in England – the system of servants-in-husbandry. Most English folk were farmers, and farm families routinely exchanged young people as workers. This exchange was institutionalized in the form of annual fairs (held during the early autumn) when servants contracted to work for a family for the coming year. The system of servants-in-industry allowed households to adjust their labor supply according to their needs – for example, families with a surplus of children sent them out to work for families that had few, or too many younger, children – and also to socialize young people into the world of work and community life. Of course this system worked better for some individuals than others – exasperated masters complained of lazy, promiscuous servants, and resentful servants railed against hard taskmasters; but at least the annual turnover of workers served as a force of moderation, and ensured that in any particular case, neither master nor servant would be forced to contend with each other for more than twelve months at a time.

As a colonial enterprise, New England deviated from patterns established elsewhere in the New World (in Latin America, the West Indies, and the southern colonies) where large groups of laborers were forced to extract precious metals from the ground or staple crops from the soil. Instead, the northern colonies closely resembled the Mother Country in climate, local economy, and labor system. New Englanders settled in villages consisting of nuclear families, and networks of these households facilitiated the bartering of goods and services and the hiring of workers. A balanced sex ratio, the Puritan value of strong patriarchal families, and the relatively healthful environment were all conducive to the growth of large households. (From 1620 to 1700, the region's non-indigenous population grew from virtually nothing at all to 90,700 souls, of whom 1,700 were black; the number of towns multipled yearly.)

In areas of New England devoted to commercial production – the rural-industrial economy of Springfield, Massachusetts, and the dairy country of Narragansett, Rhode Island, for example – servants were an integral part of the labor force. Yet large families served as the primary source of labor for the seventeenth century; servant imports to the region peaked in the 1650s and then fell off gradually after that. A family with eight children could generate as much as 100 (concentrated) years of labor, assuming that sons began to help out in the fields, and girls in the kitchen and dairy, as early as ten years of age, and that young people did not leave home until their early twenties. Fifteen or more indentured servants would have been necessary to provide an equal amount of muscle-power per work-year.

In addition, the children of a household would, presumably, be respectful of the moral standards established by its elders, in contrast to the imported servants who seemed bent on elevating laziness to a fine art. Northern indentured servants inclined to indulge in blasphemous and promiscuous behavior mightily offended their godly masters and mistresses. John Winthrop, Jr, described one servant as "being reproved for his lewdness, and put in mind of hell, answered, that if hell were ten times hotter, he had rather be there than he would serve his master. The occasion was, because he had bound himself for divers years, and saw that, if he had been at liberty, he might have had greater wages, though otherwise his master used him very well."[5] (This particular servant died while gathering oysters one day, perhaps a form of divine retribution for his "uncivil carriages" toward his master.) The relative openness of northern society, and in particular the high wages accorded scarce day laborers, provoked northern servants to run away or otherwise defy their masters. In the 1630s, a fishing master off the coast of Maine noted that the men who left his service before their times were out found decent jobs that did not require them to spend the winter months hauling stinking, slippery fish out of the freezing sea. He complained that all of his workers wanted to be "masters of themselves."

William Wood, an early New England observer, condemned the "multiplicity of bad servants" who ate their master "out of house and harbour" (that is, consumed much and produced little); Wood concluded, "he that hath many dronish servants shall soon be poor, and he that hath an industrious family shall soon be rich."[6] Accordingly, blessed with good health, the first generations of New England settlers were fruitful and multiplied, simultaneously sustaining stong families and producing more workers.

New England Puritans' quest for spiritual fulfillment found tangible expression in their devotion to an ethic of hard work. (At the same time, in the course of the seventeenth century, land speculation became an increasingly significant form of capital accumulation among prominent New Englanders.) An individual's yearning for salvation translated into industry, innovation, and self-improvement, which in turn often yielded material comfort, and material comfort signalled a godly community. In practical terms, this ideology meant that New Englanders early on began to extract a profit from their labors, spurring the development of specialized local economies throughout the region. The distinguished Winthrop family, boasting the first governor of Massachusetts Bay colony, developed iron-making and glass-making industries, and graphite mines, all in an effort to exploit natural resources as a form of stewardship of God's earthly bounty. Puritans were fond of exhorting their co-religionists to follow a "calling," declaring that all forms of labor, no matter how mean or lowly, glorified God. In fact, the notion of a calling was flexible, and permitted immigrants to cast off the trades they had followed in England and embrace new ones, and also to purchase both servants and slaves to do their work for them. Most New England families hoped to achieve a "competency," defined as economic independence (control over one's own labor), a comfortable material existence, and perhaps a few books and pewter candlesticks besides.

Although seventeenth-century New England consisted primarily of small agrarian-based villages, regional economies (based on, for example, fur trading, mining, timber, and cattle) were characterized by their own unique systems of labor. For example, the fishing industry centered in the area north of Boston relied on credit provided by English merchants; entrepreneurs financed groups of fishermen, men who were organized in independent companies and indebted for their boats and supplies of salt, cordage, canvas, and liquor. Catches of fish served as payment for the credit extended. The nature of the fishermen's daily labors, and the seasonal rhythms of their work – periods of frantic activity punctuated by months of idleness – differed from those of the farmer who tilled his own land with the help of his wife and children. In fishing communities, the men, often hard-drinking and hard-living, labored in groups of other men, and suffered from poverty and high mortality rates, in contrast to the more favorable circumstances of workers in settled farm areas.

Typically, in New England villages, husbands, wives, and children alike were responsible not only for the cultivation of crops but also for specialized skills that produced crafts and other products in demand in the area. "By-employments" included the production of textiles, candles, and soap, the brewing of ale, and the processing of food (all tasks carried out primarily by a wife with the help of her daughters). Likewise, few husbands worked exclusively as farmers; they also contributed to the community by selling or bartering their services as blacksmiths, flour millers, tanners, shoe makers, coopers, joiners, glaziers, masons, wheelwrights, tailors, carpenters, or nailers (for example). The short growing season, coupled with English-style markets and trade fairs, discouraged labor specialization. Within villages, then, households relied on the services provided by each other; no one family could be expected to own the equipment or possess the knowledge necessary for all realms of production.

The New England economy generated a series of complementary relationships that were neither rigid nor static. Within households, men and women alike served as producers, and there were no arbitrary limits on women's responsibilities (those would come later) to prevent them from engaging in a wide variety of tasks – in the fields, in the workshop, and in the tavern (especially in the absence of a husband). Indeed, one of the hallmarks of New England society was the respect it accorded women for the fulfillment of a range of duties essential to the well-being of any farming household. The housewife labored primarily within the house and its immediate area, in gardens and outbuildings; she cooked, spun thread, sewed clothes, washed laundry, milked the cows, processed garden produce and meat, and prepared the meals. As a mother she fulfilled a biological role by bearing and nurturing children, and as a mistress she supervised the daughters of neighbors who came to help her and learn from her, especially the art of textile production. Women also reached beyond their own households to engage in "swap work" with neighbors, and to minister to the ill and needy; these tasks suggested a seamlessness between laboring for one's own immediate family and laboring for the welfare of the community. Moreover, in serving as the keepers of small shops, and in hawking their butter, cheese, and ale around town, many women participated directly in the larger regional economy; though barred from town or church offices and though legally dependent upon their husbands, they were nevertheless not servile creatures. Instead, they conformed to the ideal of virtuous womanhood outlined in the Book of Proverbs (31: 27–8): "She looketh well to the ways of her household, and eateth not the bread of idleness. Her children arise up and call her blessed; her husband, also, and he praiseth her."

Two hundred years later, white women of the middle classes

would lament their loss of a productive function in the home, and romanticize the work of their colonial foremothers. (In the 1890s, one woman wrote of the long-lost arts practiced by spinners and weavers: "Firm, close-woven and pure, their designs were not greatly varied, nor was their woof as symmetrical and perfect as modern linens – but thus were the lives of those who made them; firm, close-woven in neighborly kindness, with the simplicity both of innocence and ignorance.")[7] Yet a great deal of colonial women's responsibities amounted to sheer drudgery – lugging water from nearby streams and laundering clothes in huge kettles, taking pots and other kinds of equipment off wall hooks in the morning and replacing them at the end of day, stirring stews over smoky fires, instructing their daughters in the mysteries of ale-brewing and bread-baking – all this carried out in small living spaces made ever more crowded and noisy by the arrival of a new baby every two years or so.

In their capacity as colonists laboring on behalf of the English Crown, however, women were less productive than men because they did not serve as armed soldiers defending the King's interests in the New World. For New England men at various stages of their lives, military service amounted to a significant form of work. Throughout the colonial period, young men biding their time until they could inherit the family homestead often chose to volunteer with the provincial army, a force constantly preoccupied with fending off French and Indian advances. Husbands and fathers were obligated to join village militia companies, to drill regularly and remain on alert. Within these tight-knit little communities, the convergence of landownership and military service left women and certain groups of men (Africans and Indians) marginal to the body politic. For example, by the late seventeenth century, Massachusetts readily accepted all kinds of men into its militias, "except Negroes and slaves wee arme not." The celebration of the New England musket-wielding soldier-citizen also worked against the self-respect and well-being of other groups of workers. For example, one clergyman ridiculed Marblehead, Massachusetts fishermen as "being many of them a dull and heavy-moulded sort of People, that had not either Skill or Courage to kill any thing but Fish."[8] Although many emigrants found themselves tilling the soil regardless of the skills they had acquired in the Mother Country, in general New Englanders recently arrived from Old England engaged in work that was familiar to them. However, learning how to exploit the vast forests of the northeastern seaboard represented a new and arduous challenge. At home, forests were the province of the gentry, legally off-limits to modest farmers who would have otherwise eagerly collected an abundance of firewood, or hunted down tasty deer and pheasants within them. Of early New England one observer noted with astonishment, "A poore Servant here that is to possesse but 50 acres of Land, may afford to give more wood for Timber and Fire as good as the world yeelds, then many Noble Men in *England* can afford to do." He added, "Here is good living for those that love good fires."[9]

The colonists engaged in the strenuous work of clearing the land (only over time developing the kinds of saws and axes suitable for demolishing various hardwoods), a job made even more back-breaking by the fields of rocks deposited by glaciers long ago. Though the woods thwarted the practice of large-scale agriculture, they also contained the game that became the reward of a good marksman. Again, few ordinary English farmers owned or used guns; but in the New World, firearms were a necessity, as a means of subsistence (for food) and as a means of defense. All things considered, it is apparent that middling English folk – farmers, coopers, tailors, weavers, cordwainers, carpenters, servants, and clergy – made a rather smooth transition between working in their native country, and working in the New World as armed minions of God.

Located between New England and the Chesapeake, the Mid-Atlantic colonies consisted of New York (seized from the Dutch in 1664), New Jersey (founded in 1664), and Pennsylvania (1681). The relative openness and ethnic diversity of this region inspired some settlers to pronounce it "the best poor man's country," for whites were confined neither by the religious and communal strictures characteristic of New England nor by the system of a single staple crop (monoculture) characteristic of the Chesapeake. One conspicuous exception to the rule of small landowners however was the Hudson River Valley, where estates owned by Dutch landlords (for example, Renssalaerswyck sprawled over 700,000 acres), were home to tenants, most of them recent immigrants from Western Europe.

The Middle Colonies in general soon developed a thriving regional economy based upon trade and the production of foodstuffs. In New York, merchants undercut their French competitors in the fur trade (controlled by the Iroquois Confederacy that reached from the Hudson River Valley all the way to the Great Lakes), and farmers exported grain and meat to the West Indies. Early on, this colony was home to French-speaking Walloons (people from present-day Belgium), Swedes, Portuguese, Finns, Jews, and Africans, an ethnic mix that facilitated the development of commerce and the skilled trades. Pennsylvania's founder, William Penn, recruited colonists (including Germans, and Quakers from England and Wales) by selling land at cheap prices and by guaranteeing religious freedom to all groups. Located strategically at the junction of the Schuylkill and Delaware Rivers, Philadelphia prospered as a center of trade within the Middle-Colonial "Breadbasket" of the Delaware Valley. Cultivating small holdings (an average of 150 acres), farmers grew 5–12 bushels of wheat per acre, far above the yields of New Englanders, who had to contend with long winters and rocky soils.

Landowners in the Middle Colonies relied on tenants, indentured servants, their own children, and in some cases whole immigrant families known as "redemptioners." Redemptioners arrived in the colonies hoping to be redeemed (that is, have their passage paid) by relatives; otherwise they would be sold as a unit to a master to work off transportation costs. Settlers throughout the region remained open-minded and opportunistic about the uses of various kinds of laborers. And indeed, the use of enslaved Africans was a function of supply and demand of labor, rather than the foundation of a particular socio-political system. William Penn had no scruples about owning slaves himself; he appreciated the fact that they offered a steadier and more reliable source of labor compared to indentured servants. On Long Island, landowners focused their energies on tending livestock, growing crops, and processing wool, and early on bought slaves in order to make up for a crucial labor shortage. (The lack of a threat from either Indians or outsiders there reduced the chances that Africans themselves would serve as sources of subversion.) Dutch officials in New Amsterdam alternately leased and owned slaves, and put them to work in a variety of capacities; when the English assumed control of the colony in 1664, they continued to exploit slaves as a matter of course.

To the South, Chesapeake landowners initially demonstrated a degree of flexibility in shaping a regional labor system. They began by radically altering the traditional English servants-in-husbandry institution to fit their peculiar economic needs. Within a decade and a half of intitial settlement, Virginia colonists had discovered in the lowly tobacco plant both their salvation and their curse – their salvation because the weed answered the call of English mercantilists for a crop that could be marketed for a profit in Europe; a curse because it required 15 months of back-breaking labor to cultivate it (and even then a good harvest was uncertain). Few English men or women had had experience growing tobacco in the seventeenth century, and cultivation of the crop placed a priority on stamina in the fields, rather than skill in the dairy or craft shop. These economic imperatives encouraged the formation of demographically unbalanced (some of then all-male) households called plantations, each consisting of a single landowner, perhaps an Indian hireling or African slave or two, and indentured servants – and the more the better. Seventeenth-century Chesapeake plantations included small numbers of female servants (black and white), African servants and slaves (male and female), and Indian servants, slaves, or hirelings (mostly women and children); but most of the workers were young men imported from the British Isles. During the seventeenth century, approximately three-quarters of all immigrants to the Chesapeake came as indentured servants.

In terms of their reliance on a cash crop and the extreme measures they used in order to find enough subordinate workers to grow it, elites in the southern colonies resembled their European counterparts in other parts of the New World – the Spaniards who reduced thousands of Indians to slavery in South American gold mines, the French who were beginning to rely on Africans held in bondage on West Indian sugar plantations. New England provided a discernible if at times clouded mirror image of the Mother Country; in contrast, the Chesapeake followed the labor standard set by other colonial endeavors.

As a result, English-born men and women who arrived in the southern colonies confronted a radically new world of work. Missing were the small villages characteristic of the English countryside; in their place were isolated households scattered among the inland waterways of the Virginia and Maryland tidewater region. Like their northern counterparts, southerners soon developed an intense if ambivalent view of the forests that surrounded them; these were places that abounded in game, fruits, and nuts, and yet at the same time harbored wolves and "skulking" Indians. Much of the labor performed in the seventeenth-century Chesapeake took place in the woods, and workers routinely went to their labors armed, "watching and warding" against the dangers that lurked around them.

Initially, the colonists, with the encouragement of their English sponsors, planned to exploit the fertility of the soil and the mildness of the climate by launching a variety of enterprises, some of them familiar to their countrymen and women and others characteristic of a Mediterranean economy. In 1619, eight ships carrying together almost 900 passengers arrived in Jamestown, and the newcomers' appointed tasks revealed a certain optimism on the part of English investors. Ninety "young maids" disembarked, expecting to marry and provide some social stability for the colony. Of the men, 650 would presumably work as tenants for the Virginia Company (the financial backers of the colony), and they would be assisted by 100 young boys as apprentices. In addition to the tenants came specialized workers charged with setting up iron works, rope-making shops, naval stores (pitch and tar) and salt industries, orchards of trees for silkworms, and vineyards. Nevertheless, even by this relatively early date, tobacco had taken hold as the chief staple crop of the colony, and plans to diversify were soon abandoned. Specialized workers like potters and silk-worm cultivators quickly threw their energies into tobacco, the colony's only profit-maker and its chief form of currency. More generally, English men and women who had once worked growing fruits and barley, producing cloth, and tending livestock all found themselves reduced to the common lot of weeding and worming tobacco plants.

Throughout the seventeenth century, men outnumbered women immigrants to the Chesapeake by a ratio of two or three to every woman. (As late as 1704, Maryland had 30,437 white people, only 7,000 of them adult women.) Not until the latter part of the 1600s did the white population begin to reproduce itself, so high was the mortality rate and therefore so shortlived many marriages. In the absence of wives, sisters, and mothers, men had to wash their own laundry and prepare their own meals, and they had to import their clothing and virtually all forms of liquid refreshment (beer and ale were the beverages of choice, water a last resort). The fact of the matter was that women as colonial-outpost workers were not all that efficient; if they became pregnant they might not be able to take part in a crucial stage of the tobacco-growing season, and they would bring into a precarious world new mouths to feed and bodies to clothe. Moreover, seventeenth-century Englishmen never considered arming their womenfolk, and in a colonial society that relied upon the conflation of economic and military roles, women were a luxury that the empire simply could not afford.

Even the few women who had the expertise or inclination to engage in traditional housewifely pursuits lacked the equipment necessary to those pursuits; spinning wheels and cheese baskets, among other tools of household industry, were in short supply throughout the seventeenth-century Chesapeake. Ann Tanner, who was in her mid-twenties when she arrived in

Virginia in 1621, came highly recommended as a potential wife, for she could "Spin and sewe ... brue, and bake, make butter and cheese, and doe huswifery."[10] Yet in all likelihood she was never able to fulfill the role of the industrious English housewife. Moreover, within these plantation households, customary sources of physical and emotional sustenance were conspicuous by their absence – sparsely furnished, the rude houses contained little in the way of creature comforts like beds; and there were no siblings or parents who might ease the pain of aching muscles and homesick hearts.

After a few years of settlement it was clear that women would continue to be valued as colonists to the extent that they could grow tobacco. In 1629, in the vicinity of Jamestown, the servant Dorcas Howard suffered a miscarriage soon after leaving her "worke in the grounde." Though her master later claimed that he did not know she was pregnant, it is clear that his immediate interests depended upon her capacity as a field laborer, and not as the mother of a son that would need care for many years before he would become productive himself.

If the southern male colonists too had little opportunity to engage in familiar English tasks (among traditional craftsmen, only coopers and house carpenters were in high demand), they had more than ample opportunity to sample – if not savor – new ones. The cultivation of tobacco demanded large expanses of cleared forests, and the system of crop rotation meant that exhausted lands had to be replaced with new ones continuously. The colonists learned a number of skills from the Indians, including the technique of firing a forest so that crops could be planted among the dying stands of trees, rather than going to the trouble of uprooting the trunks altogether. However, the building of houses, out-buildings, and fences necessitated the constant chopping of trees, tasks made even more unpleasant by the heat, humidity, mosquitoes, and poisonous snakes that tormented many an English laborer. Descriptions of Chesapeake drinking habits suggest that field workers routinely stumbled about the forests in a drunken stupor, their woolen clothes soaked with sweat, their fingers blistered from wielding axes and hoes for hours on end. Fortunate indeed was the servant like Roger Jones, who had the ability and the foresight to bargain for a contract that forced his master to "imploy said Servant in the Stoar and . . . not imploy him in Common workeing in the Ground."[11]

Most servants could expect no respite from their labors at night, for dusk brought yet another and new task – the dreaded beating at the mortar, which involved pounding corn until it was soft enough to be made into corn bread or hominy. More than one servant endured a beating himself for failing to exert enough time and energy beating corn.

It was not surprising, then, that indentured servants resisted "hard usage" by their masters and mistresses, and that these landowners retaliated with ever more violent forms of coercion. English householders had traditionally complained about the willful and promiscuous servants-in-husbandry under their care, but New-World economic imperatives exacerbated and rubbed raw these tensions. Ever mindful of the capriciousness of the international market for tobacco, and the unpredictability of the weather – the devastating effects of droughts, floods, and plagues of worms – landlords remained in a continuous state of anxiety, pushing their workers to plant more plants, harvest more leaves, and clear more land.

Because they faced such long terms of service, young workers devised any number of strategies to ease their lot from day to day. In Accomack-Northampton, Virginia, in the 1630s, William Ward was hauled into county court by his mistress and charged with neglecting his duty to watch over her livestock. When he was not at a friend's playing nine pins, he was "asleepe and lazing all the day." As a result, the cows ate the corn of a neighbor, and some of them "weere wronged by the dogs shamfully" – and fatally.[12] Young men and women alike vented their emotions – anger, fear, frustration, loneliness – by engaging in sex with one another, drowning their sorrows in drink, and cursing their masters and threatening their mistresses. When William Hopkins tried to reprimand his servant, the young man "struck him his Master with a Club, threatening him with many uncivill & opprobious words, with

Cursing, swearing blaspheming &c." The servant was ordered to serve his master an additional six years and to receive 30 lashes on his bare back.[13]

William Hopkins's troubles however paled in comparison with those of a Virginia master and mistress, the Cuthbert Williamsons, who were murdered in their beds by an English servant named Thomas Hellier, in 1678. Hellier emigrated to the colonies in spite of the fact that he "had heard so bad a character of the Country, that I dreaded going thither, in regard I abhorred the Ax and Haw [hoe]." Toiling for nine months on the aptly named plantation Hard Labour, he endured countless hours listening to his mistress "ever taunting me with her odious and inveterate Tongue." Before he was executed, Hellier had the presence of mind to sum up the collective shortcomings of Virginia's master class: "Conscience and Christianity sure ought to oblige them to use such Servants as their Christian Brethren, with gentleness and Courtesie, content with their honest endeavours, not Tyrannizing over Christians, as *Turks* do over Galley-Slaves, compelling them unmercifully beyond their strength."[14]

Hellier was apprehended and hanged for his treachery, but at times a young person was just not there to be punished; he or she had absconded into the woods, or down a creek in a skiff, in hope of finding a moment's peace in the swamps or a day's refuge at a nearby plantation. And runaways could wreak havoc on a neighborhood. In 1690, one local county court in Virginia condemned the "Negroe Slaves and other Servants [who] often times run from their masters, and lie in ye woods & committ divers felonies and outrages by robbing of houses killing of hogs and other offences."[15] Courts imposed penalties upon those who "entertained" (harbored or hired) runaway servants, many of whom found it difficult if not impossible to traverse the dense underbrush and intricate waterways of the Tidewater region in any case. For these reasons most servants eventually returned home, famished and covered with insect bites, but not entirely remorseful.

Whatever the relative advantages of the New England and Chesapeake labor systems – the one reliant on labor provided by families and neighbors, the other on young male English indentured servants – both were unable to deliver the large numbers of workers that their insatiable regional economies demanded. Yet in seeking out supplementary sources of labor, English settlers revealed themselves to be squeamish about incorporating "strangers" into their households, no matter how skilled or strong those workers happened to be. Within the colonies, a traditional form of English ethnocentricism – a suspicion of people who were not English-speaking, Christian, or white – melded imperceptibly with real security concerns. Colonists in New England remained in a constant state of military alert, nervous about Indian and French threats from the north and west, and the menacing Spanish and Dutch on the high seas. Southern planters too, especially those on the fringes of settlement, feared ambushes from Indians and organized raids from Spanish outposts to the South. Presumably, then, within highly militarized settlements, non-English co-habitors of all kinds were potential spies, rebels, and provocateurs – all traitors to England. Even a lone Dutch, French, or Swedish servant might remain suspect, and ordinary forms of labor resistance perceived as acts of treason or sabotage. These fears help to account for the conditional (if not at times downright paranoid) reception accorded workers who lacked either cultural or political loyalties to the English and their colonial designs.

In their roles as household heads, clergymen, sheriffs, and members of representative assemblies, landowners experimented with a number of different kinds of laboring "strangers," all of whom carried with them distinct liabilities. The earliest Jamestown settlers intended to "bring the Indians into subjection" and then force them to clear away underbrush, slay wolves and bears, serve as galley slaves, and cultivate silkworms. As we have seen, these grand plans came to little, as subsequent generations deemed Indians as warriors unfit for cohabitation with the English. Still, Indians as children were considered fit to serve as servants and slaves. For example, in Rhode Island at the end of the century, the sons and daughters of Indian men killed or captured in war were required to work for white masters for 25 years. Throughout the colonies, periodic smallpox epidemics produced large numbers of Indian orphans, who were summarily bound out as apprentices to white families.

From the British Isles were imported Scottish Presbyterians (prisoners of religious wars), impoverished Irish peasants (men and women who carried with them their own grievances against the English), and convicted but unrepentant pickpockets and murderers. Young urchins plucked off the streets of London were dispatched to the colonies with the hope that, "under severe masters they may be brought to goodness."[16] Referring to this motley assortment of workers, even an early promoter of the Chesapeake region had to admit that "The country is reported to be an unhealthy place, a nest of Rogues, whores, desolate and rooking [cheating] persons; a place of intolerable labour, bad usage and hard Diet, etc."[17]

Laborers from these outcast groups made less than satisfactory household members within either northern nuclear families or southern plantation households. Local officials in both regions showed little hesitation in sentencing criminal offenders to work as part of their punishment; Northerners might laud the redemptive effects of labor on the souls of the ungodly, while their southern counterparts were more open about just wanting a certain kind of work performed quickly and cheaply. In both regions, sheriffs and clergy alike were not above appropriating the labor of felons for use in their own households.

Seventeenth-century colonists also experimented with African slave labor; but the results were not all that promising initially. In March of 1619, 15 black men and 17 black women were already living in Virginia, a group remarkable for its balance between the sexes. During the early part of the century most people of color came to the British North American colonies via the West Indies, where they had learned a European language and in some instances converted to Christianity. Thus it is not clear that the English saw Africans as a unique kind of "stranger," distinct from the resentful and "degraded" Irish, for example. Although they performed jobs similar to those of indentured servants, slaves were often older than servants (if they had been "seasoned" in the West Indies, and lived that long), and they were more expensive than servants. On the other hand, in the Chesapeake, free black families lived in much the same manner as their white neighbors. For example, Anthony and Mary Johnson, free Negroes, lived together for 40 years and raised four children on Virginia's Eastern Shore.

Yet by the mid-seventeenth century, Virginia courts had begun to make invidious distinctions between Europeans and persons of African descent. Virginia black women were included in the list of tithables – workers to be taxed by the colony – while white women (fewer of whom were exclusively field workers) were exempt. A list of tithables for Northampton County, Virginia, in 1666, listed the full names of Englishmen, the names and ethnicity of other Europeans (Dutch, Irish, and French), but only the first name, and more often, only the word "negro" to signify workers of African descent. Black men were banned from using guns in order to defend their own households. And after 1662, enslaved men and women who converted to Christianity could no longer be granted their freedom. Although servants and slaves continued to till the soil together as bound laborers, men and women alike, only slaves grew old in the course of their bondage, and only slave women passed their own legal status on to their children – slaves for life. Eventually even free blacks were rendered impoverished, their children bound out (like orphans) as apprentices, their land stolen by white neighbors, their rights gradually drained away. In New England, blacks *qua* servants and slaves were banned from town militias. Moreover, most of the small number of free Negroes were too poor to own land, and thus they too were excluded from a kind of work that bound all whites together in common purpose – military service.

As a whole, the southern colonies moved toward slavery during the latter part of the seventeenth century. Founded in 1663, Carolina modeled its society after the English sugar colony of Barbados, and accordingly embraced the institution of bondage early and unconditionally. Within a generation, Carolina had developed a thriving frontier economy based on cattle, naval stores, and rice, but its exploitation of enslaved Africans tended to discourage white servants from settling there. By 1705 in Virginia, and a decade later in Maryland, slaves represented 20 percent of the population, a clear signal that the Chesapeake too was beginning to rely on Africans and their descendants for the bulk of unskilled labor. Thereafter the Chesapeake would follow the Carolina example and transform itself into a slave society, one characterized not only by dependence on the labor of enslaved persons, but also by a political system with bondage at its core.

By the latter part of the seventeenth century, in the southern colonies, even young men who had served their time as indentured servants found the way blocked to landownership, and with it marriage and economic self-sufficiency. Maryland masters were obliged to pay freedom dues to a servant at the end of his or her term; until 1681, these dues included a 50-Acre land warrant, in addition to the customary ax, hoe, and three barrels of corn. After that date the land grant was discontinued. Throughout the Chesapeake, the planter elite monopolized the fertile lands of the tidewater region, pushing young freemen, many of whom were unmarried and armed with guns, to the margins of colonial settlement where they remained dependent on landlords – now as tenants or hired hands – and vulnerable to the Indians. Some impoverished men and women bound themselves to a landlord in payment for a loan, in return for medical care, or as a means of getting and keeping a roof over their heads. Some pushed northward and westward, seeking out the fresh lands of western Maryland.

In Virginia in 1676, a group of English settlers residing in the western part of the colony launched an attack on the Susquehannock Indians, claiming that elites safely ensconced back in Jamestown were not doing enough to exterminate the Natives. The leader of the group, Nathaniel Bacon, a young wealthy planter, tapped into the resentments of recently freed indentured servants and others who lacked the resources to buy land. He and his followers, denounced by leaders of the colony as a "giddy headed multitude," went on to attack and burn Jamestown, forcing Governor William Berkeley to flee. Bacon died of his wounds, but 23 of his compatriots were eventually arrested and hanged.

Bacon's bloody rebellion helped to inspire the Virginia elite to elevate the status of all whites, no matter how lowly, in relation to all blacks; with the institution of slavery, even dispossessed freemen (former indentured servants) could claim some measure of equality with the wealthiest tobacco planter. Yet it is important to remember that, during much of the seventeenth century, masters and mistresses in general tended to indict members of subordinate groups *en masse*, rather than make fine distinctions (for example, those based on "race") between them. The resentful Irish or English servant, the enigmatic Indian hireling and African slave – all were condemned as resistant to discipline and feared as potentially bloodthirsty subversives, thorns in the side of the empire. In night-time bouts of drinking and carousing, these laborers commiserated with one another, their shared grievances festering like open wounds.

However, it would be difficult to argue that these workers demonstrated a kind of "class" consciousness – that is, that they thought of themselves as a unified group in opposition to masters and mistresses, and were prepared to act together accordingly. Indentured servants rightfully understood their status to be temporary, a stage of life and not a permanent condition of bondage. Though workers from Ireland and Africa or Spain and Scotland sometimes ran away in the company of each other, individuals often adhered to ethnic and religious loyalties that hindered the development of a transcendent group consciousness. Their defiance of authority tended to be unorganized and spontaneous. They got through the day by drinking, sleeping with one another, or running away, rather than by offering an explicit challenge to the master's power. In many instances their work and material condition was not much worse than that of the men and women who lorded over them; the tasks of colonization imposed a rough kind of equality on all workers regardless of legal status.

However, as the years passed, it was apparent that, in contrast to an African's dark skin, a European worker's ethnicity was, by and large, a temporal characteristic only; regardless of their grandparents' religion or native language, colonial-born workers might invoke English traditions and English rights in ways barred to persons of African descent. In 1661 in York County, Virginia, a group of white servants fomented a rebellion by claiming that they deserved to be fed meat three times a week, and by declaring that they would petition the king of England "for their Liberty," and to seek redress of their grievances. Without an English heritage, Africans lacked the standing to claim for themselves English rights (or so whites believed).

In 1700, the great dividing line between colonists was between the free and the unfree, with age a determining factor in both the northern and southern colonies, and with (increasingly) an African heritage a significant liability in the South. Yet the emergence of the system of southern slavery was not a foregone conclusion or the result of some transcendent, primal prejudice among English people; rather, it amounted to a gradual development arising from a convergence of political and economic factors. Indeed, southern planters kept a mental balance sheet that listed the trade-offs of different kinds of workers, and only over time did the large-scale enslavement of Africans present intself as a solution to the chronic problem of labor shortages. For example, the credit side of the balance sheet showed that slaves served for life, and the children of slave women inherited that legal status; on the other side, though, slaves were expensive, and in the seventeenth century, their high mortality rates made the capital investment an uncertain one at best. Enslaved Africans were marked by their color (although not all people of African descent were slaves, nor were all Europeans uniformly light-skinned), but English men and women were nervous about living under the same roof with people so different from themselves, a group of people that remained distinctive (that is, dark-skinned) regardless of their acculturation to English ways and beliefs. To control large numbers of slaves-for-life it was necessary for planters to institutionalize extreme measures of coercion, and also enlist the support of landless whites who were resentful of their landed betters. In other words, the creation of a slave system would lead to a fundamental reordering of the traditional English social structure by making the class of the very poorest people a permanent one, and by stigmatizing that group according to their skin color, African heritage, legal status as slaves, or some combination of these characteristics.

In sum, although the vast majority of emigrants to the New World, whether forced or voluntary, worked at growing crops for a substantial portion of the year, they labored within a variety of social contexts. On any one day in the mid-seventeenth century, it would be possible to catch a glimpse of all members of a Chesapeake plantation household toiling in the tobacco fields – if the head of the household was one of the lucky few to have a wife and children, the scene would include master and mistress, parent and child, black and white, bound and free, English-speaking and non-English speaking. Yet the landowner and members of his family, the Indian hireling, the several English indentured servants, and the slave or two brought to their work divergent memories and divergent expectations for the future. Drawing back our historical lens, we might compare the Chesapeake workers to farmers in New England, and contrast the all-consuming nature of tobacco production with the northern system of subsistence agriculture and domestic by-employments. Though hardly self-sufficient, New England families were much less dependent on the fickleness of the international market, and they found it easier to shift their labors between crops and crafts according to the needs of their families and neighbors. Moreover, unlike their southern counterparts, they did not necessarily consider work in the ground to be degrading – perhaps because it was associated with routine family labor, and not the brutal exploitation of servants (and increasingly slaves), as was the case in the South.

Confined within the Bradnox household on the Isle of Kent,

apparently a veritable chamber of horrors, the servant Sarah Taylor well understood the sources of her own misery – an arrogant and abusive master and mistress – and somehow she mustered the courage to confront her tormentors in court. After gaining her freedom in 1661, she disappears from the historical record – chances are good that she married (if so, her name change would have made it difficult to trace her). It was around this time that Captain Bradnox died, but his widow was determined to carry on his legacy; in 1662, she sued the Kent County commissioners, charging that they had over-stepped their own authority in freeing Sarah Taylor. A new set of judges who heard the case agreed, and awarded Mary Bradnox a judgment of "two hundred & twenty pounds of good casked Tobacco" to be paid her by each of the original commissioners as compensation for the rest of the time left on Sarah Taylor's indentures contract. Like her husband, Mary Bradnox was willing to expend considerable time and money, and risk her public reputation, in order to maintain control over the workers in her own household, and only cold hard cash (in this case tobacco) could replace that most valuable of New World commodities, an able-bodied servant.

FURTHER READING

Primary Sources

Barbour, Philip L., ed. *The Complete Works of Captain John Smith.* 3 vols. Chapel Hill: University of North Carolina Press, 1986.

Billings, Warren M. *The Old Dominion in the Seventeenth Century: A Documentary History of Virginia, 1606–1689.* Chapel Hill: University of North Carolina Press, 1975.

Bradford, William. *Of Plymouth Plantation, 1620–1647.* New York: Knopf, 1952.

Moynihan, Ruth Barnes, et al., eds. *Second to None: A Documentary History of American Women.* Vol. I: *From the Sixteenth Century to 1865.* Lincoln: University of Nebraska Press, 1993.

Tyler, Lyon Gardner. *Narratives of Early Virginia, 1606–1625.* New York: Barnes and Noble, 1952.

Secondary Sources

Carr, Lois Green, Russell R. Menard, and Lorena S. Walsh. *Robert Cole's World: Agriculture and Society in Early Maryland.* Chapel Hill: University of North Carolina Press, 1991.

Cronon, William. *Changes in the Land: Indians, Colonists, and the Ecology of New England.* New York: Hill & Wang, 1983.

Earle, Alice Morse. *Home Life in Colonial Days.* Stockbridge, MA: Berkshire Traveller Press, 1974; orig. pub. 1898.

Innes, Stephen. *Labor in a New Land: Economy and Society in Seventeenth-Century Springfield.* Princeton: Princeton University Press, 1993.

   Creating the Commonwealth: The Economic Culture of Puritan New England. New York: W. W. Norton, 1995.

Merrell, James H. *The Indians' New World: Catawbas and Their Neighbors from European Contact Through the Era of Removal.* Chapel Hill: University of North Carolina Press, 1989.

Morgan, Edmund S. *American Slavery, American Freedom: The Ordeal of Colonial Virginia.* New York: W. W. Norton, 1975.

Perry, James R. *The Formation of Society on Virginia's Eastern Shore, 1615–1655.* Chapel Hill: University of North Carolina Press, 1990.

Salisbury, Neal. *Manitou and Providence: Indians, Europeans, and the Making of New England, 1500–1643.* New York: Oxford University Press, 1982.

Silver, Timothy. *A New Face on the Countryside: Indians, Colonists, and Slaves in South Atlantic Forests, 1500–1800.* Cambridge, MA: Cambridge University Press, 1990.

Vickers, Daniel. *Farmers and Fishermen: Two Centuries of work in Essex County, Massachusetts, 1630–1850.* Chapel Hill: University of North Carolina Press, 1994.

2

"Be Sure To Come Free": Workers in the Eighteenth Century

The remarkable career of an eighteenth-century runaway apprentice revealed the expansive possibilities of late colonial America. Leaving behind his printer-master (who also happened to be his brother) in tradition-bound Boston, 17-year-old Benjamin Franklin found his way to Philadelphia, by that time a flourishing commercial center and the second largest city in the British empire. Franklin used his publishing skills and his scientific know-how to create several highly successful inventions and business ventures; of *Poor Richard's Almanac* he would later boast, "I reap'd considerable profit from it, vending annually near ten Thousand."[1] The colonists, for the most part highly literate and increasingly fond of consumer goods, welcomed the products of Franklin's genius – new means of efficient communication, and all sorts of things, from home heating stoves to eye glasses and lightning rods.

Franklin was notable for the way in which he grasped the emerging relationship among individual enterpise, economic development, and civic responsibility. He is well known for his role in founding several Philadelphia institutions that still survive in some form – the first subscription library in the colonies, a fire department, a hospital for the poor, a learned society (the American Philosophical Society) and an academy (now the University of Pennsylvania). Yet a more modest project is equally revealing. Distressed that the muddy, unpaved condition of Philadelphia's streets inhibited customers from shopping at a downtown market, Franklin located "a poor, industrious Man," who, for a modest wage paid by neighborhood residents and merchants, "was willing to undertake keeping the Pavement clean, by sweeping it twice a week." Franklin noted that, as a result, the shops did more business "as Buyers could more easily get at them," and that the merchandise was now free of "the Dust blown in" upon them.[2] Thus were linked the interests of neighborhood residents, the "poor, industrious man," and local merchants.

Benjamin Franklin was representative of an eighteenth-century spirit of enterprise that pointed toward the future, toward the eventual demise of bound labor and the triumph of free labor. As a runaway, he seized freedom for himself (a feat much more easily achieved by white servants than black slaves), and he quickly turned a skill – the printer's craft – into a marketable commodity. An early proponent of "one general government" uniting the colonies, he helped to raise volunteer armies to defend Pennsylvania's western boundaries against the French and Indians. Yet ironies abounded, both in Franklin's lifetime and within this colonial society. At times the civic leader found himself the victim of his own good fortune and his own expensive tastes, the prey of men (and women) on-the-make; in 1750, for example, his home was robbed of "a double necklace of gold beads, a womans long scarlet cloak almost new, with a double cape, a womans gown, of printed cotton of the sort called brocade print, very remarkable. . . and sundry other goods, etc."[3] Such fine goods, revealing his family's status, proved a tempting target for other men and women who shared Franklin's tastes but lacked the means to indulge them.

Indeed, the evolution of a consumer society encapsulates many of the major political, economic, and social themes of this period. The desire for more, or better, or fancier goods was at root a democratic desire, and one that bound together disparate groups of people in a common cause – to make more money in order to buy more things. The New Jersey farmer and his wife hoped to replace their wooden plates and bowls with a set of pewter, while the Boston lady yearned for a dining table adorned with sterling silver. Local carpenters, silversmiths, and merchants would all prosper accordingly. By the mid-eighteenth century, dainty china tea sets were within reach of even modest rural households, setting new standards of family well-being and social graciousness. Thus, the increasing availablity of goods of all kinds provided some people with incentives to work harder, or to explore new avenues of money-making.

Eighteenth-century workers toiled within a society that was devoted to the ideal of freedom and yet still wedded to forms of labor coercion. As settlements stabilized and as elites consolidated their power – planters in the South and merchants in the North and Mid-Atlantic – the demand for luxury goods proceeded apace, and in turn accelerated trade, the production of crafts, and the processing of raw materials. In the Declaration of Independence, Thomas Jefferson modified John Locke's conception of "inalienable rights," changing Locke's values of life, liberty, and property, to "life, liberty, and the pursuit of happiness"; happy was the man or woman who possessed property. At the same time, a traditional form of social control, the patriarchal household, persisted, and now a new form of social control, the institution of black slavery, characterized all of the colonies and came to dominate the life of a whole region, the South.

The Revolution itself had a seemingly contradictory impact on workers. At the end of the century, craft workers, now freed from restrictions imposed upon them by Great Britain, found a wider field for their labors. On the other hand, it was also clear that an increasing number of free laborers who produced a dazzling array of goods would not necessarily be able to afford to buy what they made. The egalitarian principles of the Revolution inspired large numbers of Upper-South slaveowners to free their slaves. At the same time, the hardening of the institution of plantation slavery, a system that relied upon state-sanctioned violence and terror, led to the creation of new and insidious theories about the "racial" differences between "whites" and people of African descent.

The drive to stigmatize all Africans and their descendants in the colonies – a drive that spurred the creation of racial ideologies – served to obscure the history and rich complexity of black life in the colonies. Regional economies and demographics shaped black work patterns; compare for example the lone enslaved Creole (American-born) field hand in a small town in Massachusetts with the dense networks of kin and community among recently imported low country South Carolina rice workers. Meanwhile, an emerging African-American culture, grounded firmly in the the African-American family, served to transcend the differences between Creoles and African-born slaves.

Eighteenth-century America was a multicultural society bursting at the seams of empire. By 1750 the population totaled 1.2 million people (in the Chesapeake and Lower South, four out of every ten were Africans and their descendants). Contributing to this explosive growth were the natural increase of the population, Scots-Irish immigrants who settled the backcountry from Georgia to New Hampshire, Germans – who found their way to Pennsylvania, Maryland, Virginia, and the Carolinas – and increasing numbers of Africans imported into the Chesapeake Tidewater, Georgia, and the Carolinas.

A number of regional economies testified to the overall prosperity of the British North American colonies during the first half of the eighteenth century. The Lower South produced rice for export to the Mediterranean, Portugal, and Spain. The Chesapeake gradually abandoned its reliance on tobacco and embraced a more diversified economy based on grains and crafts. New England specialized in the "carrying trade," its logging, shipbuilding, and fishing industries supplementing family-based agriculture. The Mid-Atlantic region emerged as the colonies' breadbasket, growing, processing, and marketing a variety of foodstuffs. On the western borderlands, subsistence farmers traded with the Indians, and raised cattle or made shingles, ax handles, and other products that might fetch a price in the neighborhood or an eastern marketplace.

Although social relations in the backcountry remained somewhat fluid – travellers passing through might remark upon a black blacksmith living in relative comfort with his wife, a Scots immigrant woman – eastern patterns of labor exploitation were replicated in the mountains and valleys. A backwoodsman might "glory in the stroke he could give with his ax, in the trees he felled, and the deer he shot; to conjure the wolf, the bear and the alligator,"[4] but the chances were good that he would also aspire to hire or buy a slave to work with the saw, mauls, bittles, and wedges necessary to fell trees, split rails, and construct cabins.

In New England and the Middle Colonies in particular, growth was a dynamic process, accompanied by economic diversification. Most colonists continued to labor within individual households; only the large slave plantation, and the ship – with its masters, mates, carpenters, boatswains, gunners, quartermasters, cooks, and ordinary seamen – were organized along rigidly hierarchical lines. Still, new and better tools became the stock in trade of the average Northern farmer cum carpenter or blacksmith, and the average housewife cum producer of soap, candles, and textiles. By the end of the century, flour mills were fully mechanized entities and pointed the way toward the technological innovation that would spur antebellum economic development.

Throughout the eighteenth century, a worker's legal status – as indentured servant, convict laborer, slave, or family member – continued to be more of a determining factor in his or her life than the specific kind of work he or she performed. In 1701 George Haworth, an English emigrant to Pennsylvania, wrote to his kinfolk back home, "So if any of my relations have a mind to come to this country, I think it is a very good country and that they may do well, but be sure to come free."[5] Yet this option was not available to John Aldridge, Elizabeth Armstrong, John Rogers, and Mary Row, Haworth's compatriots who were among the felons imported to the colonies (some of them branded on the hand) during the eighteenth century (Maryland received, albeit reluctantly, half of the total of 20,000).

Exploited as drudges and field workers at home, and as cannon fodder in various provincial wars, indentured servants and convicts persisted in running away in droves, and their names littered the pages of colonial newspapers published up and down the coast: desperate for freedom were young people like "an Irish servant lad named Patrick Flanley about 19 years old . . . by trade a Leather Breeches Maker and Skinner; Had on when he went away a grey homespun cloth coat, almost new, lin'd with blue shallon in the forepart."[6] Interspersed with the names of whites were those of blacks like Tony, a Virginia-born slave (who absconded from his owner in North Carolina in 1744), described as a brickmaker and "a good Sawyer," and "scarr'd on his Shoulders by Correction."[7] The advertisement for Tony ran in the *Pennsylvania Gazette*, the paper published by Benjamin Franklin.

The fate of various Indian groups also contrasted with the settled prosperity of increasing numbers of landowning and skilled whites throughout the colonies. Some tribes disappeared altogether, while others, like those in the Carolinas backcountry, regrouped and managed to carry on trade relations with whites in the process. Massachusetts and Connecticut diligently sought out Indian allies and recruits in their struggles against the French on the western frontier, although these "friend Indians" proved unpredictable. Some colonists continued to pay wages to Indian men hired to perform particularly arduous work; in 1777, Attakullakulla, Aucanestota ("the Little Carpenter"), and Pigeon, were among the 40 Cherokees who, "painted & ornamented with Feathers," appeared in Williamsburg, Virginia, "their Business here [being] to clear the Path between their Country & this, which they say has been obstructed by Weeds growing in it."[8]

Emblematic of the status of all Indians, now deprived of the ability to support themselves through traditional means – hunting, fishing, and a nomadic form of subsistence agriculture – was Hannah Freeman (1731–1802), a Lenape born to parents who were tenants in Kennett, Pennsylvania. Barred from planting corn there, and later fearful of outbreaks of violence against Indians in general, the Freeman family moved back and forth between Pennsylvania and New Jersey, and then between New Jersey and Delaware. After the death of her parents, Hannah Freeman led a peripatetic existence, "moving from place to place making baskets &c and staying longest where best used but never was hired or recd wages except for Baskets &c. . ." By this time she had "almost forgot [how to] talk Indian. . ."[9]

It would be possible to chart the history of eighteenth-century workers by noting on the one hand the eventual triumph of "free labor" in the North, and on the other the simultaneous oppression of large numbers of black workers, slave and free, in the North and South. However, this either-or approach would hinder our appreciation of a wide variety of workers – the women who played an increasingly important economic and political role as producers of textiles within their own households, and by the 1750s, within the workhouses of some of the major seaport cities; the transients who went from town to town, offering to work for a day or two and more often than not getting into trouble in the process; the children who continued to toil in the shops and fields under the watchful eye of a master, parent, or guardian; and even the home-grown pirates who smuggled goods in and out of the colonies in an effort to partake more fully of the material blessings of colonial life. It is true that the struggles of enslaved Africans and free people of color served as a most vivid reminder of the shortcomings of the seemingly progressive trajectory of American history, with its emphasis on economic freedom and small-scale agriculture (republicanism); at the same time, the fluidity in labor relations within regional economies was an equally distinctive characteristic of the eighteenth century.

Between 1700 and 1775, American society was wracked by social and political conflicts that stemmed not so much from the fact that different groups of workers performed different kinds of jobs, as from the fact that some groups of workers feared for the future while others looked forward to it with anticipation. Blacks instigated a revolt in New York City in 1712 and the Stono Rebellion in South Carolina in 1739, and, together with an assortment of Irish servants and Indian hirelings, New York's Great Conspiracy of 1741. As a result of this last uprising, for their part in setting fire to Fort

George, the governor's mansion, and the imperial armory, 13 of the conspirators were burned at the stake, 21 hanged, and more than 75 sold outside the colonies as servants or slaves. In 1737, one colonial offical in South Carolina noted ominously, "our Negroes are very numerous and more dreadful to our Safety, than any Spanish Invaders."[10] In an era wracked by a series of colonial wars fought on American soil (Queen Anne's War, 1702–13; King George's Wars, 1744–8; the French and Indian War, 1754–63), rebellious slaves were naturally conflated with spies and enemies of all kinds.

Various assortments of colonists on the western periphery of settlement – squatters, small farmers, and craftsmen – lashed out against both Indians and their social betters. Pennsylvania backcountry farmers (the "Paxton Boys") launched a campaign against the Indians in 1763; North Carolina backcountry farmers (the Regulators) attacked corrupt officials controlled by the eastern establishment in the 1760s; and tenants of the great Hudson-Valley estates engaged in violent demonstrations against their landlords around this same time. During the Revolution, urban craftsmen deflected their resentment against the Crown onto merchants. Thus the history of the eighteenth century is a story of various aspirations for the future, and the revolutionary upheaval that, depending on the group of workers in question, fulfilled, frustrated, or utterly denied those aspirations.

Where craft production and trade were most in evidence, in the North, challenges to systems of bound labor (slavery as well as indentured servitude) were most pronounced. A diversified economy mandated flexible labor arrangements, and sea captains and master craftsmen, among other employers, all needed the freedom to hire and fire workers at will. Indeed, the eighteenth-century Northern and Middle Colonies were characterized by an impressive array of tenure statuses, depending upon the nature of the enterprise and the demand for its goods or services. Thus poor German-speaking Palatines toiled as indentured servants in the New York naval stores industry, Indian whalemen labored as debt peons on the island of Nantucket, and Scots-Irish tenants worked the land of Dutch landowners in the Hudson Valley. In each particular place, landlords and employers sought the right mix of contractual statuses; the landed farmers of Chester County, Pennsylvania, for example, relied upon members of their own families, and also employed apprentices, cottagers (resident workers paid by the day or by piece-work), and non-resident day laborers. Owners of New Jersey copper mines patched together their labor forces from nearby farmers willing to work for wages in the slack season, indentured servants imported from Europe, and black slaves.

A focus on local economies allows us to distinguish among the older regions of the Chesapeake, which had turned to a grain and craft economy by the early eighteenth century; the frontier economies of the lower South; the flourishing rice economy of low-country South Carolina; and the relatively cosmopolitan seaboard towns of Charleston and Savannah. Second- and third-generation enslaved workers had become integrated into the Virginia economy, working as blacksmiths, iron-makers, and carpenters; meanwhile, the ability of black women and children to cultivate tobacco provided an incentive for Piedmont planters to encourage family life and the natural reproduction of workers. In newly settled areas of Georgia and the Carolinas, slaves grew crops, tended cattle, made boats, fished and hunted, and it was not unusual for whites, Indians, and blacks to create trade networks, some more formal than others, among themselves.

In the course of the eighteenth century, the southern labor force became both less and more diverse – less diverse because Native groups, ravaged by war and disease, virtually disappeared as sources of workers, bound or otherwise, and more diverse in the sense that the social hierarchy widened to include new classifications and tenure statuses (that is, work relationships, contractual or otherwise). By this time, the leveling of the sex ratio had produced stable nuclear families in the Chesapeake. The initial land grab on the part of wealthy first-generation colonists, and the consequent lack of available parcels, meant that former indentured servants had few alternatives but to work as tenants or apprentice themselves to craftsmen, or seek out odd jobs from landowners. Poor people, many of whom were squatting on a piece of land here and begging for day work there, reminded elites that it was more difficult to achieve a well-ordered society in fact than it was in theory. In some areas, like the eastern shore of Maryland, pockets of small landowners coexisted with great planters. And a new class of black people emerged – free people of color, descendants of blacks who had never been enslaved, or former slaves freed by their master. The complexity of the southern social structure – the white and black, slave and free craftsmen; the white and black, slave and free poor – remained at odds with an emerging planter ideology based upon supposedly immutable differences between blacks and whites.

Moreover, the largest planters alternated between different kinds of labor, depending on the cost, proximity, and tractability of certain types of workers. By the 1730s many planters were producing on their own estates what they had previously imported, and so cheese vats, bake ovens, cider presses, herb stills, spinning wheels, and looms were now becoming fixtures in the relatively well-to-do Southern household, and labor in it was becoming more specialized according to age, gender, and material standard of living. On the eve of Revolution, the largest estates resembled proto-industrial villages, with tanning and blacksmith shops, resident tailors and shoemakers, carpenters and cordwainers, some enslaved workers and some free ones. At George Washington's Mount Vernon, slaves cultivated wheat, corn, oats and rye; milled grains; and produced cloth. However, Washington also imported white craftsmen – plasterers, chimneymakers, bricklayers, millwrights, and construction workers of various kinds – and he also hired white men to work in the grain fields during the particularly busy harvest season. Throughout the region, the fortunes of white craftsmen rose and fell in relation to the specialization of the largest estates, where skilled slaves performed a variety of tasks.

Southern planters agreed among themselves that it was better to enlarge their slave labor forces than to rely on white men who resisted being "driven" in the fields, in gangs.

Founded as a free-labor colony in 1738, Georgia succumbed to a vocal pro-slavery group of landowners in 1751, primarily because white servants and hired hands proved to be such miserable workers, some adept at avoiding hard labor by feigning illness, others suffering from the real thing and carried off by various fevers. Like their seventeenth-century counterparts, white workers in 1740s Georgia wounded themselves with axes and saws, defied their masters and mistresses with curses, and ran away. Though slaves carried with them some of the same liabilities for their masters, at least they could be punished mercilessly, without the protection afforded by a code of legal rights, and at least they served for life.

Southern slaveholders gradually developed a theory of plantation management (later labeled "paternalism"), intended both to rationalize the enslavement of people of African descent, and to impose upon these workers demands for daily and seasonal work routines. The idea that slaves were in effect perpetual children, without "reason" and dependent upon the care and guidance of a (presumably benevolent) patriarch, seemed to provide justification enough for their perpetual bondage. In fact, planters were grappling with labor-management issues that their seventeenth-century counterparts (that is, masters of indentured servants) had not had to contend with – the maintenance of large numbers of children and elderly people who were not productive workers. This reality inspired many slaveowners to complain that their bondsmen and women showed them insufficient gratitude, as if these white men were providing for a group of nonworkers out of a sense of duty, and not as a calculated attempt to maintain large and self-reproducing labor forces.

Enslaved Americans in the colonial South included the newly imported, "outlandish" West African toiling in a Georgia corn field, and the acculturated Creole woman, waiting on a white family in their magnificent Tidewater Virginia estate. Over the course of the century, the locus of Southern slavery shifted from the small quarter worked by a triracial work force (Robert Carter scattered his 400 laborers among 48 small, isolated "quarters"), to the expansive slave plantations of the

South Carolina lowcountry, where large numbers of highly concentrated, recently imported Africans, combined with absentee white landowners, gave rise to a slave culture with West African antecedents. However, the relative stability of slave family life on these holdings must be juxtaposed to the high mortality rates among the workers who lived on them. A contemporary observer noted that rice cultivation necessitated "large bodies of water in reserve which being stagnant corrupt and become extremely unwholesome." At night, after a long day in the fields, slaves were forced to beat the rice in mortars, a hard task, that, carried out under the direction of a "severe overseer", "generally carries of[f] great numbers every winter."[11] Nevertheless, conventional wisdom among the planter elite held that, although other crops might be grown successfully by white people, "without Blacks . . . Rice cannot be."[12]

Slaves imported from Africa hailed from a variety of societies, some nomadic, others based on sendentary agriculture, and those societies were characterized by a variety of kinship arrangements and customs. Nevertheless, in assessing the labor of eighteenth-century Southern slaves, certain generalizations appear to be warranted. First, some enslaved Africans, like those who grew rice, herded cattle, raised chickens, wove baskets, or navigated inland waterways in skiffs they had made themselves, performed tasks with which they might have had some familiarity. In contrast, their children and grandchildren who had learned to speak English, and who had become acclimatized enough to receive instruction as gentlemen's barbers or ladies' maids, worked at jobs more distant from those of their African homelands. Regardless of the task itself, of course, few Africans had previously endured the forced pace characteristic of American slave labor.

It is not always possible to draw a clear line between the work that whites forced slaves to do and the work that slaves performed on their own behalf. By 1750, the black family had emerged as a viable institution, its extended kin binding together slaves of both sexes and all ages located on plantations within any particular area. Slaveowners began to appreciate the reproductive capacity of slave women, and to factor children into their ledger books as both future workers and solid investments. For these reasons, Southern planters (unlike their relatively short-sighted counterparts in the West Indies) consciously encouraged the development of stable slave families (as long as the economic viability of their businesses permitted them). Therefore, efforts of families to sustain themselves – the mothers to care for the children, the fathers to provide for their offspring any way feasible – also served to preserve the owner's investment in his labor force.

Some scholars suggest that all colonial Southerners, whether born in Europe, Africa, or America, shared a common worldview – that they organized their lives on the basis of seasonal rhythms, believed strongly in the power of place, perceived permeable boundaries between the spiritual and material realms, and by the time of the Revolution, embraced emotional religious revivals that broke down barriers between the races. Nevertheless, as the institution of bondage expanded, whites came to associate African culture with patterns of resistance among enslaved workers of both sexes and all ages. Though planters initially distinguished Africans according to their homeland – the Fantees compared to the Ibos, the Calabars to the Gambians – they eventually generalized about all blacks, whom they considered to be cunning, sly, and recalcitrant. George Washington complained about one of his black women workers who, he believed, persisted in feigning illness – Betty "has a disposition to be one of the most idle creatures on earth, and besides one of the most deceitful."[13] Runaway slaves were advertised as "ungrateful rogues" and "artful wenches."

Slaves throughout the South continued to adhere to certain African traditions – rituals and trading practices – and white people came to see these traditions as political acts of resistance. For instance, a Muslim named Job from Bondu, was captured and sold to a slaveowner in Maryland. Put to work tending cattle in the fields, he would often "withdraw into the woods to pray." One day he seized such an opportunity and ran off, never to return to his master.[14] When enslaved workers gathered for funerals in which whites did not take part, when they accompanied themselves on African percussion instruments during musical celebrations, when they persisted in trading the goods they had produced with Indians and indentured servants, they challenged the authority of their masters and mistresses. Moreover, whites connected specialized African skills with mayhem and subversion; for example, the elderly woman knowledgeable about the various uses of poisonous plants was especially feared throughout the (white) plantation South. Nevertheless, in the end, slaves who laid claim to freedom by virtue of their Christianity ("Releese us out of this Cruell Bondegg and this wee beg for Jesus Christs his Sake")[15] posed just as great a threat to the planters' hegemony as did those who engaged in late-night "Negro Balls," occasions when "they generally meet together and amuse themselves with Dancing to the Banjo," and singing songs about the hard treatment they received from their masters.[16]

Plantation organization directly affected the shape and welfare of slave family and community life. In the Upper South, where slave men were routinely hired out to neighboring planters for part of the year, families endured the separation of husbands from wives and fathers from children. In this region, the work of slave men as skilled artisans, especially in the towns and on the largest plantations, contrasted with the work of their womenfolk, who were confined primarily to field work and domestic service. The nature of the crop under cultivation determined whether or not family members would have the time to devote to an internal slave economy; for example, in the South Carolina Sea Islands, the task system of rice cultivation (which allowed slaves a great deal of leeway in deciding how to spend their time after they performed a specific job each day) encouraged the development of a lively market economy. Enslaved women sold their chickens, eggs, and handicrafts to blacks and whites alike in the Charleston marketplace; this relatively extensive entrepreneurial activity was unique to slaves in this part of the colonies.

Slavery exacted a heavy price in terms of whites' sense of security and safety. More particularly, the rapid increase in the number of slaves sounded alarms among the planter class. In 1736 William Byrd II advised the Georgia colonists against legalizing slavery, observing that he had learned from first-hand experience that as the slave population grew, "Numbers make them insolent, & then foul means must do [for discipline], what fair will not." Yet "these private mischeifs are nothing if compard to the publick danger. . . . And in case there should arise a man of desperate courage amongst us. . . . Such a man might be dreadfully mischeivous before any opposition could be formed against him, and tinge our rivers as wide as they are with blood."[17] In fact, the planters of South Carolina worried about this very problem – the exponential growth in the black population – and for good reason. Three years after Byrd issued his warning, the Stono rebels (eventually numbering about 100 slaves and including some newly arrived Angolan men) looted firearms and attacked white settlements on their way to Spanish Florida, and they, hoped freedom. Bands of armed whites, assisted by Indians, defeated the rebels. As many as 24 whites and perhaps 50 blacks lost their lives as a result of the uprising.

Some contemporaries, and modern historians as well, contrast the southern system of slavery to its supposedly more benign counterpart in the North. Their argument was (and is) that Northern slaves tended to be better fed and clothed, that they worked at jobs that were less dangerous and less arduous compared to those performed by Southern slaves, and that they were in general more integrated within the local Northern town or rural economy, and ultimately more integrated into the social life of local (white-dominated) communities, compared to their Southern counterparts. Yet matters were not nearly so simple. In order to assess fully the impact of enslavement upon black men and women in different areas of the colonies, it is necessary to understand the constitutive parts of their experiences – their ability to form families and partake of community life, the nature of their labor, and their material standard of living. The bottom line, of course, meant that all slaves faced the possibility that they might be sold away from loved ones, subjected to the most barbaric kinds of punishment, and worked nigh unto death – all without the benefit of legal protection.

Enslaved blacks represented a tiny percentage of the total northern population, and their value was more often reckoned in relation to that of indentured servants, rather than as a separate labor force valuable in its own right. For example, slavery reached its highest point in Pennsylvania around 1720; thereafter, the falling prices of servants encouraged the importation of German and Scots-Irish servants and redemptioners. At the end of the first century of settlement, Northerners were quick to point out the inefficiency of slave labor in relation to the Northern-based colonial enterprise. Slaves' "continual aspiring after their forbidden Liberty, renders them Unwilling Servants," noted one Massachusetts justice in 1700, and he further suggested that "there is such a disparity in their Conditions, Colour, & Hair, that they can never embody with us, and grow up into orderly Families, to the Peopleing of the Land."[18] In contrast, white servants were "serviceable" as militiamen, farmers, community leaders, and reproducers of the colonial (white) population. In the North, then, anti-slavery arguments at times stemmed from a fear of blacks as household cohabitors, as much as from egalitarianism and principles of justice.

In Northern towns, where housing was at a premium, enslaved workers were discouraged (and in some cases even forbidden) to form families; and there are cases of slave children being sold or given away so that they would not take up added space or consume additional food. One Massachusetts owner sought to rid himself of "an extraordinary likely Negro Wench, 17 years old. . . . strong, healthy, and good natur'd, [she] has no notion of Freedom, has been always used to a Farmer's kitchen and dairy, and is not known to have any failing, but being with child, which is the only cause of her being sold."[19]

In the North, slaves labored as seamen, ropemakers, carpenters, coopers, and teamsters, as well as domestic servants and farm hands. Free Negroes often pieced together a livelihood through a combination of odd jobs, wage work, craft production, and gardening. On Long Island, Venture Smith raised watermelons to sell, fished for eels and lobsters, and served on a whaling ship for seven months. Through his industry he was able to buy his wife and three children from bondage, and hire two black men to work for him. Not all free blacks boasted such success.

Slaves in the North often felt keenly their isolation from their compatriots. In western Massachusetts, an enslaved worker named Cato lived a long life (he died in 1825 in his late eighties), but the village of Deerfield afforded no real black community. Cato remained close to his mother as long as she lived; together they both accumulated trinkets such as bits of copper, brass, or glassware (his mother said she was gathering "treasures to take back to her mother land");[20] and they eagerly participated in community festivals designed to bring together members of a scattered black population, in towns and in the countryside. At times enslaved Northerners also seized the opportunity to join white churches, at least those that emphasized a brotherhood and sisterhood of the spirit.

The social isolation suffered by black workers in the North was compounded by the fact that, among white men and women, labor was more often than not a community affair. In Westborough, Massachusetts, a minister named Ebenezer Parkman and his wife Mary oversaw a procession of workers to help them and their own children with work in the fields, orchards, dairy, and kitchen – a French Acadian girl, a black slave, indentured servants, hired hands, neighbors, members of Parkman's congregation, kinfolk, and even visitors from other towns. Indeed, rural New Englanders in general encountered a variety of people in the course of their everyday work routines. Tom Hazard, a wealthy landowner in Rhode Island, bought shoes from an itinerant craftsman and yarn from neighbors, took in children as apprentices and servants, hired a woman to help his wife with the housework, and engaged tenants to alternate between chores in the field and in the craft shop.

Like their grandmothers, Northern women engaged in "swap work" with one another; they lent their daughters to neighbors who needed help with spinning or weaving, and they helped each other to pickle vegetables and slaughter pigs. These activities enhanced the independence of individual households, and surplus products sold for a profit – butter, cheese, eggs – could enable the industrious housewife to purchase a much prized piece of lace, or a fancy bonnet, or enough coffee and sugar to last the family through the winter. Though northern households were characterized by a gender division of labor, the work of both sexes was complementary, with men harvesting grain that women then brewed into beer, and men growing flax that women spun into thread and wove into clothes.

In the Northern colonies, certain household industries contributed significantly to larger trade networks. In the Mid-Atlantic, Quaker women participated in an international export economy through their production of dairy products which were then sold to the West Indies. The textiles produced by women and children in New England and the Mid-Atlantic allowed their own households and neighborhoods to remain independent of imports from England. In the late 1760s, a group calling itself the Daughters of Liberty elevated the production of homespun to a political act, exhorting their sisters throughout the colonies to double their efforts at the spinning wheel and the loom.

For most white men in the North, a stint in the army represented a kind of eighteenth-century work that was something of a departure from ordinary farm and craft-based routines (and, in a colony as menaced as Massachusetts was, as many as one-third of all the eligible men were drawn into service at mid-century); at the same time, it foreshadowed the kind of routinized and regimented labor that would become more common in the nineteenth century. Whether part of a village militia or a provincial army, eighteenth-century soldiers were supposed to adhere to strict forms of discipline that were otherwise unknown outside the slave plantation or the sailing ship. Fighting against the French in the Ticonderoga wilderness or against the Indians in the western part of Pennsylvania provided the opportunity for some young men to learn new skills, such as driving a team of horses or assisting a blacksmith, skills that might serve them well later in civilian life. Soldiers expected to earn hard currency, not just food, shelter, or the promise of being paid at some time in the future. Most agreed to serve for a stipulated amount of time, anticipating contractual arrangments with an employer, in contrast to the more open-ended terms that marked their labors for fathers or master craftsmen.

The hardships that were part and parcel of virtually all eighteenth-century military campaigns – the bitter cold endured by ill-clad men, the lack of food and the unbound wounds – inspired at least some to challenge their officers and then to go on and question the authority of the state – officials representing the colony or even the Crown. Regardless of the ordeals they faced, those who survived to return home shared with other men a bond born of hardship in the service of the Crown, a bond that was deep even as it connected white men scattered widely throughout the population. By the mid-eighteenth century, the image of the sturdy yeoman farmer, armed and at the ready, had attained political significance; he was the defender of his home, village, and practical notions of liberty.

The citizen-soldier was a farmer (a planter in the South), and more than nine out of ten colonists lived on the countryside at the time of the Revolution; but in fact it was the cities of late colonial America that foreshadowed the future. As commercial centers, northern and southern seaports boasted more variegated occupational structures compared to rural areas, and spawned classes of free workers and impoverished workers, two groups that often overlapped. Out of 100 male workers in a typical port city like Philadelphia or New York, 15 were bound workers of some kind (slaves or indentured servants); one-quarter of the total worked as seamen; 40 were artisans; and five people made their living in trade or service, or as merchants, small shopkeepers, colonial officials, or professionals such as clergymen or lawyers. In the cities, unlike on the farm or plantation, married women worked apart from their husbands, toiling as seamstresses, domestic servants, laundresses, spinners, knitters, or peddlers. Most urban folk worked for money, and the bustling commercial economy depended upon a flexible labor force that was more conducive to wage labor than to bound labor.

Colonial cities were hard hit by the imperial and provincial wars that plagued eighteenth-century American society. Refugees from the frontier, many bereft of kin and resources of any kind, made their way to towns. Military conflict in the backcountry or on the high seas disrupted trade, making the life of a sailor or teamster or dockworker even more precarious. An underground economy based on theft and the fencing of stolen goods flourished, and drew upon the initiative and resentments of a multicultural laboring class consisting of Irish indentured servants, black slaves, and Indian hirelings. In the cities, then, congregated the wandering poor, servant and slave runaways, widows and orphans – groups comprising as much as a third of the urban population.

The depressions and epidemics that periodically swept through these cities proved devastating to those already destitute. Public-sponsored efforts to provide employment for such men, women, and children were not always successful. In Boston, poor women resisted forced labor in the public workhouse where they were put to spinning. A few years later, in 1748, these women made it clear that they preferred to stay at home with their children, and spin what they could there, rather than go into a manufactory. In the coming years, the impoverished spinster, together with her sister, the weary needlewoman, would represent the dark side of "free labor" – women workers not bound to any master, father, or husband, and vulnerable to the vicissitudes of the urban marketplace.

Indeed, more generally, the intracolonial social and political tensions of the mid-eighteenth century were revealed in new and different kinds of poor people, workers and would-be workers. Certainly the first century of settlement had afforded numerous examples of men and women who could not provide for themselves or their families. In 1700 in Bristol County, Massachusetts, John Baker was forced to throw himself on the mercy of the court and beg for aid. Drafted into the army when he was a young man, he suffered a debilitating injury to his arm, but after returning home did his best to eke out a living as a weaver. Impressed into service once again, he soon found himself penniless and indebted to his doctor: "I have nothing to help my selfe withall."[21] He begged Bristol County authorities for relief from taxes.

However, by mid-century, a new kind of worker had appeared on the scene – the able-bodied adult who could not find employment, and, perhaps like John Barret, a Philadelphia baker, was "in and out [of the almshouse] as often as the number of his fingers and toes."[22] In eastern parts of New England, the continuous subdivision of family homesteads over the generations meant that the children of large families had little land to inherit, and they were forced to migrate north or west, the men to seek out fresh lands or to follow new kinds of trades. Those who remained behind turned to day work or public charity. In the Chesapeake region, landless men and women worked as tenants for great planters, but an unlucky growing season could spell disaster and force them to rely on the uncertain favors of their betters. Some of the poor survived by their wits and disrupted households and whole communities in the process. A former blacksmith's apprentice in New York, John Jubeart became a transient, and "being badly paid for his work, had reduced him so low that he was greatly in want of linen and several other necessaries." Where other men in his circumstances turned to robbery, Jubeart became a counterfeiter, pursuing his new career "with great assiduity and hard labour."[23]

Northern merchants came to look upon seaport cities as sites of civil disorder, places where Indians, Irish servants, and slaves came together within a larger transatlantic community of workers. Southern elites also harbored strong suspicions of cities; with its population of 12,000 about equally divided by whites and blacks, pre-revolutionary Charleston, South Carolina, swelled with an influx of indigent whites, including the widows and children of soldiers and 1,000 French-Canadian refugees. A perceived "crime wave" in the late 1760s heightened fears that slaves and poor whites were colluding (they often met together in "tippling houses") and trying to make a living on their own apart from white elites – through stealing, prostitution, and trafficking in pilfered goods. Representative of suspect urban workers were slaves who "hired their own time" and remained outside the control of whites. Free Negroes followed a variety of occupations, as carpenters, hucksters, and fishermen, mocking the notion that blacks were fit only for menial labor in the fields. For example, Thomas Jeremiah, who worked as a fire fighter, a fisherman, and harbor pilot in Charleston, was accused of plotting an insurrection and sentenced to death. One white man denounced him as a "forward fellow, puffed up by prosperity, ruined by Luxury and debauchery and grown to an amazing pitch of vanity and ambition."[24]

Yet the seaports were also home to a group of workers whom Thomas Jefferson called "the yeomanry of the city" – self-employed skilled tradesmen who owned their own tools and businesses, and presided over lively shops that produced custom-made goods of various kinds. Laboring within the largest shops were journeymen who possessed skills but not property, apprentices in the process of learning the trade, and at times the children and wife of the master. Unlike the factories that would appear later in the century, the shops of tanners, blacksmiths, printers, hatters, tailors, carpenters, and coopers (among others) were characterized by informal work relations (at times based on kinship) and flexible hours, rather than time-oriented wage labor.

Artisans (sometimes called "mechanics") took pride in their skills and their status as independent producers of goods, and they resented attempts by the British Crown to regulate the colonial economy, attempts that intensified after the French and Indian War of the 1760s and provoked depression in the cities by the early 1770s. In their opposition to the Mother Country these craftsmen were joined by seamen, dock workers, and ship workers of various kinds (represented collectively by the name "Jack Tar"), groups that languished, waiting in dockside taverns, while American ships remained empty and moored in harbors up and down the Eastern seaboard.

The sailors in particular, long victims of Britain's impressment policies on the high seas, represented a multiracial, multiethnic revolutionary force throughout the Atlantic basin.

Accounts of the American Revolution often highlight the role of the patriotic Paul Revere, a wealthy silversmith; but in fact ordinary workers served as the backbone of the rebellion, especially in the cities. For example, in Boston, the men who fell under the fire of British muskets in the Boston Massacre in 1770, and the men who, disguised as Indians, dumped tea in the harbor three years later, included sailors, ship's mates, journeymen leathermen, and rope-makers, as well as other artisans. Among the city's "Loyal Nine" (a forerunner of the Sons of Liberty) were John Smith, a brazier; Thomas Crofts, a painter; Benjamin Edes, a printer; and George Trott, a jeweler. In the course of the conflict, artisans and day laborers would alternately ally with and struggle against the prominent lawyers and merchants who were becoming increasingly anxious about the revolutionary potential of the "people in the streets" (mobs and other spontaneous demonstrations against the Crown and against privilege in general).

The genius of the American Revolution was its rhetoric of freedom and liberty that could be appropriated by so many different kinds of workers for so many different purposes. The coopers who joined the Philadelphia Sons of Liberty, the Charleston merchants beholden to Scottish creditors, the tenants of the Van Rensalear estate in the Hudson Valley region of New York, the slaves of the great planter Landon Carter in Virginia – all of these groups could call for "liberty" and "freedom" within strikingly divergent contexts, and for strikingly divergent ends.

Nevertheless, the Revolution itself exposed the social faultlines within American society. Merchants who had stockpiled goods before the war benefited from the disruption of trade with England, and native artisans enjoyed a whole new market for their hand-crafted goods. Laborers in war-related industries like glass, powder, salt, paper, and iron found their services in great demand, yet teamsters and seamen suffered for lack of work. Throughout the emerging, war-torn nation, slaves claimed their won freedom both apart from, and as part of, the struggle waged by their masters. These were the 100,000 enslaved men and women who ran away and joined the British forces (in many cases, finding only disease and forced labor).

In contrast, small numbers of enslaved Indians and blacks in New England gained their liberty by helping to fulfill the quotas imposed on towns by conscription authorities. The revolutionary heritage claimed by black war veterans echoed through the generations. A slave named Silvia Dubois – the daughter of a slave who served as a fifer at the battle of Princeton – fled from her mistress in Pennsylvania, striking out on her own and declaring to whites who sought to impede her journey, "I'm no man's nigger – I belong to God – I belong to no man. . . . I'm free; I go where I please." When she recorded her story later in life, she made special mention of her father, linking his fight for freedom to her own.[25]

Thus it is not surprising that, from the perspective of many different kinds of workers, the founding of the new republic was an inherently contradictory development. With the elimination of British restrictions on both trade and territorial expansion, regional economies grew and local populations migrated west. For the owner of a glass-blowing manufactory, and for the land-poor Vermont farmer, the Revolution wrought measurable changes in their opportunities to prosper. Some members of certain groups – Hudson-Valley tenants and slaves in the Upper South – reaped tangible rewards from the new ideology of egalitarianism, which yielded land grants to the former group, and emancipation for the latter.

Craftsmen could point with pride to their own role in initiating and sustaining revolutionary fervor throughout the war and into the early national period. Yet in the process they came to identify themselves increasingly in negative terms; they were not women, not children, and neither the slaves nor the grandsons of slaves. In this regard white men used the rhetoric of Revolution to reinforce their own sense of exclusiveness, their own sense of superiority (and ultimately political and economic privilege) in relation to other kinds of workers.

In the South, ideologues like Thomas Jefferson glorified the tilling of the soil, and proclaimed the yeoman farmer the backbone of an enlightened citizenry; yet Jefferson and other planters consigned the tilling of their own soil to the lowliest of southern workers, the slaves. And other ironies abounded: Attempting to create a dignified place for wives and daughters in the new order, elite men and women exalted the public role of the "republican mother," though she remained deprived of the vote and property rights that would have allowed her either to establish her own independence or to protect herself from a domestic tyrant in the form of an abusive father or husband. Poor women were accorded no such rhetorical idealization, but instead were supposed to labor under the watchful eye of public officials and private employers – to work and avoid becoming burdens on local charities. For example, the owners of a cotton manufactory in New York City in the 1790s noted the critical labor shortage provoked by the fact that even immigrant workers quit their place at the looms as soon as they were able, so eager were they to own a piece of land and thus "arrive at independence." In their place the owners engaged women and children, the women receiving two dollars a week, the children bound as apprentices until the age of 21.[26] Many workers – for example, almost all who were children – contined to labor under ancient, patriarchal strictures, and the Revolution did little to change their responsibilities in field or workshop.

Finally, a significant segment of free workers included the propertyless workers of seaport cities – disabled soldiers, scavenging in back alleys and scouring the docks for work; emancipated slaves who offered to work for their former owners in return for subsistence only; teamsters who relied on the arrival of a ship in order to be able to feed their families; and recently freed indentured servants pressed into service on a whaling ship bound for the South Pacific. All of these workers were "free" of the traditional constraints imposed by masters, fathers, and slaveowners; but they were also "free" to suffer the vagaries of an unpredictable marketplace, "free" to be fired at a moment's notice, and "free" to fall into any number of exploitative labor arrangements.

Benjamin Franklin himself found it difficult to reconcile these apparent contradictions within an emerging liberal society. No doubt the foundation of economic prosperity was an achieving people, yet in his view not all groups of people could be relied upon to share this vision of the good life. He denigrated Indians as lazy, aspiring only to a life "of freedom from care and labour." In addition, he claimed that the "Majority" of blacks were "of a plotting Disposition, dark, sullen, malicious, revengeful and cruel in the highest Degree." That Franklin later in life helped to found the Pennsylvania Abolition Society, and served as its first president, suggests that his primary aim was to rid white households of the subversives who lived within them, "as every Slave may be reckoned a domestick Enemy."[27] Franklin was convinced that Africans and their descendants were dangerous to the social order because they were enslaved; at the end of the eighteenth century, white elites would begin to claim that Africans and their descendants were dangerous because they were black.

Stinging from the criticism that American slaveholders were hypocritical in their quest for liberty from Britain, Franklin pointed out that there existed a whole host of "free" but degraded workers within the empire – the Scottish "Wretches that dig coal for you," sailors impressed into service on the high seas, and soldiers conscripted into the army.[28] In the eighteenth century, a man or woman who immigrated to America (especially to the North) and "came free" possessed a multitude of possibilities within the world of work; but in the decades after the Revolution, more and more workers would discover that freedom was not absolute, and carried with it its own uncertainties and liabilities.

FURTHER READING

Primary Sources

Allison, Robert, ed. *The Interesting Narrative of the Life of Olaudah Equiano, or Gustavus Vassa, the African.* Boston: Bedford Books, 1995.

Cott, Nancy F., et al., eds. *Root of Bitterness: Documents of the Social History of American Women.* Boston: Northeastern University Press, 1996.

Klepp, Susan E. and Billy G. Smith, eds. *The Infortunate: The Voyage and Adventures of William Moraley, An Indentured Servant.* University Park: Pennsylvania State University Press, 1992.

Smith, Billy G. and Richard Wojtowicz, eds. *Blacks Who Stole Themselves: Advertisement for Runaways in the Pennsylvania Gazette, 1728–1790.* Philadelphia: University of Pennsylvania Press, 1989.

Wallett, Francis G., ed. *The Diary of Ebenezer Parkman, 1703–1782.* Worcester, MA: American Antiquarian Society, 1974.

Secondary Sources

Horn, James. *Adapting to a New World: English Society in the Eighteenth-Century Chesapeake.* Chapel Hill: University of North Carolina Press, 1994.

Littlefield, Daniel C. *Rice and Slaves: Ethnicity and the Slave Trade in Colonial South Carolina.* Baton Rouge: Louisiana State University Press, 1981.

Moss, Richard Shannon. *Slavery on Long Island: A Study in Local Institutional and Early African-American Communal Life.* New York: Garland Press, 1993.

Rediker, Marcus. *Between the Devil and the Deep Blue Sea: Merchant Seamen, Pirates, and the Anglo-American Maritime World, 1700–1750.* Cambridge, MA: Cambridge University Press, 1987.

Salinger, Sharon Y. *"To Serve Well and Faithfully": Labor and Indentured Servants in Pennsylvania, 1682–1800.* Cambridge, MA: Cambridge University Press, 1987.

Schultz, Ronald. *The Republic of Labor: Philadelphia Artisans and the Politics of Class, 1720–1830.* New York: Oxford University Press, 1993.

Smith, Billy G. *The "Lower Sort": Philadelphia's Laboring People, 1750–1800.* Ithaca: Cornell University Press, 1990.

Spruill, Julia Cherry. *Women's Life and Work in the Southern Colonies.* New York: W. W. Norton, 1972; orig. pub. 1938.

Ulrich, Laurel Thatcher, *Good Wives: Image and Reality in the Lives of Women in Northern New England.* New York: Knopf, 1982.

Usner, Daniel H., Jr. *Indians, Settlers, and Slaves in a Frontier Exchange Economy: The Lower Mississippi Valley Before 1783.* Chapel Hill: University of North Carolina Press, 1992.

3

Crosscurrents of Slavery and Freedom in the Antebellum South

Born a slave in Talbot County, Maryland, in 1818, Frederick Douglass later in life emerged as the country's most eloquent proponent of "free labor," and most eloquent opponent of slavery, his critique of the latter institution informed by 20 long, hard years of first-hand observation. Douglass was the son of an enslaved woman and a white man, and his mixed parentage exposed the "racial" basis of bondage as a strategy of social control, rather than a physical fact. Though he labored within a diversified Upper-South economy, he felt the full effects of the system's brutality. Noting the principle of terrorism that undergirded slaveowners' treatment of their slaves, he suggested that the most vulnerable blacks – the elderly, the infirm, and children – were those most likely to be victims of their masters' (or mistresses's) wrath. All his life he remembered the sight of his own aunt, tied to a pole, and whipped "upon her naked back till she was literally covered with blood."[1] Further, Douglass claimed that the custom of allowing enslaved workers to indulge in "sports and merriments" at certain times of the year – "playing ball, wrestling, running foot-races, fiddling, dancing, and drinking whiskey" – were in fact "among the most effective means in the hands of the slaveholder in keeping down the spirit of insurrection."[2]

Slaveholders claimed to preside over a labor system superior to free labor in the North, superior because all slaves, and not just productive ones, remained under the benevolent care of their master. Yet, as Douglass shows in his *Narrative*, enslaved workers concocted a variety of strategies to carve out a sphere of individual and collective autonomy for themselves. In the Chesapeake Bay region, able-bodied men, women, and children eschewed dependence on whites, and fished for oysters and otherwise scrounged for food to make up "the deficiency of their scanty allowance."[3] Even a mistress who began to instruct the young Douglass in the alphabet could not ameliorate a system characterized by the routine separation of families, and the unremitting toil extracted from black people of both sexes and all ages: "Work, work, work, was scarcely more the order of the day than of the night."[4]

Before he escaped to the North, Douglass encountered a variety of white people as co-workers; though the Southern caste system relied upon stark dichotomies between blacks and whites, in fact there existed no explicit "racial" division of labor. As a youth Douglass traded bread for reading lessons while he worked as an errand boy in the company of "poor white children" in Baltimore.[5] Later, he toiled in wheat fields alongside two hired white men, and eventually, as a skilled ship calker, he labored together with whites of the same trade. Inspired by Patrick Henry, Douglass won his freedom by degrees – by reclaiming his "long-crushed spirit" in a fistfight with his master, by colluding with other slaves in an aborted escape attempt, and by gaining permission to hire himself out, an arrangement that enabled him to begin "the work of making money."[6] In 1838, thus emboldened by a wider view of the world, and possessed of the requisite money and courage he needed to make his escape, Douglass found his way to New Bedford, Massachusetts.

The most prosperous southern slaveholders (the men at least) never worked with their hands, but they did labor ceaselessly to protect and advance the peculiar labor system that served as the basis of their wealth and political power. In seeking to justify the enslavement of millions of people within an otherwise liberal and increasingly democratic Western society, planters emerged as accomplished mythmakers, for their generalized and self-satisfied view of the South remained at odds with the complex social relationships embedded in everyday life. In the planters' view, the constitutive parts of Southern society fitted together as neatly as jigsaw pieces, interlocking and revealing a mosaic of whites and blacks, males and females, adults and children, rich and poor, existing in symbiotic relation with one another. The pivot on which this idealized society turned was the responsible citizen, the benevolent patriarch. In 1845, the South Carolina planter and ideologue James Henry Hammond proclaimed, without apparent irony, "I have no hesitation in saying that our slaveholders are kind masters, as men are usually kind husbands, parents, and friends – as a general rule, kinder."[7] In this schema, then, the richest white men assumed responsibility for the welfare of everyone else, while everyone else accommodated themselves to working on behalf of their masters, husbands, fathers, and well-to-do neighbors.

In the course of the antebellum period, the southern elite became a more concentrated and more wealthy group with larger average holdings of slaves. Around the time of the Revolution, 35 percent of the South's free white population were slaveholding families; on the eve of the Civil War, that percentage had dropped to 26 (though the figure was 52 percent in the Cotton South). In 1860, 11,000 Southerners (only three-quarters of 1 percent of all whites) owned more than 50 slaves; 2,358 owned more than 100. Still, the majority of enslaved workers lived on holdings of 20 slaves or more, and on the largest plantations labor was highly specialized, for masters had the luxury of distinguishing between house servants and field hands, and in general were able to parcel out various work assignments on the basis of gender, skills, and age. It was on these estates that black men and women were likely to find mates for themselves, and their families were likely to enjoy some degree of stability, at least until (in many cases) the life-cycle among whites took its horrible toll, a process by which black husbands, wives, and children were given (as "gifts") or bequeathed to young masters and mistresses and thus separated from one another.

Yet not every white Southerner could realistically aspire to become a "lord of the lash," reigning over prosperous, self-sufficient villages devoted to staple-crop production, handicrafts, and extractive industries (like timber and naval stores). In 1860, fully half of all slaveholders owned fewer than five slaves, and in contrast to their social betters, modest slaveowners labored in the fields with their bondsmen and women, and literally could not afford to uphold fine distinctions between the work of whites and blacks. During the last few decades of the antebellum period, the prosperity of rural industries in the Upper South, coupled with a booming cotton economy in the Lower South, pushed the price of slaves ever higher and led to the out-migration of small Black-Belt farmers who could no longer afford to hold onto their land or hire a slave or two during the busy harvest season.

Within this highly stratified society, the very definition of productive labor was varied, but invariably politicized. Indeed, on the plantation, deep in the countryside, and in the cities, different groups of Southerners daily challenged the slaveholders' contention that the mark of an honorable man was his freedom from manual labor. (Some critics in the South charged that elites took this view so far that they ranked even school teaching "among the MENIAL employments," to be shunned by native whites as a group, and left to northern interlopers.)[8] Slaveholding women contended with the irony of their own status; they were "ladies" but hardly leisurely, responsible for managing large households and reproducing the planter class at a furious rate. As free people of color and as slaves, African-American men and women insistently, some boldly and others surreptitiously, resisted the planters' demands that they work well and faithfully to enrich the white household, and instead attempted, with varying degrees of success, to work well and faithfully on their own behalf. In the upcountry, yeomen farmers and their wives toiled to preserve a degree of independence from all of the encumbrances that defined the planter elite – the international staple-crop market, internal improvements, and credit institutions to facilitate transportation and commerce. In cities like New Orleans, Charleston, and Baltimore, boisterous groups of immigrant workers, transient seamen, and slave artisans attempted to pursue their respective self-interests, clashing with each other and with members of the elite – whites who were torn between securing services cheaply on the one hand and ensuring public order on the other. And throughout the South were scattered impoverished people who, bolstered by the the arrogance that came with a white skin, refused to work like slaves.

In fact, the fundamental tension within southern society itself centered upon the planters' frantic attempts to manipulate a number of different labor sources, and not just slaves, in the most efficient way possible. Soon after the War of 1812, textile mill owners initiated a lively discussion among themselves debating the merits of black (slave or free) versus free white laborers as mill operatives. In Virginia on the eve of the Civil War, the northern journalist Frederick Law Olmsted interviewed a tobacco planter in the Tidewater area of Virginia; though a slaveowner, the planter had hired a group of Irish laborers to reclaim swamp land for cultivation because he did not want to risk the health of his slaves on such dangerous work. Some slaveowners engaged in brutal forms of punishment in order to extract compliance from their enslaved workers, while other white men experimented with incentives and rewards to coax slaves to worker harder and produce more. Masters enjoyed the profits earned for them by skilled slave artisans, but they feared the disruption and commotion caused by quasi-free blacks who tried to go about their own business in towns and cities.

The plantation was the core economic unit of southern society and economy, and the plantation existed to organize workers to grow crops and process other natural resources like timber and turpentine. In the Black Belt (the cotton-growing region between the Piedmont and the coastal plain), most workers were enslaved men, women, and children, though, depending on the crop under cultivation and the surrounding local economy, non-elite whites might labor on plantations routinely or sporadically. Some Louisiana sugar estates employed white tenant farmers. Planters at times relied upon the services of white craftsmen for fine woodworking, or white seamstresses for fine needlework. Some planters derived a great deal of power and influence within their local communities in their role as creditors to their poor-white neighbors, and at times debtors could make good on financial obligations with a stint in the fields, picking cotton or harvesting hay. Planters might even take pity on the wife of a local ne'r-do-well, and offer her and her children the chance to work during the busy harvest season in exhange for a small amount of cash. Still, a white man who spent his time hunting and fishing, and allowed his wife to "go in with the niggers and pick," was not considered a working man at all; he and his family were labeled "vagabonds" by their social betters.[9]

In the Black Belt, where large planters held sway over the economic and political life of the community, bonds between whites of various classes coalesced around the rhythms of the cotton-growing season, the shared experience of religious services and political electioneering, and kinship ties. Thus white men of widely divergent statuses might perceive each other as kindred spirits, raising families within a staple crop economy, praying to the same God, making use of the labor of black people to the extent they could afford to do so – in other words, adhering to a "Southern" way of life.

Nevertheless, everyday reality often intruded into this placid view of community and labor relations. For example, the managerial mainstay of the plantation, the overseer, was always a white man. Though he might benefit from association with a prominent planter, every overseer understood that in the South status derived from landownership, and that a white man with any gumption soon moved on to lord over slaves of his own. High turnover rates among overseers, coupled with the fact that they more often than not came from the class of tenants and yeomen farmers, contributed to their problems with their employers. It was not surprising, then, that with their enslaved work forces numbering in the hundreds and sometimes even in the thousands, lowcountry South Carolina rice planters sought to choose their overseers with great care. On James Henry Hammond's Silver Bluff Plantation, a new employee was handed a list of rules and regulations, stipulating that he must never be absent from the plantation without his employer's permission, he must remain in the company of the hands in the fields at all times (though he "will never be expected to work in the Fields"), he must check up on families in their quarters at night, avoid the use of all spiritous liquors, and "cheerfully and faithfully carry into effect the views of the Employer," even though he might disagree with those views.[10] High on the list of overseers' shortcomings were chronic drunkenness and absenteeism, cruelty to slaves, and a general carelessness in discharge of duties. Presiding over expansive plantations in the vicinity of Charleston, John Ball, Sr, once declared "I have not an overseer that is intrinsically worth the hominy he eats."[11] In contrast to their employers, overseers saw the management of slaves as an aggravation, and not as a way of life.

Plantation mistresses gladly appropriated and eagerly helped to promote the overblown rhetoric that glorified their own work within a slave society, but in some respects they fulfilled roles not unlike those of white overseers. On the largest plantations, white wives were essentially managers, coordinating the cooking, cleaning, gardening, and textile-producing activities of slave women; the jumble of keys they carried (to cellars, storehouses and smokehouses, linen closets and silver chests) represented the breadth of their responsibilities. Writing in her diary in 1860, a South Carolina slaveholding woman noted,

> A Plantation life is a very active one. This morning I got up late having been disturbed in the night, hurried down to have something arranged for breakfast, Ham & eggs. . . wrote a letter to Charles. . . had prayers, got the boys off to town. Had work cut out, gave orders about dinner, had the dinner feed fixed in hot water, had the box filled with cork: went to see about the carpenters working at the negro houses.[12]

Like others of her class, this woman worked mainly as a manager, her tasks listed in the passive voice: She had something arranged for breakfast, she had work cut out, she had dinner fixed and the box filled with cork. The workers who carried out these tasks went unnamed.

On the smallest plantations, white wives retained a great deal of authority, but they reddened their own necks with picking cotton or worming tobacco plants in the fields, and coarsened their own hands slaughtering pigs, elbow-to-elbow with enslaved workers. Interviewed when he was 84 years old, Charlie Moses, a former slave living in Brookhaven, Mississippi, recalled that his master, Jim Rankin, worked everyone on the plantation "like animals." Rankin "had a right smart plantation an' kep' all his Niggers, 'cept one house boy, out in the fiel' a-working.'" In Charlie Moses' eyes, the proof of Rankin's rapacity was the role he assigned to his own wife and children: they "had all the work in the house to do, 'ause he wouldn' waste no Nigger to help 'em out."[13] Under the watchful eye of her husband above her, and tormented by the willful resistance of black men, women, and children below her, more than one mistress melodramatically declared herself a "slave of slaves." Yet even the most beleaguered white women understood that their relative comfort and well-being, and their absolute position as members of a superior caste, rested firmly upon the foundation of slavery.

Although the actual tasks performed by enslaved Southerners varied according to their gender, age, and the crop economy within which they labored, it is possible to delineate three kinds of work that virtually all of them did to some degree or another – first, the tasks imposed upon them by a white person, either the master, mistress, overseer, or even at times the masters' (white) children; second, their domestic labors on behalf of their own family members; and finally, "overwork" that might take the form of either petty commodity production or paid labor that the master condoned, or illicit trade that he did not.

The size of a plantation and the degree to which it was specialized profoundly affected all of the work performed by any particular group of slaves. On the largest holdings, male slaves in particular fulfilled highly skilled tasks, and identified themselves as (for example) fulltime shoe-makers, carriage drivers, basket-makers, blacksmiths, carpenters, saddlers, "mechanics" (makers and repairers of tools and machinery), and boatmen. (Along the coast, this last job might be broken down according to the vessel manned – a shallow-draft flat, canoe, lighter, or rowboat – and the position served on it.) Women worked as midwives, seamstresses, weavers, laundresses, maids and cooks, and at times they produced starch, dyes, candles, and soap as well as textiles.

In contrast to the northern and midwestern farm households that were relying increasingly on store-bought supplies, many Southern plantations aspired to self-sufficiency. Charles Hayes, who grew up on an Alabama plantation before the Civil War, remembered that its slaves produced "Most of de things us used," including "beds, buckets, tools, soap, brogans, breeches an' chairs." His parents were typical in the work they performed: "My mammy was a fiel' han' an' my pappy was a mechanic an' he use to be de handy man aroun' do big house, makin' eve' thing f'um churns and buckets and wagon wheels."[14]

Slaveholding men and women had a vested interest in keeping their workers employed year-round regardless of their gender or age. Children were put to work early, and forced to gather kindling wood, tend livestock, keep birds out of the fields, and weed gardens as soon as they were able. Elderly enslaved women at times had responsibility for caring for babies while their mothers were working in the fields. In the Upper South, where extractive industries and grain processing intensified the demand for seasonal labor, masters leased their slaves to owners of mines, mills, and forges for part of the year. Regardless of the local economy, many slaves spent the winter months mending fences, clearing fields, and performing other kinds of maintainence work.

The particular crop economy characteristic of a specific region in the South determined the way that slaves were organized in the fields. Cotton cultivation spread westward and southward after the Revolution, and the invention of the cotton gin in 1791 eliminated a bottle-neck in the processing of the raw fiber. Cotton slaves were worked in gangs, large groups of men and women under the direction of either a black driver or a white overseer. Along with their menfolk, enslaved women prepared fields for cultivation in the spring time, wielded heavy iron hoes (made that way so they could not be easily broken) during the "chopping" season, and moved slowly, stooped over, down the rows at harvest time. Their work days in the fields began at "first light" (dawn) and continued until sundown.

The routines associated with rice planting were markedly different, with daily labor delineated by the task – for example, a quarter of an acre to be hoed, a certain length of a ditch to be dug, a specific number of rice sheaves to be cut and tied. On the largest holdings a predictable gender division of labor pertained outside the fields, where men worked as carpenters, drivers, and mill hands, and women predominated in the jobs of servants and cooks. However, women and men alike labored as prime field hands. Along the coast of South Carolina and Georgia, on large plantations with absentee owners, slaves pushed themselves to complete their assigned task, putting in up to nine hours of strenuous labor by early afternoon, and devoting the rest of the day to tending their own plot of rice around their cabins, fishing for shrimp and other kinds of seafood, tending chickens and hogs, and marketing eggs and meat to the master, to other slaves, or to poor whites in the area. By the late antebellum period, some lowcountry slaves had accumulated modest amounts of property that they then bequeathed to their heirs, a feat that earned them the respect of their families and neighbors.

Louisiana sugar slaves represented an intermediate group of sorts, between cotton workers on the one hand and rice workers on the other. The expansion of the Louisiana sugar industry was marked by the increase in the number of slaves who labored within it – from 20,000 in 1824 to 125,000 in 1861. During this period, small plantations gradually disappeared, and large estates consolidated their holdings in land and slaves. Sugar slaves labored in gangs, men and women alike engaged in the strenuous field work of cutting cane, and, at the end of the season, they spent 18–20 hour days grinding the cane in sugar mills. Nevertheless, enslaved laborers on sugar plantations also worked for themselves, on Saturdays and Sundays, cutting wood that they then sold to the master for use in the mill; collecting and drying Spanish moss to be sold (for mattress stuffing) in a nearby town; marketing vegetables, poultry, and hogs both within and outside the plantation.[15] With the money they earned slaves bought clothing, housewares, pipes, and tobacco. A flourishing underground economy in the Lower Mississippi Valley relied on the bold slaves who stole everything from food to pieces of iron machinery from their masters, and the resourceful white traders who plied the river in boats, offering whiskey and cash in return.

Theoretically, tobacco cultivation, with its intensive 15-month cycle, allowed less room for alternative employments among slaves; however, by the nineteenth century, few large Chesapeake plantations grew the weed exclusively. Instead, small farmers in North Carolina and Virginia cultivated modest amounts of tobacco and also participated in regional economies that relied upon the hiring out of slaves to various proto-industrial enterprises – salt-making and iron-making for example.

After the Civil War, among members of the former slaveholding class and their descendants, the loyal house servant, together with the elderly slave "mammy," became shrouded in the mists of romantic nostalgia. Yet in fact relatively few enslaved women labored their whole lives as the so-called favored domestic servants. On the largest plantations, little girls catered to the whims of fastidious mistresses and their daughters, while older black women worked as nurses, cooks, and maids. Still, only the most elaborate estates could divert the energies of able-bodied women to the kitchen, and out of the fields. In any case, the testimony of former slaves suggests that work under the watchful eye of a mistress carried with it certain difficulties, and even dangers. Domestic labor, which included washing and ironing clothes, preparing meals for large numbers of people, and carrying heavy loads of wood, water and laundry, was arduous. Mistresses varied widely in their attention to detail; some reacted swiftly and violently to the most minor infraction, wielding the nearest weapon at their disposal – a pot of boiling water, a pair of scissors, a knitting needle – and inflicting lifelong scars on the women who displeased them. Domestic servants often slept in the Big House, on call 24 hours a day and thus forcibly separated from family members back in the slave quarters. And finally, younger enslaved women in particular remained vulnerable to fits of jealousy and outbursts of temper on the part of a white woman who suspected, rightly or wrongly, that her husband was sexually abusing a black woman – either the object of her immediate wrath, or someone else. For these reasons, it is clear that the conventional view of house servants – as pampered, well-fed and even smug workers relative to their kinfolk in the fields – is a considerable distortion of their actual duties and the highly charged social context under which those duties were carried out.

Black men and women drew a clear line between the work they performed for their masters and the work they performed for themselves. Slave wives, mothers, and daughters were responsible for child care, food preparation and laundry within the quarters, and in many parts of the South they spun and wove cloth late at night after they had completed the tasks assigned to them by their mistresses. Much of this work was performed in groups. In contrast to slave mothers, who more often than not lived with their own children, slave fathers were more likely to live on a nearby plantation. There is evidence that these "abroad" fathers took their family responsibilities seriously to the extent that they were able, bringing to loved ones a tasty squirrel, possum, or fish (indeed, any game or fish that could be caught without the use of a gun), or fashioning furniture out of pieces of wood.

Together, men and women within the quarters fulfilled roles that remained outside the purview of their masters and mistresses. The opening of the Old Southwest to cotton cultivation spurred the forced migration of enslaved workers from the Upper South to the fresh lands of Alabama and Mississippi; it has been estimated that of the 68,000 black Virginians thus removed during the decade before the Civil War, fully 75 percent were separated from all family members. On the receiving end, black men and women stepped into the breach and served as fictive kin, laboring to integrate the newcomers into a new community of slaves. Moreover, an elaborate hierarchy of status could shape the largest communities – vying for influence and prestige were male preachers and female conjurers and fortune tellers.

While the distinctive meanings of work for whites – in contrast to work for the slave family – seem self-evident, the larger implications of "overwork" are less clear. The general sustenance of slave families constituted a kind of work that ultimately benefited the slaveowner (by helping to preserve and prolong his initial investment), and the opportunity to perform "overwork" often served as an incentive for slaves to work harder, or at least more quickly, at their appointed task. Moreover, some owners deliberately withheld supplies, meting out a paltry ration of food each week, a single pair of shoes for the season, or a threadbare blanket to be shared by family members, thereby encouraging men and women to earn money that could be spent on compensating for such stinginess – an extra portion of flour, new shoes for the children.

With the exception of lowcountry South Carolina slaves, few enslaved African Americans were able to carry on the pervasive, institutionalized trade characteristic of their West Indian counterparts during the first half of the nineteenth century. Yet slaves all over the American South engaged in clandestine trade relations among themselves and poor whites in their immediate vicinity. At times this trade became routinized, as when "chicken thieves" – boats of white traders and scavengers – traveled up and down the Mississippi River, docking at riverbanks under the cover of darkness, and offering their slave suppliers liquor in return for any ill-gotten gain plundered from nearby plantations. More often, individual slaves took their chances and bartered the fruits of their own labor, or a chicken surreptitiously plucked from the henhouse, or a ham carefully appropriated from the smokehouse, to anyone who could offer them something in return.

Planters throughout the South condemned this form of slave initiative, involving as it often did some form of collusion with poor whites, and some form of theft. In the eyes of the master, the illicit appropriation of goods was immoral, an act defying the biblical commandment "Thou shalt not steal." In contrast, as otherwise uncompensated laborers, slaves considered theft an extension of legitimate forms of "overwork"; they were merely claiming their due. By the late antebellum period elites tended to see proto-abolitionists lurking everywhere, and it was always difficult to tell whether a late-night encounter between a slave and a white tenant farmer involved the exchange of whiskey, or a more nefarious exchange of news from the fanatical, abolitionist North.

Gradually then, the trading that slaves had routinely engaged in during the colonial period was redefined as "trafficking" with poor whites and increasingly identified with political subversion. A white woman, Mrs Francis M. Dougles of Hanover County, Virginia, became suspicious in the summer of 1821 when she spied two vegetable peddlers, one an "elderly white man with red whiskers," and the other "an old tall and very black negro man" talking together. The two men were apparently taking the opportunity of exchanging cabbage in order to discuss "in a very low tone" how "they were all of Adams race or words to that purport."[16] In Mrs Dougles's view, the cabbage was only a pretense while the two men conspired. In 1846, planters in the vicinity of Augusta, Georgia, formed the Savannah River Anti-Slave Traffick Association, a group dedicated to halting slaves from "plundering" the countryside at night, an evil supposedly akin to a "serpent knawing at society's vitals."[17]

In assessing the nature of black people's resistance to slavery, it is possible to interpret virtually every form of "self-activity" as proto-political behavior. Indeed, simple acts of family nurturance could stand in stark contrast to the slaveholder's crass calculations about the market value of any one black person. Working slowly or carelessly, breaking farm implements, letting the cows stray into the corn, burning the biscuits, spilling coffee in the lap of an honored guest – the opportunities for aggravating the master and mistress were endless, if ultimately dangerous to the well-being of a particular slave. Planters varied in their responses to these kinds of behavior. The shrewdest kept families together and offered incentives for individuals to do their work quickly and well. The most short-sighted engaged in sadistic forms of punishment – whipping pregnant women who were laid face-down in a trench in the field – and separating family members out of spite.

Everyday acts of resistance blurred the lines among family life, work, and culture as these factors shaped the lives of black people in the quarters and in the fields and Big House. Therefore, we might place discrete kinds of behavior, or cultural sensibilities, on a continuum, with overt acts of violent rebellion – Nat Turner's revolt of 1831, for example – at one end, and diverting one's energies to attend to one's family at the other end, with a whole realm of experience, from creating and maintaining African-American religious practices to instances of informal sabotage, somewhere in the middle.

Historians have debated the profitability of slavery as a labor system; while it is true that planters provided for the subsistence of workers who were not yet, or not any longer, productive (infants and the disabled elderly), it is also true that by the late antebellum period the price of cotton had pushed the price of slaves to unprecedented highs. Although a very few of the wealthiest slaveowners lived extravagantly (and the ones who did often relied on massive amounts of credit), many others lived in more modest circumstances, and they and their wives and children routinely worked in the fields. Nevertheless, it is important to keep in mind that slavery was not only a method of organizing labor; it also amounted to a means by which the elite organized their world, one in which the strong had a duty to oversee the lives and labor of the weak. Therefore, the profits white men derived from this world cannot be measured in financial terms only, for these profits were also political.

Every planter-husband considered the best uses to which his wife, slaves, debtors, and hirelings might be put, and few of those decisions were set in stone, or irrevocable. Indeed, as we have seen, in times and places where cotton prices were especially high, a household head might decide to concentrate the energies of his slaves in the fields, and assign his wife the more traditional domestic duties that had been performed by black women the week before; or an owner might arrange to hire a group of white men to perform particularly onerous tasks in the fields. These examples serve as reminders that the margins of labor on any plantation were fungible – that in most instances slaves provided the bulk of manual labor, but that white wives (or white hirelings and overseers) might be called upon to work with their hands at any particular time. In addition, a sudden reversal in a planter's fortunes, or routine events in family life, such as marriages and deaths, could result in the sale of or bequest of slaves; the plantation was not a fixed entity but a fluid process, always changing in response to labor supply and demand at the most immediate level of any white family. These examples of flexibility in labor roles and labor availability were not exactly what planters had in mind when they marveled at the harmonious innerworkings of Southern society.

Since slavery was an inherently aggressive system in both political and economic terms, the planter elite was forced to remain ever vigilant, ready to defeat the designs of antislavery Northerners in Congress, ready to seek out new and fresh lands to replace their old and exhausted ones. Yet not all white rural households shouldered such momentous responsibilities. For the modest slaveholder, or the nonslaveholding yeoman farmer, work consisted of keeping his family alive and contributing to community networks of exchange not unlike those in the eighteeenth-century rural North. (Yeomen, who constituted at least half of all white families in the antebellum South, owned fewer than 150 acres of land and less than ten slaves.)[18] In the upcountry, farmers produced more corn than cotton, and their wives did their own spinning and weaving. A yeoman farmer might own a slave or two, or he might lease one for the season, producing the striking sight of a white wife and her daughters laboring in the corn fields next to an enslaved man or woman.

Though seemingly innocuous forms of household maintenance, these tasks performed by the farmer working his own
land and the wife spinning thread and weeding corn fields
assumed heightened political significance within the antebellum South, for by the 1850s the expansive cotton economy of
the slaveholders had already begun to encroach on the Piedmont, bringing with it banks, railroads, and crop liens. The
yeomen continued to prize their "independence," but it was
independence from neither toil nor economic uncertainty –
rather a tenuous aloofness from a worldwide staple-crop
economy that was bound to show no mercy to hardworking
nonslaveholders and their families.

At the bottom of the southern white social structure were
landless white men and women who moved from place to
place, and did their best to eschew the hard labor that was
the lot of every slave. These were squatters who lived off the
land and preferred to pursue wild turkeys rather than hoe
and chop cotton. In their material standard of living they lived
lives similar to those of slaves and the poor class of free
people of color; they were whiskey-besotted, superstitious and
promiscuous (so went the charge leveled by their social betters), neither producing nor consuming, refusing to hire themselves out to work, akin to "the wild Indian of the forest, or
the European gypsy."[19] Throughout the rural South, impoverished white and free black women were in constant danger of
being declared "unfit mothers," and their children seized by
local courts and bound out to landowners as "apprentices."
Indeed, pressed to describe the poor people of either color,
slaveholders could find precious little to recommend them either as neighbors or as workers.

In fact landless whites did labor, though not necessarily in
the field and according to the forced pace that the planters
demanded. Some, in the South's Wiregrass region along the
Atlantic or Gulf coast, herded cattle, and their seemingly
nomadic way of life masked a livelihood that was modest
but not necessarily impoverished. Others boarded travellers
and sold firewood to their neighbors; their wives made
clothes and sold them, or performed domestic service for the

well-to-do. Some white men made a living one step ahead of the law, as highwaymen, cattle rustlers, and slave stealers.

It was not unusual to see blacks and whites working together, at the same task, throughout the rural South. Among the most racially integrated worksites of the antebellum South were those rural industries that relied upon flexible labor systems from one season of the year to the next. The construction of transportation networks like canals and railroads claimed the energies of black and white men working together. In addition, by the late antebellum period the Southern backcountry was dotted with small-scale operations of various kinds, most of them dependent upon local natural resources – naval stores in North Carolina, coal mining in Virginia and Alabama, the salt industry in the western part of Virginia, lumber rafting along the Mississippi river, rock quarries in western North Carolina, gold mines in Georgia, sugar mills in Louisiana, and sawmills scattered throughout the region. These enterprises at times attracted white farmers looking for wage work during the slack season, or itinerant laborers who sought out day work wherever they could find it. In the 1840s, a Virginia coal mine boasted a diverse work force consisting of 130 free Negroes, "several newly arrived laborers from England," and "old Virginians, also, of the white race. . . although their countrymen looked down upon them at first for associating with such companions."[20]

Rural nonagricultural industries were complementary to plantations; that is, slaveowners might operate a mill on their own, or lease their slaves to one in the neighborhood, during the slack season. When cotton prices were high, leased slaves were expensive, if not impossible to procure. Moreover, owners at times hoped to find employment for slaves they considered superfluous – children and the elderly, for example. In this sense, tobacco-processing factories and textile mills served to absorb otherwise unproductive workers. On the other hand, slaveowners remained alert to the dangers posed by certain kinds of work and balked at hiring out their slaves to owners of coal mines, iron forges, and salt works. Some employers of leased slaves were notoriously lax about their health and safety, prompting an owner to insist on contracts that prohibited certain kinds of work for their slaves: In 1856, a Virginia salt company signed a lease for "The negro Jim [who] is not to be worked in Coal Bank or as a kettle-tender, nor to be compelled to work on Sundays."[21]

As they pieced together their labor forces, rural industrialists and other kinds of managers (like railroad construction officials) confronted a variety of trade-offs. Tasks that were dangerous or otherwise unappealing attracted few white wage-earners; on the other hand, the slaves leased for those purposes were quick to complain to their owners about dangerous working conditions, and in turn owners were loath to risk such valuable property in such hazardous situations. White men of the landless classes were notoriously difficult to discipline; they staged walk-outs if disappointed with their paychecks or angered by a foreman's curses, they came to work drunk and left early to go fishing. For these reasons many textile mill owners preferred black slave labor to white free labor – not because of any essential differences between whites and blacks, but because slaves were more easily disciplined and kept on site, compared to white operatives regardless of their gender, age, or marital status.

The problem of women's textile work in the antebellum South suggests the ways that social context might transform the larger significance of any particular task, no matter how routine or mundane. The poorest Southern households lacked the bulky spinning wheels and looms that were so ubiquitous throughout the colonial North, equipment rendered increasingly superfluous in that area of the country by the onset of industrialization. The inability of these poor Southern women either to make their own cloth or to purchase (much of) it signified the dire straits in which they found themselves within a society supposedly divided between two groups – enslaved blacks and landed whites.

In many instances, enslaved women and the wives of slaveholders and yeoman farmers all had access to the means of textile production, but the political economy of the South invested their labors with contasting meanings. Women on modest homesteads in the Black Belt, the Piedmont, or the mountains of Kentucky and Tennessee contributed to family economies that remained outside the staple-crop marketplace dominated by large planters. In these cases, spinning and weaving (like the growing of corn) served to preserve the autonomy of individual households – or rather, local networks of exchange – in opposition to the staple-crop economy, which relied on elaborate systems of finance and marketing.

Enslaved women perceived their own labors spinning thread and weaving cloth in quite different ways. Forced at the end of a long day to spin a "cut" of thread or weave a set number of yards (eventually to be sewn into clothing for the master and his family), black women saw this kind of work as an extra burden to be shouldered. On the other hand, allowed the time to work on behalf of their own families, they worked with a sense of purpose – perhaps not happily, but at least secure in the knowledge that their families would derive some benefit from their toil. In contrast, slaveholding women delegated textile-production tasks to their slaves whenever they could afford to do so; to a woman of wealth, or a woman who aspired to wealth, such labor represented a thankless job better foisted upon slaves.

And finally, diverse groups of women textile operatives working machines no doubt brought any number of sentiments to bear on their own labors, depending upon whether they were enslaved women relieved to be released from the rigors of field work if only for a short time, or poor white women chafing under the stigma of wage work within an overwhelmingly agricultural society. The antebellum period affords numerous examples of blacks and whites working together in the small textile mills that dotted the fall line through the Piedmont sections of South Carolina and Georgia. At the same time, some white entrepreneurs were convinced that the mills should serve as a means of "domesticating" the white poor; in this view "every cotton mill established in the South [is] a *machine* for the conversion of many to favor the domestic industry of the country – by seeing the good effects of such mills . . . in affording employment to the labouring poor."[22]

William Gregg of Edgefield District, South Carolina, took this view to its logical conclusion and by the late 1840s was employing 300 "white laborers, native to the soil," most of them young women, in his mill.[23]

Some observers argued that the all-white textile mill force was one of economic convenience rather than political principle – slaves were becoming increasingly expensive and confined to work in the cotton fields, and poor whites were the only untapped labor source in the rural South. In any case, employers complained bitterly about the high rate of labor turnover among the young white women, their lack of loyalty to any one employer, their nasty habit of turning out for higher wages and better working conditions. Before the Civil War at least, the debate among Southern elites over the relative viability of black and white textile workers – blacks could be driven hard and paid nothing at all, but whites were better off living in mill villages than scrounging for food on the countryside – remained unresolved.

If textile mill villages confounded the neat, idealized world of the planters, where all blacks were field workers and all whites prospered as a result, labor patterns in Southern cities also bore little resemblance to the organic society of master-class lore. In a region otherwise characterized by (white) religious and ethnic homogeneity, Southern cities were relatively diverse; in a region marked by the extensive use of blacks as agricultural laborers, cities relied on black workers, slave and free, male and female, in a variety of capacities; and in a region ruled by an elite determined to maintain black–white distinctions, cities were raucous and disorderly places, where white mechanics clashed with their slaveholding betters, and where slaveholding elites disagreed among themselves about the proper limits of black life and labor.

There existed no overarching racial division of labor in the antebellum South, though blacks predominated in certain trades and crafts in certain cities. In cities like Baton Rouge, Mobile, Charleston, and New Orleans, foreign immigrants (primarily from Germany and Ireland) constituted a substantial proportion of both skilled and unskilled working men.

These newcomers jockeyed with two distinct groups – slaves and free (often skilled) Negroes – for a foothold in the Southern urban economy. Charleston affords a useful example of the rivalries that smoldered between free and enslaved, white and black workers in antebellum Southern cities. In Charleston, Irish immigrants managed to displace slaves from unskilled and semi-skilled day-labor (nondomestic) jobs in the construction and transportation industries and in mills, iron foundries, and leather-tanning industries. The overall immigrant population of Charleston constituted 40 percent of the city's white population by 1860; in contrast, the black population declined by 5,000 during this period, as slaveowners diverted their labor forces from urban trades to cotton-picking in the expanding Southwest. Once again, then, white employers chose their work forces on the basis of supply – which workers were available – rather than on some preconceived notions of what all black people, or all white people, should do.

In Charleston, the Irish enjoyed dramatic success in forcing blacks out of the drayage trade. (A similar dynamic applied in New Orleans.) One local Charleston judge remarked in 1855, "I am afraid there is an inclination to make war upon the Negro. Not many years since one of the only two Irishmen who drove drays in the city . . . was tried . . . for knocking out the eye of a slave, his competitor."[24] Within the space of a decade, from 1850 to 1860, the Irish share of drayage jobs in the city increased from one-seventh to two-thirds.

Moreover, the Irish came to constitute a sizable proportion (one-third) of the city's police force, affording them a measure of upward mobility, this of course in the absence of competition from blacks, slave or free, who were barred from such a position. Yet these white immigrants had less luck in competing directly with certain black workers – those men who had formed an integral part of the city's skilled laboring population for generations. Free black men continued to predominate as carpenters and butchers, though they faced stiff competition from the Irish as coopers and painters and plasterers. Irish workers exhibited high rates of geographical mobility, and lacked the political clout to force the city's leaders to exclude black workers from specific kinds of jobs. Their status as menial hirelings garnered them little in the way of respect from white employers. In 1855, a group of Irish railroad workers went on strike for higher wages; the police rounded them up and threw them in jail.

Each city exhibited a unique division of labor among native-born whites, immigrants, slaves, and free Negroes. New Orleans boasted large numbers of skilled free black workers as carpenters, masons, cigar makers, shoemakers, and tailors. In Baltimore members of the same group predominated as stevedores, grain-measurers, coal handlers, and warehousemen. The tobacco factories of Richmond and Petersburg relied upon the labor of enslaved men, women, and children.

In the South, the class of free Negroes belied the notion that all free men were white, and all blacks were slaves. Concentrated in the Upper South, most free rural blacks were poor, forced to scratch together a living through day work or domestic service. In 1860, about 13 percent of all Upper-South blacks were free; one-third lived in cities, as opposed to only 1.5 percent of blacks living in the Lower South. Still, the majority of the country's free Negroes lived in the South in 1860 – 262,000 in contrast to the North's 226,000 (the former figure represented 3 percent of the South's free families). In the urban South, free black men and women created enduring community institutions, founded and sustained by individual livelihoods that were either poorly paid or becoming increasingly tenuous in the course of the antebellum period. Savannah women worked as seamstresses and dressmakers, washerwomen, and cooks, but managed to play an active role in supporting the city's three African Baptist Churches. Like Catherine Baty, pastry cook, some women managed to save their earnings and purchase real estate – in Baty's case, property on Pierce Street worth $1,150 in 1860. A few daring souls persisted in teaching school for black children.

Throughout the urban South, free Negroes possessed skills that earned them the respect of their communities, and imbued in individual men and women a profound sense of pride and self-worth. The evolution of a class of highly self-conscious, skilled urban slaves served to enrich their owners, but not all white city folk were convinced that the economic benefits were worth the risks. And at times it was difficult to draw the line between enslaved and free black workers, so potent was the danger both groups posed to the social order. In Charleston in 1822, a skilled, literate, well-traveled free black man, a carpenter named Denmark Vesey, drew upon a collective, revolutionary consciousness among black men who labored together in shops and mingled in taverns after-hours. Chafing under a system that denied him his family (his wife and children were still enslaved), the fruits of his own labor, and even the freedom to worship in the church of his choice, Vesey cited the Bible in a call to arms: "Behold the day of the Lord cometh, and thy spoil shall be divided in the midst of thee. For I shall gather all nations against Jerusalem to battle, and the city shall be taken." He and his co-conspirators devised a plot that was nearly a nightmare come true for the city's white citizens; they apparently intended to attack the city's arsenal and guardhouse, and then flee the country. Yet before they could carry through with the plan, they were betrayed by an informer. Eventually, thirty conspirators were hanged and many more were deported.

In the aftermath of the Vesey conspiracy, the white citizens in Charleston expressed a well-founded fear of all skilled blacks who controlled their own work lives; "Irregularity of habits is thus acquired," a group of whites wrote in a petition to the state legislature, and "this irregularity produces restlessness of disposition, which delights in mischief and detests quiet." Petitioners called for the exclusion of all blacks from "the mechanical arts," the abandonment of the practice of letting slaves hire their own time, and, just for good measure, the banishment of all blacks to the countryside: "In this manner we will exchange a dangerous portion of our population for a class of persons [white mechanics] 'whose feelings will be our feelings, and whose interests our interests.'"[25]

Charleston elites understood that the urban mix of transient whites, free blacks, and enslaved blacks posed a constant threat to social stability. Between voyages, black and white seamen languished in the ports of New Orleans, Savannah, and Charleston, at times looking for day work, at other times looking for trouble. This group of men played a key role in urban underground economies of stolen goods, including weapons of various kinds. Their social-demographic profile – mostly young, unmarried men without much in the way of landlubbers' skills – meant that they were a prime target for law enforcement officials ever vigilant to perpetrators of crimes like disturbing the peace, fencing stolen goods, and patronizing prostitutes.

Urban elites worried with some justification that black people who performed specific kinds of work posed a hazard to social order generally. In 1810, the city council of Richmond passed an ordinance barring blacks from the jobs of teamster and drayman, apparently on the assumption that such workers routinely transported stolen goods. South Carolina sought to bar free black seamen from the port of Charleston, on the assumption that such workers transported from the North or Europe the subversive ideas of the abolitionists. Black men put to work on street construction projects had the opportunity to collude among themselves in plotting any number of misdeeds. Slaves given the run of the city served as messengers in underground communication networks. Slaves working on or near the water faced the constant temptation to run away, and eagerly learned of possible escape routes from people of their own race or from "no-account" whites. Slaves who, pokerfaced, waited on white diners, overheard indiscreet conversations and also possessed unique opportunities to poison food. Ultimately, then, virtually every black urban worker posed a potential threat to white supremacy. Echoing his counterparts in Charleston, one Virginian noted, "nothing will more effectually counteract projects for insurrection than to devote the labors of slaves and free blacks to agriculture; there might be a few exceptions, but the circumstances to warrant them ought to be very strong."[26]

Slaveowners *qua* public officials fully understood the political imperatives that mandated urban slaves be monitored closely and barred from certain kinds of work if at all

possible. But slaveowners *qua* profit-seekers were more tolerant of the autonomy of their hired slaves (if not of free Negroes). Thus demands like the one from a white man in Athens
in 1838, on behalf of white bricklayers and joiners, to "make
it penal to prefer negro mechanic labor to white men's" – fell
on deaf ears. In 1858, two hundred mechanics and laborers
in Atlanta petitioned the City Council to ban slave mechanics
owned by absentee masters, black men who "are of no benefit to the city" and in their quasi-free state stood to gain to
the degree that white men lost their sources of livelihood.[27]
White working men as a group learned soon enough that the
color of their skin was a less significant factor in finding and
keeping work than the wages they were willing to work for.
In 1847, a group of skilled white iron puddlers employed in
the Richmond Tredegar iron works withdrew from work when
the first black puddlers made their appearance. The white men
were fired and replaced by all black workers, in the process
learning a harsh lesson about the triumph of class interests
over caste sensibilities.

In 1837, Frederick Douglass was working as a hired slave
in a racially integrated shipyard in Baltimore when suddenly,
one day, "the white carpenters knocked off, and said they
would not work" with him. For years, white and black (both
free and enslaved) ship carpenters had labored side by side
without apparent animosity. Now apparently the whites feared
that it was just a matter of time before the blacks took "the
trade into their own hands, and poor white men would be
thrown out of employment." Soon too the white apprentices,
youths of Douglass's age, "began to put on airs, and talk about
the 'niggers' taking the country, saying we all ought to be
killed." They proceeded to beat him bloody with a brick, a
handspike, and their fists.[28] The black man recovered, and he
soon set about plotting his escape. Within a year he had fled
to the North.

In New Bedford, Massachusetts, Douglass embarked on a
new life; but when he "went in pursuit of a job of calking . . .
such was the strength of prejudice against color, among the
white calkers, that they refused to work with me, and of course

I could get no employment." The journey north to freedom meant that Douglass the skilled enslaved workman would now become Douglass the free hod carrier and chimney sweep. He had exchanged the calker's tools for the saw and the shovel. And he once again encountered white men who feared, for much less reason than their Southern counterparts, that the appearance of a lone black worker meant that inevitably, "poor white men would be thrown out of employment."

FURTHER READING

Primary Sources

Commons, John R., et al., eds. *A Documentary History of American Industrial Society*. 10 vols. New York: Russell and Russell, 1958.

Faust, Drew Gilpin, ed. *The Ideology of Slavery: Proslavery Thought in the Antebellum South, 1830–1860*. Baton Rouge: Louisiana State University Press, 1981.

Mullin, Michael, ed. *American Negro Slavery: A Documentary History*. Columbia, SC: University of South Carolina Press, 1976.

Olmsted, Frederick Law. *A Journey in the Back Country, 1853–1854*. New York: Schocken Books; orig. pub. 1860.

Rawick, George P. *The American Slave: A Composite Autobiography*. 19 vols. Supp. series I: 12 vols. Supp. series II: 10 vols. Westport, CT: Greenwood Press, 1972–9.

Secondary Sources

Berlin, Ira. *Slaves Without Masters: The Free Negro in the Antebellum South*. New York: Vintage Books, 1974.

Bolton, Charles C. *Poor Whites of the Antebellum South: Tenants and Laborers in Central North Carolina and Northeast Mississippi*. Durham: Duke University Press, 1994.

Cecil-Fronsman, Bill. *Common Whites: Class and Culture in Antebellum North Carolina*. Lexington: University Press of Kentucky, 1992.

Dew, Charles B. *Bond of Iron: Master and Slave at Buffalo Forge*. New York: W. W. Norton, 1994.

Genovese, Eugene. *Roll, Jordan, Roll: The World the Slaves Made*. New York: Vintage, 1976.

Hudson, Larry E. *To Have and to Hold: Slave Work and Family Life in Antebellum South Carolina*. Athens: University of Georgia Press, 1997.

Jones, Jacqueline. *Labor of Love, Labor of Sorrow: Black Women, Work and the Family from Slavery to the Present.* New York: Basic Books, 1985.

Joyner, Charles. *Down by the Riverside: A South Carolina Slave Community.* Urbana: University of Illinois Press, 1984.

McDonald, Roderick A. *The Economy and Material Culture of Slaves: Goods and Chattels on the Sugar Plantations of Jamaica and Louisiana.* Baton Rouge: Louisiana State University Press, 1993.

Reidy, Joseph. *From Slavery to Agrarian Capitalism in the Cotton Plantation South: Central Georgia, 1800–1880.* Chapel Hill: University of North Carolina Press, 1992.

White, Deborah Gray. *Ar'n't I a Woman? Female Slaves in the Plantation South.* New York: W. W. Norton, 1985.

4

The Northern Laboring Classes at Odds with One Another, Before and During the Civil War

At the beginning of Louisa May Alcott's 1873 novel *Work*, Christie Devon, the earnest young heroine, is an orphan living in the home of her aunt and uncle somewhere in New England. Aunt Betsy is a kindly person, but Christie chafes under the authority of Uncle Enos, a farmer "whose soul was wrapped up in prize cattle and big turnips," a man, then, "whose soul was in his pocket."[1] In a bid to fulfill her ambition "to be a useful, happy woman," and to earn "the possession of a brave and cheerful spirit," Christie leaves the farm of her guardians and embarks on a picaresque journey through the world of antebellum New England work. She begins by scorning the employment that consumed the energies of countless other unmarried women – "no humdrum district school to imprison her everyday" – and takes a position as a servant instead. However, the mistress of the house where she works "took no more personal interest in her servants than if they were clocks, to be wound up once a day, and sent away the moment they get out of repair."

Christie continues her quest for a satisfying position: "I like to work for people whom I can respect." A stint as an actress provides an outlet for her creative talents, but she leaves the theatre troupe just in the nick of time, before she can become "selfish, frivolous, and vain." Next, as the governess for the children of a wealthy, shallow couple, she endures the opprobrium of their fashionable friends – "she's a dowdy thing, always trailing round with a book and those horrid children" – and turns down the chance for a "promotion" in the form of a marriage proposal from an aristocratic gentleman. Christie's suitor seems to be a generous and kind-hearted man, but she is lucky enough to catch his "tone of unconscious condescencion" toward her, and she flees, contemputously turning her back on "vanity, ambition, and the love of pleasure." A year tending an invalid girl leaves our heroine "weary but well satisfied," and she goes on to accept a job as a seamstress. Yet here in the crowded workshop she resents the unreasonable demands of a mean-spirited employer. Declares Christie on her way out the door, "I'll do slop-work and starve, before I'll stay with such a narrow-minded cold-hearted woman." Apparently (according to Alcott), New England was full of Christies, young women "willing to work, yet unable to bear the contact with coarser natures which makes labor seem degrading, or to endure the hard struggle for the bare necessities of life when life has lost all that makes it beautiful." Christie eventually marries a young man named David Sterling; he is more akin to a brother surrogate than a love-interest, and Alcott quickly takes him out of the picture by sending him off to fight for the Union cause, "for the gun fired one April morning at Fort Sumter told many men like David what their work was to be." David Sterling's young widow, now a mother, finds a new career for herself as a speaker on behalf of women's labor reform, and she achieves a modest economic self-sufficiency through the cultivation of flowers and fruit; of her own labors and those of her friends Christie tells her aged Uncle Enos, "We don't make bargains, sir; we work for one another and share everything together." Alcott leaves her heroine bereft of a boss but possessed of the pride that comes with productive labor that finds its ample reward in the form of self-satisfaction, if not cash – perhaps "a hopeful omen, seeming to promise that the coming generation will not only receive but deserve their liberty."[2]

In *Work*, Alcott intended Christie Devon to represent Everywoman, buffeted by the dramatic transformations that were reshaping the antebellum New England society and economy. In fact, however, Alcott had a specific group of women in mind when she chronicled the tribulations of this particular woman worker. Among the middling landowning classes of the rural North, women were losing their function as household producers and assuming a new role, that of consumers in the marketplace. Hired servant girls were no longer "help" working as adopted daughters within the households of neighbors; now they were wage earners, their social position considerably diminished in communities where cash counted for more than character in shaping the social structure. A foreign visitor to the United States in the late 1850s noted that the prevailing opinion among native-born whites seemed to be that "white men ought to trade and cultivate farms, and that white women are their proper helpmates, and should scorn to serve, save in their own households and in behalf of their own husbands and children."[3]

The out-migration of men into the Midwest and Far West created a whole new class of women workers – maiden aunts, "spinsters," dependent on their kinfolk and (like Alcott herself) yearning for a kind of "usefulness" that would transcend the routine drudgery of domestic chores. Some women turned their attention to the world outside their homes, to "social housekeeping," in an effort to infuse a "female" moral sensibility into an increasingly crass society. Yet in some respects, Alcott's Christie Devon is the female counterpart to the journeyman shoemaker of the same period, a man who took pride in his craft but found himself displaced – in this case, by machines – and forced to work for wages while someone else enjoyed the benefits – in this case, the profits. Historians have chronicled in detail the process by which skilled artisans in certain trades underwent forced de-skilling when they took on new factory jobs that reduced production to a series of incremental, simple steps performed by employees who needed little in the way of experience or formal training. Thus the colonial craftsman, working in a household-shop with the help of his wife, children, and assistants, yielded to the factory worker deprived of a competence (that is, the ability to support his family, own his own tools and land, and control his own livelihood).

This view of antebellum Northern workers possesses an elegiac quality. It is true that the plight of formerly independent workers now reduced to the status of employees serves as a reminder that the historic processes of economic change in general and technological innovation in particular often leave whole groups of people behind, and in some cases even renders them poverty-stricken. And it is true that, with the rise of a bourgeois society in the North, certain traditional values – the respect for women as producers as well as nurturers, the economic interconnectedness of neighboring households – gradually faded, to be replaced by a society characterized by the glorification of individual (male) workers pursuing opportunities wherever they could find them and earning a "living wage" (that is, enough money to support a family).

At the same time, a single-minded focus on displaced craftsmen (or displaced productive housewives) is misleading for several reasons. First, it romanticizes the lives and labors of colonial workers, a simplistic view of any group in the past. Second, it obscures the fact that many different kinds of workers embraced wage-earning as an alternative way of life from that of working for father-patriarchs on the farm, English landlords in Ireland, and masters and mistresses of all kinds of servants. Third, by positing a single male working class, or a single group of Northern housewives, this view flattens the antebellum social landscape and leaves many other different kinds of workers historically invisible. We should consider a whole range of working classes, male and female, immigrant and native-born, if we are to gauge the effects of the Northern political economy on workers in general. And finally, an emphasis on the process of labor displacement hinders our understanding of African-American workers, who faced nearly insurmountable legal, political, and economic barriers in their struggle to adequately provide for themselves and their families. Denied the right to vote and the opportunity to move in search of better jobs and to send their children to public schools, many blacks in the Northern states became scapegoats, easy targets for white men anxious about their own futures. Ultimately, the once-proud shoemaker now reduced to working as a cog in a factory retained a kind of political power that the African-American worker did not. For many aggrieved white workers, their loss of status was purely relative.

Although the New England village began to lose its insularity as a collection of interdependent households, the North as a whole continued to demonstrate a corporate ethos, symbolized most dramatically by the rise of state-sponsored public school systems. (Nevertheless, it is significant that most forms of employment required informal on-the-job training, rather than formal schooling.) Workers in a variety of industries launched craft-based labor unions, most of which lacked long-term staying power but nonetheless countered to a modest extent the ideal of (white male) individualism that pervaded the North during this period. A new ideology of middle-class womanhood posited the stability and universality of "women's sphere," a source of moral ballast in a rapidly changing world. In addition, the emergence of a whole host of professional classes – combined with the rise of political parties and the appearance of a dense network of moral-reform organizations – spurred the growth of horizontal associations and thereby knit together various groups of people throughout the region.

The facts of population growth, territorial expansion, and dynamic economic development exist in striking contrast to the themes of loss and degradation suggested by certain contemporaries and historians who focus only on the children and grandchildren of colonial middling folk. The migrants who spilled out of New England and into western New York, Ohio, and the upper Midwest, and who trekked as far as California and Oregon, began their journeys with a sense of the possibilities inherent in a vast and sweeping landscape. The emergence of an integrated national market – with the East producing manufactured goods, the South staple crops, and the Midwest grain and cattle – was facilitated by revolutions in the technology of transportation (steamboats and railroads) and communication (the telegraph and a national print culture). Whole new job categories made a dramatic appearance, now that workers were needed to produce everything from sewing machines and canal barges to farm implements and ready-made clothing.

Eastern merchants shipped a variety of goods west, and those goods were made in a variety of settings, including garrets, artisans' shops, factories, homes, barns, and sweatshops. The diversity of work settings mirrored the diversity of workers – widows sewing in tiny attic quarters, child workers tending textile looms in factories, young women braiding straw hats at home, native-born men laboring in machine shops, and Irish immigrants and black people working as teamsters and canal diggers.

Technological innovation proceeded unevenly (by the time of the Civil War, only the shoe and textile industries were fully mechanized), and high rates of residential mobility among many Americans (especially the poorest) inhibited the development of a single, unified "working class." Instead, working classes (including self-consciously literate white housewives, and African Americans with a common historical memory, no less than the white male members of skilled-trades associations) proliferated throughout the North, and in their divergent work experiences they remained fragmented and alienated from one another. Moreover, various working classes reconfigured themselves over time, as shifting forms of self-identification involving race, ethnicity, gender, religion, and pride of craft yielded the core of social identity among men and women in the North. Loyalties – to a particular job, church, or kin group – were ever changing in response to political, social, and economic developments.

In fact, although workingmen's trade organizations and political parties made a tentative appearance during the antebellum period, conflicts among different groups of workers were often more raw and bitter than those between workers and their employers. In urban areas especially, intra-class animosities took the form of street performances, and black people, who were likely to work out of doors, proved vulnerable to the wrath of immigrants and declining tradesmen who sought to retain, or win, group advantages within this new, roiling economy. Northern workers, then, represented a variety of group identities, and those identities could assume a violent, almost tribalistic, quality.

During the period between the Revolution and the Civil War, wage-earning – that is, working for people other than kin, for money – overtook farming as the most common form of labor outside the home. In 1855, 82 percent of New York City's working population worked for wages. Even New England farms registered the effects of economic change; after 1830, farm hands tended to be young transients, largely poor; in ever greater numbers, native-born boys (and girls), from the mountains of New Hampshire to the undulating hills of Pennsylvania, considered the farm to be a bleak place, and chose to work in mills, find jobs as store clerks, or follow a trade instead of toiling for their fathers in the fields (or their mothers in the kitchen).[4] At the same time, the New England farm was becoming a more productive place compared to its colonial counterpart, as a plethora of new consumer goods spurred individual farmers to earn more money by clearing and improving more of their land, and concentrating their efforts on specialized crops or livestock, or on household manufacturing.

During this period, thousands of New England farming men moved west, eager to escape from the rocky land and high mortgages of their family homesteads. In contrast, wives and mothers were often reluctant to abandon their circles of kin and to embark on an uncertain journey which in many cases exacted tremendous personal sacrifice. The way west demanded of women both traditional kinds of labor in terms of cooking and child care, but also new and arduous responsibilities – helping a wagon ford a stream or scale a rocky ledge, collecting buffalo chips for fuel, bearing children far from home, and burying some of those children along the trail. As one woman who had travelled the Overland Trail recalled: "It strikes me as I think of it now that Mothers on the road had to undergo more trial and suffering than anybody else."[5]

Nevertheless, western life did not produce "new men" or "new women" so much as it intensifed the materialistic impulses that characterized workers back home in the East. Pioneers in Michigan, Wisconsin, and Oregon worked to build a new life for themselves and their families, but they hoped that that new life would resemble the old one represented by newly purchased rocking chairs, books, and fashionable clothing.

This migration movement had its human costs. The settlement of "frontier" territory led to the immiseration of the native peoples who inhabited it, and a radical change in the lives of large numbers of Hispanic people who had formerly made their living off the land. In California, Spanish missionaries and large landowners exploited the agricultural labor of indigenous peoples (called by the derogatory name "Diggers") and landless migrants from Mexico.

The Midwest and the Far West remained sites of uneasy accommodation among many different ethnic groups and social classes. By the 1850s, immigrants from western Europe, including Germans, Swiss, Belgians, and Scandinavians were streaming out of eastern port cities and into the Midwest. In their new homes, they clashed with their Yankee neighbors over the propriety of putting wives and daughters to work in the fields (the Germans approved of such a practice, transplanted New Englanders did not). In California, native-born and West-European-born gold miners expressed their bitter resentment of Chinese immigrants who hoped to reap a windfall from the riches buried in "Gold Mountain"; discriminatory tax legislation passed in that state in the 1850s relegated the Chinese to the kind of work otherwise performed by women – as cooks and laundry operators.

Pioneers quickly found themselves enmeshed in a commercial economy that was as unpredictable as it was full of promise – in other words, similar to the economy of the Northeast. Those who were best able to take advantage of the opportunities the new territory afforded included migrants fortified with a reserve of cash. William Seyffardt, a German immigrant who settled in Michigan in the early 1850s, capitalized on the fact that he "could not get grain ground for months without going 20–30 miles," and so he "thought that I could start a small mill, as my neighbors would come to me if I could grind halfway well." With loans from his parents back in Germany, Seyffardt invested in land and a wood sawing machine, and built a prosperous business; but early one winter morning in 1860 the mill burned to the ground and he and his family were forced to move to town (Sagninaw) where he took up work as a butcher and a hardware store owner.[6] Likewise, Yankee-born women might parlay their modest savings into entrepreneurial ventures in the West. One energetic boarding-house operator in Nevada City, California, recalled that "Each man put a dollar in my hand and said I might count on him as a permanent customer. I called my hotel 'El Dorado.'"[7]

The rapid maturation of Midwestern local economies meant that family farmers in that area of the country were drawn into an orb of commercial development that mandated increasingly sophisticated kinds of agricultural machinery, as well as reliance on railroads and grain operators and other middlemen. The invention of the steel plow (by John Deere in 1837) enabled individual farmers to cultivate many more acres than previously, and Cyrus McCormick's mechanical reaper, which made an appearance in 1841, allowed a single person to harvest as much as could 14 field hands. Speculators pushed land prices upward, and bankers facilitated the growth of one class of landed creditors, and another class of landless debtors. As early as the mid-nineteenth century, a rural proletariat emerged in the Midwest – men, women, and children who worked their whole lives as tenants or day laborers.

It was during this period that a particular kind of worker – the farmer dependent on the labor of his wife, children, and a hired hand or two – assumed overt political significance, as northern migrants became the standard-bearers of a "free labor, free soil" ideology. Faced with the prospect of competing with slaveholding neighbors, these family farmers elevated their own form of household organization to a political ideal. This view carried with it no incipient support for black civil rights; although it represented a form of anti-slavery ideology, the "free soil" movement as a whole remained hostile to the possibility that black people might migrate to the west and, as free men, serve as a source of cheap labor for large landowners. Therefore it was not incongruous for free-soil men (and after 1854, leaders of the newly formed Republican Party), to call for the abolition of slavery on the one hand and legislative restrictions on black migration and job opportunities on the other.

Indeed, the plight of black workers throughout the antebellum North foreshadowed the legal and institutional barriers that southern blacks would face after the Civil War. After emancipation, Northern black craftsmen found it difficult to make a living without white customers and without the financial resources that would enable them to invest in new tools and expanded shop space. Black seamen, heirs to a proud tradition of seafaring stretching back to early colonial times, faced increasing competition from white sailors beginning in the 1830s. Likewise, for black teamsters, chimney sweeps, waiters, carriage men, and other manual laborers, their hold on even low-paying jobs became increasingly tenuous in a labor market flooded by immigrant workers (especially after the 1840s). Laws barring the in-migration of blacks into Midwestern states, and laws barring black parents from sending their children to school, and black men from voting in local, state, or national elections, meant that many black people had to struggle to piece together a living, without the benefit of a political voice. In rural areas, black workers were likely to be transient paupers, threshing oats, planting turnips, swingling flax, and cutting wood for daily wages. In cities, the majority of men performed odd jobs and women worked as laundresses, servants and hucksters. An 1847 survey of the black population in Philadelphia found that nearly half of the men were laborers, and the rest were mechanics, seamen, carters, waiters, and hairdressers. Most black women worked as washerwomen, domestic servants, needlewomen, and cooks. Others were scavengers, searching for rags and bones that they could sell for a few cents each day.

Within this realm of stunted economic opportunity, modest entrepreneurs like barbers and caterers rose to positions of prominence within their own communities, and the most resourceful cobbled together a living from a variety of sources. Elleanor Eldridge, born in Rhode Island in 1785, managed to accumulate enough money to build an imposing house. In the course of her long worklife, which commenced at the age of ten, she washed clothes, wove carpets and coverlets, and labored as a dairywoman until she was able to open her own "miscellaneous business," which included weaving, spinning, nursing and laundry services, boiling soap, white-washing, papering, and painting. Nevertheless, her house was eventually repossessed by creditors, and she found herself unable to reclaim in court her due, because, in the words of a sympathetic observer, *"THE OWNER OF THE PROPERTY WAS A LABORING COLORED WOMAN."*[8]

Significantly, a disproportionate number of black workers were included in the ranks of Northerners caught up in the last vestiges of bound labor. These included "shanghaied" seamen forced by "crimps" to serve on merchant ships; debt peons exploited until they could work off their financial obligations; whole families victimized by slave catchers, men whose "business . . . [of] hunting up runaways"[9] was supplemented by kidnapping free blacks and selling them south into slavery; poor people's children, bound out as "apprentices" to white employers; and men and women convicted of petty crimes and "sold" at auction to the highest bidder.

Northern black leaders claimed for themselves a public voice disproportionate to their small numbers. David Walker, a Boston black who issued his fiery tract, an "Appeal," in 1829, was equally outraged by the southern system of slavery, which made black people into *"beasts of burden,"* and the Northern so-called free labor system, which reduced black men and women to the point where they expressed gratitude to be able to shine white people's boots or wash their dirty laundry. Frederick Douglass, too, issued an indictment against the Northern merchants who professed to sympathize with the abolitionist cause but refused to hire blacks as clerks or bookkeepers. It was during this period that African-American lawyers assumed the role of civil-rights activists. Robert Morris, Sr was admitted to the bar in Suffolk County, Massachusetts, in 1847, and played a key role in launching (unsuccessful) legal challenges to both the segregated Boston public school system (in 1848) and the Fugitive Slave Law of 1850.[10]

Black people's economic marginalization was compounded by the process of technological innovation, which was eliminating some jobs, changing the shape of others, and creating many new ones at the same time. As new jobs and job categories appeared, employers (in some cases aided and abetted by their own workers) began to identify certain demographic groups with certain kinds of work. These developments varied according to region and industry or craft. For example, flour milling had utilized water power and a series of gears and pulleys from the eighteenth century, and textiles were among those products mechanized before the Civil War, but many jobs, like ship-building, glass-blowing, paper-making, and machine-making relied on a combination of unskilled and highly skilled workers. In Berkshire, Massachusetts paper factories, women continued to perform low-skilled hand-sorting work, while men assumed the new jobs of machine operators, positions that required a great deal of strength, intelligence, and skill.

Predictably, the social composition of each industry's workforce derived from a combination of factors. An unbalanced sex ratio in New England (the result of the outmigration of young men to the west) provided the demographic foundation for the textile mill labor force. Moreover, the role of women and children in colonial household textile production eased the way of young Yankee farm girls into the mills of Lowell, Massachusetts, and children into the mills of Pawtucket, Rhode Island, in the 1820s, for example. Finding themselves in the business of attracting young women to the mills, and forced to depend on the willingness of fathers and mothers to release their daughters from home, mill owners attempted to create a paternalistic work and living environment and thereby distance themselves from their British counterparts who operated the "dark Satanic mills" of Birmingham and Manchester. Ironically, though, the fellow feeling that developed among a group of young women from similar backgrounds spurred labor organization; for example, in Lowell in February, 1834, 800 women workers "turned out" (that is, left work) to protest the recent wage cuts that assaulted their dignity as workers and threatened their ability to support themselves. In the 1840s, women textile workers were in the forefront of the (ultimately unsuccessful) ten-hour day movement. By this time mill owners were eagerly casting about for more compliant workers, ones who could not, on a moment's notice, abandon their place at the loom and head back to the home of their parents in the hills.

The Yankee mill girls were an historical aberration of sorts, a transitional group of textile producers situated between colonial housewives and late antebellum immigrants. Scholars tend to regard as more representative of Northern workers the New England shoemakers, men and women who traditionally worked together under a single roof and took pride in their skills as skilled craft workers. For this group of workers, the incursion of the factory transformed not only their jobs but also their family relations. Gone now was the father who presided over a "ten-footer" (workshop) and the work of his journeymen, apprentices, wife, and children, a man who valued a "competence." In his place was the factory employee responsible for a small piece of the production process, and vulnerable to speed-ups, lay-offs, wage decreases, and abusive and arrogant bosses.

It was not uncommon for a specific immigrant group to locate a job niche for itself within a specific regional economy. Germans made inroads into the skilled trades in Buffalo and Milwaukee, while Norwegian and Swedish farmers staked their claims to family homesteads in Wisconsin and Minnesota. The thousands of Irish who fled their homeland in the 1840s and 1850s challenged the small number of black workers scattered in the drayage, construction, and domestic service trades throughout the East and Midwest.

Small establishments utilized workers wherever they could find them, offering employment to immigrants and the native born, and to men as well as women and children. Farmers desperate to meet their mortgage payments, and youngest sons fearful of prolonged dependency, might try a stint in the mills without committing themselves to this type of work permanently. Indeed, it would be a mistake to draw a strict dividing line between farm work on the one hand and factory work on the other. Not only did some people divide their time between the two in any one year, but much manufacturing took place on the farm, as part of a system known as "outwork," whereby young women might weave, sew collars, or braid straw hats during the long winter months. Therefore, many young people who moved to the city had had some previous experience doing piecework or working for wages. And the distributor of outwork goods – the merchant capitalist – was a fixture on the urban scene as well.

Each antebellum Northern city had a unique character; for example, Boston remained the province of petty proprietors, while Philadelphia emerged as a great manufacturing center, and New York claimed dominance for its mercantile houses. It was in the cities that ambitious (white) workers of all kinds might reasonably expect to improve their lot, or the lot of their children in life. Upward mobility often came in increments, and so a store-keeper might aspire to become a merchant, an artisan a manufacturer in the same craft, a tailor a clothier, an innkeeper a grocer, and a carpenter a cabinetmaker. For women, this process might be even more modest; a domestic servant might gauge her own success according to the wealth of the family for which she worked. Some workers might reckon their own well-being not according to their status as a skilled or semi-skilled worker, but according to their ability to own their own home, or allow a younger child to forego wage work at an early age in favor of schooling.

Historians have documented the high rates of residential mobility among Americans in general during this period, and city dwellers in particular; it is estimated that families moved on average once every five years, and those in urban areas once every three years. Mobility varied according to wealth; in Boston, for example, the native-born persisted at a rate three times that of the foreign-born. As workers moved in search of jobs, they often broke ties with a particular kind of job, and reconstituted ties with their kin, their co-religionists, or specific ethnic communities. In this way a person's cultural allegiances superseded his or her allegiances to to a specific workplace or trade.

In the midst of this population "churning," what were the ligaments that held Northern society, or at least certain groups of workers within it, together? We might begin by noting the significance of several forms of social cohesion, including a "separate spheres" ideology that supposedly bound together all women; various workingmen's organizations (including the Democratic Party); and the many different political agendas that came under the broad rubric of "moral reform."

Political parties brought together disparate groups of white men regardless of ethnicity or nativity, but women of all kinds remained conspicuous for their absence from formal partisan activity. The separation of workplace from homeplace revealed in practical terms a sexual division of labor among the emerging bourgeoisie. By the 1830s or 1840s, Northern ideologues – including clergymen, mill owners, politicians, and writers – began to view the world in gender-specific and (less overtly, class-specific) dichotomous terms. According to this view, women's work was centered in the home, where wives and mothers engaged in (or oversaw) food preparation and the nurturing of children. "Women's sphere" advocates (including many women who welcomed this new productive role) attributed to women a whole host of temperamental traits which presumably reflected and furthered their specific tasks – women were "naturally" more pious, self-sacrificing, and attuned to the needs of other people, in contrast to their enterprising menfolk, who supposedly possessed in abundance the requisite character traits for a workplace marked by ruthless competition.

As cash wages and salaries became the standard by which all men's work was measured, the compensation for women's housework appeared to be limited to the realm of overblown rhetorical glorification and their own (varying) sense of self-satisfaction. Once again, social context was everything;

washing clothes and feeding babies were kinds of work that conveyed status only when performed by a woman who remained dependent upon her employed husband; the wage worker who performed these same tasks for persons outside her immediate family in return for cash or some other material compensation bore the stigma of servant.

It is apparent that few antebellum women could conform to "separate spheres" strictures, and indeed the black washerwoman, the starving needlewoman of New York City, and the Irish textile operative were left out of this ideological construct altogether. Furthermore, in rural areas of the North and newly settled West, some women kept alive the spirit and mysteries of household industry perfected by their great-grandmothers; they remained outside the emerging industrial economy, where women's work included consumption in the marketplace. Moreover, even the Northern middle classes could not always afford to exempt their wives and daughters from paid labor of various kinds. Young women might spend their years before marriage at home as outworkers, or boarding in a distant village as textile workers or school teachers.

Indeed, perhaps as many as one-fifth of all native-born white women in certain parts of antebellum New England served as schoolteachers at some point in their lives. During the colonial period, the village school was a haphazard affair, vulnerable to the mood of the taxpayers and the availability of a young seminary or law student who was willing to teach for part of the year. By the 1820s, New Englanders (and New England migrants to the Midwest) became receptive to the importations of school reformers like Horace Mann, men who extolled the social value of a standardized education for all children, all over the country, and who pointed out that unmarried women could teach as well or better than their male counterparts, and at bargain rates. Teaching rapidly became the province of young women who had finished a modest amount of schooling themselves, and before they married.

Despite the "feminization" of the common school teaching force, in general the development of formal training and certification standards associated with certain professions related to law, medicine, and organized religion further isolated women from mainstream economic activity. And in some cases, these new standards stripped specific groups of women of an informal social influence that had traditionally accrued to skilled (and even revered) practitioners of various kinds, like midwives. In post-revolutionary Hallowell, Maine, a midwife named Martha Ballard was busy delivering babies and providing medical care to much of the town's population. Yet the future of obstetrics was represented by one of Ballard's contemporaries, the physician Daniel Cony, a member of the newly formed Massachusetts Medical Society (based in Boston), and president of the Kennebec Medical Society (founded in 1797). Increasingly, men's work of all kinds – in the delivery room as well as in the counting-house – took the form of waged labor, while much of women's traditional work remained unwaged and therefore, increasingly undervalued or devalued.

Within this fledgling capitalist-industrial economy, gender-specific roles among the emerging middle class stood in symbiotic relation to each other; husbands were responsible for the accumulation of capital, regardless of its price in labor exploitation, while their reformer-wives busied themselves with smoothing over the worst excesses of a profit-based system. The lowly seamstress, paid a pittance for each day's work, might appeal to a local Ladies' Aid Society, and, if she possessed the appropriate credentials testifying to her respectable nature, might receive enough in the way of support, financial or otherwise, from her employer's wife to continue to sew another day and further enrich her employer. In New York City, the Society for the Relief of Poor Widows scrutinized the moral character of the homeless and widowed women who applied for aid, searching for the "proper objects" of their benevolence, but rejecting those who were unable "to sustain as good a character as was hoped" – even if that meant casting pregnant or ill women back into the street.[11]

This example suggests some of the class and gender dimensions of moral reform characterized by the creation of a vast network of temperance and missionary societies throughout the North. (Here we should not confuse moral reform with more radical forms of activism, like the black-sponsored state conventions that called for the lifting of laws that prohibited blacks from voting, attending the public schools, and moving from state to state.) The ladies bountiful of New York City were careful to screen the objects of their benevolence to make certain that these widows and children qualified as the "worthy poor" (prostitutes and petty thieves need not apply for aid). For women of more modest means, ministering to the poor and faithless constituted a "splendid work"[12] that extended their sphere outside the household and into the larger community. Some women's groups took up the temperance banner, claiming that the husband who drank up his weekly paycheck at the neighborhood tavern represented an assault on the physical well-being of families all over the country.

At the same time, antebellum workingmen's organizations – especially those consisting of native-born men – embraced the call for moral reform in an effort to distance themselves from their rivals in the workplace. An 1843 procession sponsored by the Washington Temperance Society in New York City featured the founders of the organization, including a carpenter, a coach-maker, a tailor, a blacksmith, a wheelwright, and a silver-plater. Fraternal orders representing specific groups of workmen condemned the alleged moral turpitude characteristic of immigrants, African Americans, and impoverished workers – the Germans who enjoyed a beer with their noontime meal; the Irish who worked in the slaughterhouses that despoiled otherwise respectable neighborhoods; the black "nightmen" who emptied chamber pots and advertised their services in a raucous way; and the "idle poor," often conflated with criminals and diseased persons. By adopting a stance of moral self-righteousness and stressing sobriety and industry as the highest virtues of a worker, then, native-born Protestant workmen might lay claim to privileges (that is, the good jobs) that other groups supposedly did not deserve. Thus the canal digger from County Cork, and the black chimney sweep, remained outside the realm of workingmen's "virtue."

Historians remain intrigued by the processes of class formation that characterized the North during the antebellum era, but the fluidity of Northern society makes it difficult to pinpoint those processes with much precision. A major component of class of course was group self-consciousness, and it is not certain that people who performed the same kind of work under the same conditions considered themselves part of a unified group in ways that had political consequences. Even white male shoemakers in Massachusetts, who early on created a relatively formidable union (the Knights of St Crispin), took pains to hold themselves aloof from other workers employed in the same industry – women stitchers, outworkers who labored in their own homes and not in the factory, and farmers who hoped to pick up a little cash during the slack season. Other fledgling unions created barriers against Catholics, and Chinese or Irish immigrants, especially to the extent that those workers derived employment from the mechanization of certain crafts.

Exacerbating raw prejudice was the fact that many manual laborers organized their lives inside and outside the workplace around specific and ultimately narrow loyalties based on kinship, ethnicity, religion, and skin color. In New York City, groups of male workers as members of gangs and fire companies, some Protestant, some Catholic, engaged in pitched battles with each other during the 1830s and 1840s. If certain groups of white workers indulged in melodramatic forms of masculine camaraderie, they also often went out of their way to proclaim their contempt for black people, most of whom were poor and tainted with a legacy of bondage.

Different groups of workers found their respective collective voices through a variety of means, institutional or otherwise, but none of these means represented the general interests of workers *per se*. In Eastern and Midwestern cities, the Irish rapidly integrated themselves into the Democratic Party, a move that produced immediate, tangible payoffs in the form of municipal and state legislation aimed at eliminating opportunities for black workers (as voters, as migrants, as municipal licencees). For Irish men in general, long-term gains came in the form of political patronage jobs (in building construction and law enforcement, for example).

However, depending on the region, politicians felt compelled to reckon with a multitude of groups of workers who exerted influence via their large numbers and, more often than not, boisterousness in the streets. Indeed, Northern politicians of all stripes remained sensitive to the power wielded by the "mobocracy," rioters who were as likely to protest the arrival of black interlopers as a cut in wages. In the end, the constituency of the national Democratic Party was too diverse (including as it did Southern slaveholders) to allow it to speak on behalf of the white working classes who, in any case, spent little time debating the interests they all had in common.

The series of anti-black riots that punctuated the history of the antebellum North from the 1820s through the Civil War revealed the raw conflicts that pitted worker against worker, class against class, and white against black. A petition to the Connecticut legislature submitted by New Haven's white workingmen in 1834 revealed the overlapping levels of anxiety that gripped this group and impelled them to turn their anger toward the small number of impoverished black people in their midst. The efforts of black abolitionists and their allies to secure schools for blacks in the city and in nearby towns prompted fears that black people would eventually hold an advantage over white men who were just barely able to support their families. The fact that black people constituted only 5 percent of the New Haven population in 1830 did not deter whites from seeing them as a terrible threat:

> Whenever [blacks] come into competition, therefore, the white man is deprived of employment, or is forced to labor for less than he requires. He is compelled to yield the market to the African, and, with his family, alternately becomes the tenant of an almshouse, or is driven from the state to seek a better lot in the Western wilds . . . banished from home and kindred for the accommodation of the most debased race that the civilized world has ever seen.[13]

The petitioners failed to account for the apparent fact that members of this most "debased race" could pose such a formidable challenge to the industrious, sturdy sons of the (white) North. In any case, by promoting the abolition of slavery, blacks, as well as a few prominent whites of the professional and merchant class (as the white workers alleged), were in effect encouraging the mass migration of black people out of the South and into Northern cities, where they would presumably work for far less than any self-respecting white man. The argument was, then, that any gains made by black people in the workplace must necessarily come at the expense of whites; abolitionism, and all forms of black civil rights agitation, was a ploy to reduce white families to beggary.

Among the most formative developments that shaped the history of American work was the exclusion of African Americans from machine work in the antebellum North. While few Northern factory managers went out of their way to create a theory of black inferiority, a number of forces converged to keep factory labor forces lily-white. The seemingly endless supply of Northern children and women, and after the 1840s, Irish immigrants, provided little incentive for employers to hire black operatives, especially when such policies presumably would mandate expensive innovations to accommodate the racist proclivities of white workers – separate housing, separate washrooms, separate eating places. Martin Robison Delany, a black man who wrote about the condition of black people in the North, contrasted technological marvels of city life – "the trading shops – the manufactories . . . the operations of the various machinery . . . the railroads interlining every section, bearing upon them their mighty trains" – with the traditional forms of labor to which almost all black people were confined: "Our fathers are their coachmen, our brothers their cookmen, and ourselves their waiting-men. Our mothers their nurse-women, our sisters their scrub-women, our daughters their maid-women, and our wives their washer-women." Concluded Delany, until black people posssessed the chance to rise above "drudgery and menial offices . . . it is useless, it is nonsense, it is a pitiable mockery, to talk about equality and elevation in society."[14]

In sum, by the 1850s, several different groups gained a sense of collective (if illusory and ultimately fleeting) political purpose by setting themselves in opposition to blacks in general, and to black workers in particular. The Irish claimed that the true mark of citizenship was a white skin, thereby choosing to ignore the political ramifications of their own poverty and their own history of oppression at the hands of English colonial landlords. Native-born white workers anxious about losing their jobs to cheap-labor competitors agitated for restrictions on black tradesmen and legal barriers to black geographical mobility. (Those whites belonging to a nativist political party called the Know-Nothings denounced immigrants of all kinds, in addition to African Americans.) The Democratic Party excoriated blacks for their historic allegiance to the Federalists, and later the Whigs. And the majority of urban merchants and textile mill owners, in some instances related by kinship to southern slaveholders, and reliant on the products produced by slave labor, provided rhetorical if not material support for anti-abolitionist mobs.

It was no surprise, then, that there existed no single working-class consciousness in the North and Midwest. Those workers who had the most to gain by committing themselves to a labor organization were the most mobile, reluctant to cast their lot with groups that needed long-term leadership in order to survive. The emerging pattern of ethnic, religious, and racial diversity within the northern working classes represented a shock to the sensibilities of native-born Protestant white workers, who clung to ideologies of superiority wherever they could find them, and whenever they could manufacture them. Uneven processes of technological development meant that the deskilled shoe makers had little reason to associate with the semi-skilled makers of wheat threshers, and that native-born, white skilled harness workers would continue to view their semi-skilled Chinese co-workers with fear and suspicion. Even the grown sons of respectable families often followed peripatetic careers, moving off the farm and into wage work, but not settling for any length of time in a particular job. The fact that literate, native-born Protestants came to predominate the burgeoning middle-level job stratum of bookkeepers, clerks, and managers, offered some confirmation of the idea that wage-earning was only a temporary condition for anyone with enough intelligence and ambition to succeed. For many unskilled workers, petty proprietorship (in the form of owning a shop or a farm) beckoned as an ideal, and the traditional pride of craft was rendered irrelevant within industries where tools and job descriptions changed with dizzying speed.

The Civil War, the greatest political crisis in the history of the Republic, claimed over 600,000 lives in an effort to resolve the antebellum "labor question." With the future of family homesteads in the terrritories at stake, Northerners realized that "free labor" carried with it the power of moral imperative. At issue was not the routine of work so much as people's ideas about the future of work – their own and that of other groups. Would the Midwest provide a haven for the hard-pressed farmers of Vermont and New Hampshire, or a fertile field for slaveholding aristocrats and their degraded bondsmen? For their part, radical abolitionists stressed two particular evils embedded in the slave system – the denigration of slave family life and the fact that workers were denied the fruits of their labor – but members of the Northern white working classes were apprehensive that freed slaves would eventually flood the urban labor market.

The Civil War provided final and bloody proof that work-based collective identities would remain submerged under forms of political and cultural allegiance. The majority of Northerners and Southerners were landowning farmers, and despite differences in climate and marketing structures in the two regions, most men and women followed seasonal rhythms in their work and depended on the soil for their livelihood. Yet the farmers of Massachusetts found no common political ground with their counterparts in Georgia, though both groups shared the enterprise of tilling the soil. In the end, that enterprise was fraught with divergent meaning for people in the two states, and among groups (black and white, landed and landless) within each section, North and South.

The war itself exposed the faultlines of antebellum society based on ethnic, class, gender, and racial antagonism. In the North, the economic burdens of the war were borne by dockworkers thrown out of work as a result of cessation of international and interregional trade, and by all kinds of laborers who staggered under the effects of wartime inflation. Women workers frantically tried to piece together a living in the absence of their soldier-husbands. In Boston, Irish workers assumed that each and every slave freed by the Union army would hasten north to deprive honest white workingmen of the chance to make a decent living. In New York City, whites took advantage of the turbulence of the times to oust black men from their jobs as teamsters and dockworkers. In both of these cities, the riots prompted by Lincoln's draft law of 1863, and directed against defenseless black men, women, and children, boded ill for any national labor movement that would claim to represent the interests of all workers.

Approximately 180,000 black men served as soliders in the Union Army, but many were denied the role of armed freedom fighter. As the war dragged into its second long, bloody year, some Northern politicians concluded that black men might well serve the cause of the Union as cannon fodder and ditch diggers. The distinguished combat record of the Massachusetts 54th Regiment (for example) notwithstanding, most black men who volunteered for service found themselves relegated to digging trenches, chopping firewood, constructing fortifications, and washing and cooking for white soldiers. Under the command of white officers exclusively, and denied equal pay with their white counterparts, black soldiers soon came to the bitter realization that the work of war bore a striking resemblance to their labors in the civilian labor force.

In contrast, the war represented a watershed of sorts in the history of women professionals, specifically nurses, teachers, and government workers, though the medical, educational, and government bureaucracies continued to be organized hierarchically, along racial and gender lines. Young New England schoolteachers volunteered to go south to teach the freedpeople; like Jane Hardy of Shelburne, Massachusetts, "cooped up all her life in such a still old town," freedmen's teaching represented a "great thing" in their lives.[15] At times these young women locked horns with the men who were their superintendents and bureaucratic superiors as the teachers attempted to carve out for themselves a "sphere of usefulness" and to maintain a modicum of professional independence in the process. (The freedmen's aid societies also tended to employ Southern black women as servants in their mission homes, and to turn away applications from black men and women who sought to obtain teaching commissions on their own.)

Women nurses, trained and organized by the reformer Dorothea Dix, chafed under the highhanded authority wielded by male surgeons determined to preserve their prerogatives in the operating room and throughout the hospital. The Union army employed an estimated 20,000 women in a variety of capacities – white women as nurses and matrons, and black women as cooks and laundresses in military hospitals. (As one northern nurse who doubled as a spy for the Union army wrote: "I could only thank God that I was free and could go forward and work, and I was not obliged to stay at home and weep.")[16] Still, though the war opened the door to relatively well-educated white women as workers in the "helping professions," the conflict did little to advance the idea of a more inclusive notion of citizenship that would acknowledge the labors of either black men and women or white women.

In the South, the wartime mobilization of manpower and *matériel* provoked a crisis over the most efficient use of black labor, slave and free. Many planters resisted the injunction of their Confederate leaders to suspend the cultivation of cotton in favor of foodstuff production; at the same time, the heavy hand of Confederate impressment agents, combined with the profitablity of certain wartime industries like munitions, led to the large-scale diversion of slaves from field work to military fatigue duty or factory work. Southern military officers disagreed among themselves about where the routine labor of white recruits should leave off and where the routine labor of enslaved workers should begin. But the fact of the matter was that slaves were not always available to spare young white men the rigors of cooking their own food or washing their own clothes.

Throughout the war, blacks worked at tasks that whites feared possessed inherent subversive potential, whether they labored with Unionist sympathizers in North Carolina salt mines or as orderlies in Confederate hospitals far from home. The managing and housing of enslaved workers off the plantation presented obvious problems of social control. And no wonder: the sudden or gradual loosening of bondage's chains – when both a master and an overseer went off to war, when slaves were put to work tending machines instead of cotton fields, when whole families sought refuge behind Union lines – signalled new patterns of work for whites and blacks alike. Seizing opportunities, blacks abandoned the fields of their masters in favor of tending their own gardens or raising their own chickens; they sought autonomy as workers as well as autonomy as church members or parents.

Non-elite southern whites resented the fact that they placed their own lives in danger on the battlefield while members of the slaveholding elite bought substitutes or wrangled exemptions for themselves and their sons, and enslaved men and women continued to toil far from harm's way, back home or safely ensconced behind the trenches. Decrying what many came to perceive as a rich man's war, yeoman farmers and poor whites resisted military discipline, and showed themselves to be poor "workers" in the process. The much vaunted ideology of Southern individualism proved to be a poor foundation for organizing an army, and nonelite whites hid themselves from conscription agents, and then, if they were caught, deserted from the army whenever the heat of battle, or the cries of loved ones back home, became too great for them to bear. In the years after the war, Southern landowners would confront similar problems when they attempted to rein in whole families of poor whites, subject them to the pace of forced labor in the fields, and expect deference from them in return.

In sum, the tumult of wartime revealed the contradictions in a Southern system that pitted the interests of all white people against those of all black people. Slaveholders railed against the irresponsibility and laziness supposedly inherent in all slaves, but in the service of the Confederate nation poor whites appeared no more reliable or industrious. The great planters initiated a war to preserve the institution of slavery, but so great was their attachment to it that they could not relinquish their bondsmen and women even temporarily to preserve it. The war itself unleashed the forces of emancipation – not government decrees, but sporadic chances for enslaved men and women to seize their own freedom and flee the plantation. And finally, as skilled workers and as freedom fighters, Union spies and traitors at home, blacks belied the antebellum image that portrayed them as docile and obsequious drudges.

The Civil War left intact the broad outlines of blacks as dependent agricultural laborers, but the conflict also dramatically transformed the work of Southern black men and women within the realm of family and community life. As networks of kin coalesced after the war, groups of freedpeople set about creating the basis of an institutional life that amounted to an extension of the "overwork" they had performed under slavery. Although the vast majority would continue to labor in the fields – husbands on a regular basis, wives and children when their help was needed – the maintenance of black churches, schools, mutual aid societies, and political organizations would constitute a significant form of work within African-American communities for the generations to come.

Nevertheless, among elites, and white men in particular, nonwaged forms of labor like the maintenance of family and community life failed to qualify as productive work at all. Louisa May Alcott understood this fact of mid-nineteenth-century life as well as anyone. During the Civil War, she volunteered to work in a Union hospital in Washington, DC ("I've enlisted"); men fought their battles with guns, while women like Alcott contributed to the cause by bathing and feeding patients and dressing their wounds, administering medicines, changing linens and bandages, and comforting the dying. At the hospital, her work took her to places that were "cold, dirty, inconvenient, up stairs and down stairs, and in everybody's chamber." As a reward for her mission of mercy – to "soothe and sustain, tend and watch" – Alcott received little in the way of either money or glory (and in fact, she contracted a severe case of mercury poisoning that left her weakened for the rest of her life).[17] To Alcott and others, the larger meaning of her labor of love was evident: Now that work had come to be defined ever more narrowly in terms of cash wages, the soul of the United States would be lodged ever more firmly in its pocket.

FURTHER READING

Primary Sources

Berlin, Ira, et al., eds. *Freedom: A Documentary History of Emancipation, 1861–1867.* Series I, vol. 1: *The Destruction of Slavery.* Series I, Vol. 2: *The Black Military Experience.* Cambridge, MA: Cambridge University Press, 1982–90.

Blassingame, John, et al., eds. *The Frederick Douglass Papers.* 4 vols. New Haven: Yale University Press, 1979.

Cottrol, Robert, ed. *From African to Yankee: Narratives of Slavery and Freedom in Antebellum New England.* Armonk, NY: M. E. Sharpe, 1998.

Eisler, Benita, ed. *The Lowell Offering: Writings by New England Mill Women, 1840–1845.* New York: W. W. Norton, 1977.

Hazard, Thomas A. ed. *Nailer Tom's Diary, Otherwise the Journal of Thomas B. Hazard of Kingstown, Rhode Island, 1778 to 1840.* Boston: Merrymount Press, 1930.

Rock, Howard B., ed. *The New York City Artisan, 1789–1829: A Documentary History.* Albany: State University of New York Press, 1989.

Secondary Sources

Bernstein, Iver. *The New York City Draft Riots: Their Significance in American Society and Politics in the Age of the Civil War.* New York: Oxford University Press, 1990.

Blewett, Mary. *Men, Women, and Work: Class, Gender, and Protest in the New England Shoe Industry, 1780–1910.* Urbana: University of Illinois Press, 1988.

Boydston, Jeanne. *Home and Work: Housework, Wages, and the Ideology of Labor in the Early Republic.* New York: Oxford University Press, 1990.

Dublin, Thomas. *Transforming Women's Work: New England Lives in the Industrial Revolution.* Ithaca: Cornell University Press, 1994.

Gilje, Paul. *The Road to Mobocracy: Popular Disorder in New York City, 1763–1834.* Chapel Hill: University of North Carolina Press, 1987.

Ignatiev, Noel. *How the Irish Became White.* New York: Routledge, 1995.

Lott, Eric. *Love and Theft: Blackface Minstrelsy and the American Working Class.*

New York: Oxford University Press, 1993.

McGaw, Judith. *Most Wonderful Machine: Mechanization and Social Change in Berkshire Paper Making, 1801–1885*. Princeton: Princeton University Press, 1987.

Roediger, David R. *The Wages of Whiteness: Race and the Making of the American Working Class*. London: Verso, 1991.

Shelton, Cynthia J. *The Mills of Manayunk: Industrialization and Social Conflict in the Philadelphia Region, 1787–1837*. Baltimore: Johns Hopkins University Press, 1986.

Way, Peter. *Common Labour: Workers and the Digging of North American Canals, 1780–1860*. Cambridge, MA: Cambridge University Press, 1993.

5

Ideologies of Race in a Modernizing Economy: The Cases of African-American and Chinese Workers

Around 1900, one Mississippi farmer observed that, for poor folk, "times don't never get no different." To a certain extent, that observation did indeed hold true for workers who remained outside the burgeoning industrial economy in the late nineteenth and early twentieth centuries. In this regard, the trials and tribulations of the Holtzclaws, an African-American family in Alabama, were representative. During the 1870s, all of the members of the household, including both parents and the children, worked as cotton sharecroppers on a white man's land. At the end of each year they received no cash for their labors, for the landlord told them they had already "eaten" their share of the proceeds from the sale of the cotton in the form of "advances" of credit and supplies. After the crop was "laid by" at the end of the planting and hoeing season in the summer, the white man routinely cut off the family's "furnishings," and all of the family members had to scramble to make ends meet. The mother went to work as a cook for the "white folks," and the children spent hours in the nearby swamps and marshes, "wading in the slush above their knees" in search of the hog potato, which, together with the persimmons, nuts, and muscadines they managed to scrounge up, kept "body and soul together during those dark days." Toiling in the company of poor white men from the area, the father hauled logs at a sawmill for 60 cents a day until the mill moved out of the neighborhood in search of fresh timber. Then the elder Holtzclaw left the family behind for a year and found a job working on a railroad 50 miles from home, returning every three months to deliver his wages ($40 or $50) to their landlord; each penny went to pay for the advances consumed by the family in his absence.

In 1880 the family managed to rent a 40-acre farm and purchase a mule, a horse, and a yoke of oxen, thereby making a bid for a kind of economic independence that sharecropping did not allow. Yet a series of natural and human catastrophes crushed their hopes. The mule became ill, one of the oxen suffered an accident and could no longer work, and the horse was "so poor and thin he could not plow." The father injured himself when he stepped on a stub of cane in the field one day, and then their "splendid" crop of corn, gathered by the other family members and carefully piled in heaps, was washed away after a storm. It was this last blow "from which we were never wholly able to recover," recalled one of the sons, William.

His father, by this time barely able to walk, took a job off the farm. But after four years all this effort yielded only a monstrous debt that prompted the family's creditors to "clean them out" – "they came and took our corn and finally, the vegetables from our little garden as well as the chickens and the pig." At the end of the year the Holtzclaws "applied to a white man for a home on his place – a home under the old system," and the father was never again able to raise himself out of the ranks of sharecropping.[1]

The struggles of workers who remained marginal to the emerging industrial economy are as revealing of its political contours as are the struggles of those who were central to it. The Holtzclaws, and the majority of African Americans at this time, remained barred from the consumer culture that was the hallmark of "modernization." In an era when paid labor was becoming associated almost exclusively with the individual wage earner, the Holtzclaw family worked together as a productive unit. In a period when increasingly sophisticated kinds of technology dictated the structure of the workplace, the Holtzclaws tilled fields and foraged in the forests in ways similar to those of their forbears on the Southern countryside. They lived outside the cash economy, ultimately reduced to the status of debt peons, their geographical mobility severely circumscribed by the machinations of creditors nearby and the racial prejudice of employers in Southern cities and up North.

The forces that conspired to keep the Holtzclaws dependent on their landlord persisted in the rural South well into the twentieth century. In 1920s Alabama, Ned and Viola Cobb struggled against formidable odds to make a living for themselves and their children. Mired in a political economy that rendered landless blacks and whites alike perpetually cashless, the Cobbs "scuffled" to earn some cash. Ned Cobb was a good cotton farmer, a hard-working man, and in addition to tilling the land he whittled ox handles, wove baskets, caned chair bottoms, and hauled lumber. A proud man, he disapproved of his wife working for whites in the fields or in the kitchen; Viola contributed to the family income by raising hogs and peddling butter, syrup, and eggs. As tangible proof of their success within the narrowly circumscribed plantation economy, the Cobbs boasted two large mules, fat and well-fed, and by the 1920s, Ned Cobb had purchased a brand new Ford, a rare sight indeed on the bleak landscape of the Jim-Crow South. Nevertheless, Ned Cobb was the first person to acknowledge that many of his neighbors led lives devoid of ambition in the modern sense. These were men and women like his brother Peter, a person who "made up his mind that he weren't goin to have anything, and after that, why nothin could hurt him."[2]

African Americans were not the only group to suffer constricted employment opportunities (and political rights) because native-born whites of all classes developed racial ideologies that served to subordinate them; on the West Coast, Chinese immigrants too faced a kind of prejudice that made them vulnerable to the exclusionary sensibilities of employers, labor unions, consumers, and public officials. Together, the work histories of African Americans in the South and

Chinese immigrants in California tell us much about the structure of the late nineteenth-century labor force and the political forces that shaped it. Though blacks and Chinese had strikingly different histories – the Chinese consisted primarily of men who had left their families behind at home – both groups inspired racial ideologies that were essentially strategies used by white men to protect their own precarious superiority within a turbulent political economy. After the Civil War, these strategies became wrapped in the mantle of scientific objectivity, as both African Americans and Chinese immigrants were branded members of "infantile races": "They are beardless children, whose life is a task, and whose chief virtue consists in unquestioning obedience."[3] The violence directed at both groups assumed a ritualistic quality, the shootings, burnings, and lynchings revealing of a collective cartharsis among white men desperate to hold onto privileges they increasingly came to identify in "racial" terms.

Relegated to "traditional" kinds of work (primarily domestic service and agricultural labor), their womenfolk denigrated, and their chances for advancement within the workplace stymied, blacks and Chinese devised strategies (with varying degrees of success) to live their lives on their own terms. Nevertheless, the reality of the situation meant, in the words of one contemporary, the black porter "may be an educated man, as ambitious and as intelligent as the baggage agent or the conductor; but he must keep his place, and that place is at the bottom, and his color fixes it."[4]

The vulnerabilities of black and Chinese workers were compounded by structural changes in the late nineteenth-century United States economy. In a drive for efficiency, companies eagerly installed labor-saving mechanical devices, displacing workers at the lowest rungs of the occupational ladder – the shovellers at a steel mill, the sweepers at a textile factory. African-American entrepreneurs found it difficult to compete within a new economy that favored large enterprises capable of appealing to the tastes of newly fastidious consumers; an established but small class of black caterers in Philadelphia reluctantly yielded to their white counterparts, men who could afford to emulate European styles and also locate their offices in a fashionable section of the city. Many black people worked as servants and many Chinese men worked in laundries, not because they had cultural proclivities in those directions, but because alternative forms of employment were closed to them. In the long run, however, their jobs became foregone "cultural" conclusions, as conventional wisdom among whites held that black people were incapable of serving as machine operatives, and that both groups were "particularly suited" for domestic work.

In the South, the end of the Civil War sparked a four-way debate over the "labor question," a debate that spilled over into terrorist attacks upon the former slaves initiated by whites of all classes. White landowners professed the belief that black people would not work unless forced (by threats or violent intimidation) to work; they interpreted attempts by the freedpeople to recover long-lost loved ones and to seek independence from their former masters as evidence of laziness and "vagabondizing." Poor whites, now stripped of the legal superiority that elevated them relative to the enslaved black population, emerged from the war desperate to maintain an upper hand *vis-à-vis* the freedpeople at all costs, in the labor market and at the polling place.

For their part, the Northern conquerors – whether as officers of the military occupation, agents of the Bureau of Refugees, Freedmen, and Abandoned Lands, members of the carpetbagging Republican Party in the South, or teachers of the freedpeople— urged black men, women, and children to return to the fields and continue to toil under the direction of their former masters. In an address delivered to the black population in the Orangeburg District of South Carolina in June of 1865, Captain Charles Soule, a white officer stationed in that state after the war, exhorted his listeners: "Remember that all your working time belongs to the man who hires you: therefore you must not leave work without his leave not even to nurse a child, or to go and visit a wife or husband. When you wish to go off the place, get a pass as you used to . . . Do not think of leaving the plantation where you belong."[5]

Deprived of the credit and other resources that might have enabled them to buy land (had whites been willing to sell to them), black people sought to carve out a measure of household and community integrity for themselves within exceedingly narrow boundaries. Together, they demonstrated a determination to cultivate gardens, and to fish and forage rather than return to staple crop production – whether cotton, rice, or sugar – in the postbellum South. Recently freed, black people near Mt Pleasant, South Carolina, showed considerable ingenuity in providing for themselves; in the words of a federal official, these "idle, vicious vagrants, whose sole idea consists in loafing without working" were subsisting on green corn, pond lily beans, and alligator meat, and also appropriating from the estates of their former masters what they believed to be their due: "Lead pipes taken from wells and cisterns, Harness from stables, cotton from the fields and even the iron from the cotton gins and engines." Whatever their other shortcomings, these freedpeople were hardly "idle."[6]

Despite the widespread destruction of property and the overall devastation of war, the Southern staple crop economy survived the conflict intact. Elites perceived the black quest for autonomy to be a challenge to their own political and economic self-interests, and they attempted to impose a quasi-slavery, gang-based system of labor organization on the black population, beginning in the summer and fall of 1865. However, to the consternation of elites all over the South, black women attempted to exercise their prerogatives as freed women, and withdraw from field labor to attend to their families if they could afford to do so. In the 1870s, a Northern reporter surveying conditions in rural Lousiana observed that black women did not regularly work in the fields, though they might earn wages for limited time during the harvest season. Noted the reporter, "If the colored laborer is forehanded [ie., has enough children to work] he prefers that his wife shall not work in the field."[7]

The general resistance of black people to the system of gang labor contributed to the emergence of squads, kin groups of workers that contracted together with a landlord for the year.

Ultimately, the desire of planters to grow more cotton, and the desire of black people to organize their energies as families, or households, led to the system of sharecropping, a system characterized by the chronic indebtedness of the workers in it.

The stark black–white dichotomies posited by the postbellum southern economy obscured regional variations in local economies, and the efforts of blacks to support themselves and their communities apart from the demands of whites. On the Sea Islands off the coast of South Carolina, blacks resisted the gang system of labor in favor of the task system characteristic of antebellum rice cultivation. In the dozen or so years after the Civil War, workers in the rice districts located on the Sea Islands off the coast of South Carolina failed to provide the predictable and compliant labor that large landowners considered their due. Bitterly resentful of the federal government's decision to renege on a promise of land redistribution after the war, African Americans tried to alternate work in the rice fields with cultivating their own crops, or seeking wage work off the plantation in railroad construction camps or phosphate mines. The fact that black men were voting in large numbers made their bid for self-direction in the fields doubly threatening to whites. In 1876, a series of strikes proved devastating to the interests of rice growers, and gradually more and more workers abandoned day-labor in the fields in favor of cultivating small plots on their own. By the end of the century, the locus of the rice economy had shifted from South Carolina to Louisiana.

All over the South, freedpeople attempted to carve out a space of productive labor that would free them from the watchful eyes of white landlords and supervisors and yield at least a modest amount of cash in the process. During the winter along the Virginia and Georgia coasts, black men gathered oysters, their children and womenfolk working as oyster shuckers. In the summer, the men farmed, the women went to work for whites as domestic servants, and the children picked berries. Nevertheless, throughout the South, in small towns and cities, black women searched for alternatives to domestic service, which they had come to regard "as a relic of slavery and as degrading ... [they] only enter it from sheer necessity, and then as a temporary makeshift."[8]

White housewives issued routine, plaintive laments about the "unreliablity" of such workers, and indeed the image of the "faithful" cook or servant notwithstanding, turnover rates in domestic service remained extraordinarily high. Black wives and mothers resisted the demand that they work long, regular hours each day, preferring to arrive late and leave early. They quit their jobs when there was cotton to be picked in nearby fields, when their husbands had earned enough cash to support the family for a few months, when an ill child or infirm elderly relative needed long-term care. They skipped work to attend funerals and revival meetings, to particiate in church outings, to see the travelling circus when it came to town. If the summer's heat or their employer's sharp tongue became unbearable, they took a few days off, no matter that the guests of a grand dinner party were left to fend for themselves.

Turnover among domestics had its counterpart among share-croppers – the tendency of families to pick up and move every couple of years or so in search of a better landlord, a larger cabin, a place closer to the neighborhood school or church. Sharecroppers rarely stayed in any one spot for very long, but they did not gain much in the way of upward social mobility by moving so often. Instead, they "shifted" within the narrow confines of the local plantation economy, their decision to leave or to stay dictated by a matrix of factors related to the family life-cycle and the temperament and whims of individual landlords. Contractual arrangements between landlord and laborer did not vary much over the years, though white landowners tried to erode the bases of self-sufficiency that black people struggled to retain – small garden plots, the ability to keep pigs, chickens, and cows. In the Mississippi Delta, black sharecroppers were enjoined from growing their own food, a policy that had devastating consequences for the health of family members forced to subsist on fatback, cornbread, and molasses without the requisite nourishment that a more varied diet of fruit and vegetables would have provided.

Thus, throughout the Cotton South, black families defied the injunction of landlords that they should remain immobile, confined to a single plantation for years on end, and direct all of their energies toward the growing of a staple crop. They seized bits of time to engage in petty commodity production, selling eggs and chickens, and trading and bartering the fruits of their labors conducted outside the fields – hunting, fishing, weaving baskets, making hats. The small amount of money earned by these activities helped to build schoolhouses and sustain black churches and mutual aid societies all over the South.

Moreover, black fathers and sons responded to the slack season in crop production (in the winter and mid-summer) by pursuing wage-earning opportunities off the plantation. Like William Holtzclaw's father in Alabama, black men found work in saw mills or flour mills, on railroad construction projects or in cotton gins, in lumber mills and turpentine camps, in coal mines and on river levees. Indeed, the plantation and proto-industrial sectors of the rural South complemented each other, though neither one afforded black workers a living wage.

Not all sharecroppers were black. During the late nineteenth century, increasing numbers of Southern white farmers became mired in debt. Their homesteads damaged or destroyed by the war, their land, homes, and out-buildings lying in ruins, they had little choice but to seek out loans and credit from local lenders, men who insisted they grow more cotton and less corn. In 1868, John D. Williams, a planter in the Laurens District of South Carolina, prepared a labor contract to be signed by all of his hands. The contract stipulated that workers who left the premises without the employer's approval would forfeit one dollar the first time, and all of their interest in the crop the second time. They were forbidden from keeping firearms or alcohol, and could be discharged for a variety of offenses, including "want of respects or civility to me or my Agent or my Family or any elce." Signing this document, which was notable for both its detail and its open-endedness, were two groups of people – five blacks (three men and two women), and seven white men. The five black workers and two of the white men "made their marks" – that is, they signed their name with an "X" because they could not write.[9]

Rates of white landlessness increased thorughout the late nineteenth century. Gradually, in parts of Texas and North Carolina, Georgia and Florida, rural poverty wore a white face. Nevertheless, poor whites retained seemingly modest but in the long run significant advantages over their black counterparts. White men possessed the right to vote and serve on juries, and derived some satisfaction, and some concrete gains, from participating in Democratic politics. Whites predominated in the categories of tenants and renters, steps above the sharecropper and day-laborer rungs on the rural tenure ladder. Proportionately more white than black families managed to buy a mule, the dividing line between the enforced dependency of the cropper and the modest amount of self-direction enjoyed by the tenant. Though backward compared to the North's system, Southern public education overwhelmingly favored white pupils, and denied to black children the resources – teachers, books, and schoolhouses – that were due them.

Even the few Eastern-European immigrants who ventured South and found themselves working stooped over in the fields managed to parlay the modest amounts of cash they earned into life possibilities more promising than those of black field hands. In 1890, 960 Italians were working on the sugar plantations of five Louisiana parishes, and ten years later the number had climbed to 5,000. Planters lauded these workers as "hardy, thrifty, tireless" peasants and predicted that they would someday dislodge "irresponsible" black workers who resisted the forced pace of field labor. Yet convinced that the future held some promise for them, Italian workers on a cotton plantation in Arkansas planted the crop on every available square inch of land, picked it frantically (at times by moonlight), and saved the little they earned. Eventually they managed to leave the fields and many opened small businesses, mostly grocery stores, in New Orleans.[10]

At the same time, other immigrants suffered the fate of young African-American men and women forced into virtual servitude in the swamps and forests of the "New South." These included recent arrivals at Ellis Island, mostly young Italians or Greeks, who were lured south with false promises of high wages and easy work. Instead, these workers found themselves held at gunpoint in snake-infested railroad construction camps, or knee-deep in water in phosphate mines, or in isolated timber or turpentine camps. A federal investigator looking into the plight of Ed Sanders, a black man held in a lumber camp in the eastern district of Louisiana in 1910, reported that such worksites "in this neighborhood are many of them quite lawless places, and by reason of fear and intimidation, it is difficult to obain witnesses" about the plight of the peons who toiled in them.[11] Southern authorities colluded to keep these workers hard at work. For example, Bessie Edwards, a young black woman, applied for a job through an employment agency in Durham, North Carolina, in 1906. Though the agency had promised to place her as a cook for a mining or railroad construction camp, she found herself on a Mississippi plantation forced to labor for the owner. Six years later railroad agents were refusing to accept the money her mother tried to send to her so that she could buy a ticket and return home. Local law-enforcement officials, including sheriffs and judges, routinely tolerated and in some cases actively promoted such forms of labor exploitation.[12]

Peonage predominated in industries marked by heavy, dangerous, or otherwise disagreeable kinds of work that laborers of all kinds avoided if they could possibly afford to do so. Some farm workers charged that virtually every plantation amounted to a "peon camp," for employers felt free to brandish guns and whips against workers who resisted neoslavery forms of discipline. In addition, the South's notorious penal system amounted to a great funnel that channelled mostly young black men off the countryside and into various workplaces. In the 1870s, Southern prisoners worked on plantations and in far-flung sawmill camps and coal and iron mines. By the end of the 1890s, convict laborers had become a lynchpin in the New South's "good roads" movement, a "Progressive" reform that sought to further efficient communication and travel throughout the region, but relied on the brutal exploitation of vulnerable black workers in the process. Indeed, a case could be made for the argument that convict laborers were treated more harshly than their slave forbears, for convicts were cheap and available in almost unlimited supply. Prisoners endured beatings with whips encrusted with sand, and hours or days in "sweatboxes" under the Southern summer sun. Women were not immune to these brutalities; in 1888, an Alabama state investigating committee heard testimony from black women prisoners who were whipped for "sassing" guards and falling short of their daily quota for cotton picking. Flora Adams was punished for "dancing while the preacher was here on a Sunday."[13]

The case of Southern coal mines reminds us that there existed no fixed or even single "racial" division of labor. Still, the better jobs outside the mines were reserved for whites, who also had more opportunities to ascend the internal ladder of occupational mobility within each worksite. West Virginia coal mine operators deliberately fashioned mixed workforces by hiring some blacks and also sought employees from a variety of ethnic groups (in 1915 the state had 28,583 foreign-born miners and 49,458 workers in the industry born in this country) – in order to forestall the fellow feeling among laborers that might ultimately lead to unionization.

Southern employers' efforts to discourage biracial unionism were not always successful, and in some turn-of-the-century integrated worksites, blacks and whites challenged Jim Crow in its most basic form. In places where black workers were already established and numerous in certain industries, whites had little choice but to incorporate them into emerging industrial unions. Examples include the United Mine Workers in the mineral district near Birmingham, Alabama; the International Longshoremen's Association on the docks of New Orleans; the Brotherhood of Timber Workers in the forests of Louisiana; and (beginning in 1919) the International Union of Mine, Mill, and Smelter Workers in the phosphate mines of Florida. Even most integrated unions were organized into segregated locals, however, and white leaders insisted that black men not be allowed to supervise whites, earn job promotions, or operate sophisticated kinds of machinery. These exclusionary principles meant that black workers would regard even relatively egalitarian unions with a well-founded degree of skepticism.

The fact that black people constituted less than half of the Southern population meant that there were very few jobs performed by black men, women, or children exclusively. As we have seen, blacks and whites labored within the New South's staple-crop economy, although they rarely labored side by side. (In North Carolina tobacco fields, whites who found themselves elbow-to-elbow with blacks refrained from singing with their darker-skinned co-workers, in a bid to distance themselves from them.)

Nevertheless, some manual labor jobs remained – or evolved into – the exclusive province of whites. In contrast to the enterprises established in the antebellum period, the textile mills that sprang up along the fall line from South Carolina to Alabama during the 1870s and 1880s reserved the position of machine operative for white women, men, and children, thereby draining off the countryside some of the discontented white farmers and (it was hoped) defusing the possibilities for biracial challenges to the politics of white landlords and employers. In fact, the textile-mill case reveals the way employers could manipulate the racial composition of workforces for political ends.

Still, the social division of labor amounted to a rather fluid and unpredictable process shaped by a variety of local factors as well as longstanding (or, in the case of the textile industry, mythical) "custom." For example, a journalist who visited Jonesboro, Georgia, in the 1890s found that the few employers who gave preference to blacks in nonagricultural employment "because of their sense of the injustices practiced against the race" tended to be "men of the missionary type, whose broad human creed cannot be narrowed by the feeling of those about them." More often, though, whites simply hired whites if they were available; noted one barrel manufacturer, "People don't think it right to employ negro labor when there is white to be had." This view was so widespread among the farmers of Jonesboro that they had in recent years refused to sell lumber to a factory owner who used black employees (he was forced to sell his business as a result). The journalist noted that a boycott where men "refused to sell is novel in our annals. . . . It was pure self-sacrifice [on the part of the timber sellers] in behalf of a cause."[14]

In other instances, too, diverse groups of whites clashed over the proper sphere of black workers. On Southern trains, black firemen (who stoked the engines) traditionally worked under the supervision of white engineers, and the whites regarded the deference accorded them by black underlings to be an integral component of their own jobs. White firemen objected to this custom, however, and complained that the low wages paid to blacks undercut their chances for employment. At the same time, employers justified the higher wages paid to white firemen performing the same task as their black counterparts: "The colored fireman is paid less than the white fireman. That would naturally follow from this circumstance, if no other: There are white firemen always on the road who are candidates for promotion to engineers. These white firemen outrank, so to speak, the colored firemen."[15]

Throughout the postbellum South, the class of black tradesmen and artisans faced stiff opposition from their white counterparts and found it increasingly difficult to pass their skills onto their sons. This process of displacement was similar to the one characteristic of Northern cities after emancipation, when race-based restrictive employment legislation was implemented in the late eighteenth century. In both sections of the country, black men *qua* slaves worked at a diversity of tasks, but black men *qua* free men were severely constricted in their range of employment opportunities. In New Orleans in 1870, a total of 3,460 black men labored as carpenters, cigar makers, painters, clerks, shoemakers, tailors, bakers, blacksmiths, and founding hands. By 1904, not 10 percent of that number remained in those trades combined. In some Southern cities black men managed to retain a niche in the building trades (as plasterers and bricklayers for example), though they often confronted the opposition of white unions that sought to monopolize a particular kind of work in any one city.

In the iron industry, Southern white workers launched more aggressive campaigns to retain their privileged position in the workplace, and white employees conspired with their employers to relegate black men to unskilled positions. In Birmingham, iron manufacturers chose to import skilled white workers from the North rather than train indigenous black men for tasks above those of sweepers and loaders. The marginalization of black workers thus provided the basis for white men to predominate in better paying jobs, ones that provided (relatively) well for their families, and also to link their own favored status to larger tenets of white supremacy. In this endeavor they received the enthusiastic support of "New South" Democratic politicians.

Yet in parts of the South (as in other areas of the country) black men managed to gain a foothold in skilled jobs when they entered the workplace as strikebreakers. In the late nineteenth century, the emerging steel industry came to rely on large numbers of semiskilled operatives. As a result of a strike by whites in Birmingham in 1907–8, black men were hired as strikebreakers and used as skilled workers for the first time; by 1917, 14 percent of Birmingham's skilled steel workers were black, and in 1920 that number had increased to 22 percent.[16]

The black men and women who faced the least opposition from whites at the highest echelons of the employment ladder were those ensconced securely within positions that served their own (black) communities. In the South, black undertakers, bankers, and lawyers joined members of more longstanding black professional classes – the preachers and the teachers – in representing the pinnacle of the black labor force. In general, the black social elite was drawn from classes of workers considered to be relatively modest within the more elongated white labor structure. For example, Mamie Garvin Fields, a seamstress and school teacher, together with her husband Robert, a bricklayer, built a secure life for themselves in early twentieth-century Charleston. Together, the Fields, as pillars of the city's African-American community, "went purposefully in and out the front door of their life," while "the blasts of 'Dixie'" – the intrusiveness of Jim Crow – played "like a background Muzak unlistened to."[17]

Outside the South, too, local economies and their peculiar mix of "custom," demography, and politics, dictated the kinds of jobs that black people were permitted to do. For example in early twentieth-century Los Angles, the small black community competed with European immigrants for jobs as janitors and waiters, and with Mexicans for jobs as common laborers. In that city, a clothing manufacturer rationalized the exclusion of black women as employees by citing the "great expense" involved in rearranging his machinery and workspaces in general so that members of the two races would not have to work or eat in close proximity to one another.

Turn-of-the-century local Northern economies mocked the desperation of black family members to enter the modern industrial labor force. Pittsburgh offered employment to black men as laborers in blast furnaces and rolling mills, but black women found few opportunties apart from domestic service. In most Northern cities, black migrants who had followed the trades of coopers and blacksmiths now found that there was little demand for their services in an economy where these kinds of jobs were becoming mechanized. Moreover, the large numbers of immigrants limited the employment opportunities of black children as well as adults; in Pittsburgh, for example, white boys exclusively, as young as ages nine or ten, dominated all of the work in glass factories that was designated as children's labor. The fact that the working-class neighborhoods in the vicinity of factories were off-limits to black residents meant that most black workers faced long commutes to work each day, further eroding their meagre wages.

In his study *The Philadelphia Negro* (published in 1899), W. E. B. DuBois noted that trends toward business consolidation and technological innovation worked against small craftsmen and entrepreneurs, both white and black, but black men and women remained at a disadvantage in finding new "modern" jobs within an expanding economy. Noting the displacement of black barbers by skilled men from Germany and Italy, DuBois wrote, "the application of large capital to retain business, the gathering of workmen into factories, the wonderful success of trained talent in catering to the whims and taste of customers . . . the economic condition of the day militates largely against the Negro."[18] Moreover, the city's large manufacturing sector systematically excluded black people in virtually all positions above the unskilled level, illustrating a fundamental principle of Northern labor-force management – that employers preferred to hire Eastern-European workers as a group, but sought out Southern African Americans as strikebreakers in times of labor strife.

Together, Southern black field laborers and skilled workers entered the ranks of the northern urban proletariat, taking the jobs (as one contemporary in Milwaukee put it) that "even Poles didn't want" – those that were particularly dangerous, dirty, and disagreeable.[19] In Chicago's meatpacking industry, black men and women worked in departments that produced fertilizers, hides, and sausage casings. Glue stripping – a job that white women rejected because it was "greasy, oily, dirty, and smelly" – remained the province of black women employees. An investigator for the Women's Bureau reported that, "The work of Negro women was usually in the wet, slippery part of the establishment where unpleasant odors filled the air and where marked variations in temperature and humidity made the surroundings hazardous to health."[20] In contrast, only white women were employed in slicing bacon, a job that required workers to handle the product, and a part of the meat processing business that was often prominently featured in the company's promotional literature and during tours of the plant.[21]

Two intriguing exceptions to this general rule pertained. In Philadelphia, black men found jobs in the Midvale Steel plant; the company employed 1200 men in 1895, one-sixth of whom were black and the rest evenly divided between first and second-generation immigrants from Western Europe. Frederick Winslow Taylor, a scientific-management expert and consultant to some of the era's most prominent industrialists, told an interviewer that the plant's hiring policy was designed to counter "the clannish spirit of the workmen and [their tendency] to form cliques." Taylor objected to ethnic enclaves of men who set their own piece-rate goals and refused to adhere to an employer-imposed pace of industrial discipline. The integration of black men into these enclaves had produced favorable results, he reported: "Now our gangs have, say, one Negro, one or two Americans, an Englishman, etc. The result has been favorable both for the men and for the works. Things run smoothly, and the output is noticeably greater."[22] In this case, the racial integration of the workplace represented a specific anti-union strategy on the part of management.

In Detroit, a somewhat different political dymanic pertained when Henry Ford broke ranks with his fellow auto manufacturers and hired black men, relying on the personal recommendations of local black clergy. Ford sought to secure a workforce that was grateful for the opportunities that industrial work provided, and for a while at least he was largely successful, since the other car makers who refused to hire any blacks did so out of stubborn principle. Nonetheless, the black men who worked for Ford were segregated in the foundry and enjoyed little or no mobility within the overall complex.

During this period, labor unions became more active and aggressive in their role as "gatekeepers" guarding entrance into the skilled trades. The career of Lewis Henry Douglass, a son of Frederick Douglass, revealed the reasons why so many skilled black workers were forced to renounce their trades altogether. A veteran of the Union army, Lewis learned the printer's trade by working for his father's paper, *North Star*, in Rochester. After the war, no white printer would hire him, and so he moved to Denver, where he found work on the Denver *Daily Gazette*. However, the local printers' union refused him membership because he was "a colored man," and he left for Washington, DC, and became a compositor at the Government Printing Office. The Columbia Typographical Union, no. 101, refused him membership because, they noted, he had worked previously as a non-union printer. In the 1870s

Lewis, along with his brother, Frederick Jr, became publishers of their father's new paper, the *New [National] Era*.[23] Like other relatively well-educated African-American workers, Lewis Douglass found skilled employment only within the confines of the black community.

The convoluted political and economic forces that assigned African Americans their "place" in the workforce, in the South and in Midwestern and Northeastern cities, had parallels on the West Coast. The history of nineteenth-century California in particular reveals how groups of whites invoked the idea of racial difference in order to limit the opportunities of certain prospective wage-earners, and how whites aimed to further their "class" consciousness at the expense of workers defined in exclusively "racial" terms. At times Anglos might identify Mexicans and Asians as members of distinct "races," but these whites also took pains to distinguish among social classes of Spanish-speaking peoples, and between Chinese and Japanese immigrants. In the late nineteenth century, the small number of Japanese immigrants posed little threat to the white working classes, and hence whites tended to perceive members of this group in a relatively favorable light: The Japanese, it was claimed, "seem to have an instinctive knowledge of our institutions. . . . They stop at hotels, etc., and live like Americans." As one California Protestant clergyman observed, "I am utterly amazed at the difference between the Japanese and the Chinese."[24]

In some cases, clusters of African Americans also sought to manipulate anti-Chinese sentiment in claiming for themselves the banner of responsible United States citizenship. Nevertheless, a comparison of anti-black and anti-Chinese rhetoric and political activity during the latter half of the nineteenth century suggests the limits of a targeted group's "culture" – their so-called "preference" for menial labor – as a major factor affecting the structure of the work force. Instead, patterns of economic change and technological innovation go a long way toward accounting for a particular social division of labor.

In 1869, Frederick Douglass delivered a speech in Boston on the subject of "composite nationality," drawing the attention of his audience to the political economy of the West Coast, where a variation on eastern "racial" conflicts was emerging. Douglass contended that poverty and overcrowding would continue to push the Chinese out of their native country and into the United States, and yet "Already has California assumed a bitterly unfriendly attitude toward the Chinaman. Already has she driven them from her altars of justice. Already has she stamped them as outcasts and handed them over to popular contempts and vulgar jests. Already are they the constant victims of cruel harshness and brutal violence." Douglass noted that, "In all this there is, of course, nothing strange." In supporting the rights of Chinese to immigrate to the United States, to find justice in the courts, and to enjoy the blessings of American citizenship, Douglass drew upon the principles of equality and freedom that he had honed over many years in support of black civil rights. He noted that, in California, workingmen had created associations to keep Chinese out of certain workplaces – in other words, already had "popular prejudice . . . [been leveled] against the weak and defenceless." Concluded Douglass, equal treatment under the law was the best policy to be applied to the immigrants, for "Right wrongs no man."[25]

The history of Chinese labor in California is the history of male workers' engagement with successive sectors of the economy. Drawn to "Gold Mountain" (their term for the United States) by the opening of California gold mines, the first immigrants toiled as independent placer miners during the Gold Rush of 1849 and into the 1850s. However, hostility from native-born (white) rivals – expressed through violence and discriminatory tax legislation – forced Chinese men into work on the transcontinental railroad. Employers welcomed them as strikebreakers in 1865, and they replaced whites protesting the grueling hours, low pay, and dangerous conditions that prevailed on a line that traversed hundreds of miles over mountains and across deserts and rivers. The railroad was completed in 1869, and some Chinese workers returned to mining, now as wage-earning lode miners, while others went into the largest cities to work in shoe, cigar, and textile factories. The few Chinese women immigrants were relegated to prostitution and to homework in the garment industry. At the same time, increasing numbers of Chinese men found jobs as domestic servants, as vegetable peddlers and truck farmers on the countryside, and as operators of hand laundries.

By the mid-1870s, anti-Chinese sentiment had reached the proportions of a major political movement in California, and the rhetoric emanating from that movement bore a striking resemblance to anti-black discourse in the East during the antebellum period and beyond. In neither instance did whites as a group charge that members of the other "race" were incapable of performing certain jobs; rather, the arguments against expanding job options for Chinese (as for blacks) rested on issues related to "unfair competition" and perceived immorality of the vulnerable group. Of the Chinese too it was charged, "Hewers of wood and drawers of water they have been since they had a country, and servile laborers they will be to the end of time." [26] Most Chinese men came to the United States as voluntary immigrants, but whites persisted in calling them "coolies," assuming that they were enslaved to unscrupulous labor brokers and thus the ultimate in "cheap labor." As single men, the Chinese could afford to work for much less than (native-born) family men, or so the argument went; just as black workers were supposedly satisfied with fatback and collard greens, so the Chinese "require only rice, dried fish, tea, and a few simple vegetables" to keep them alive. Whites went further to decry the Chinese in general as "a nation of thieves," they charged that Chinese women ("by the cheapness of their offers") in particular existed as sources of disease and moral pollution for susceptible American boys.[27]

Proponents of immigration restriction claimed that Chinese domestics had pushed American women and girls from their rightful employment, and that Chinese factory workers had plunged native-born male breadwinners into poverty and despair. In this view, servile labor rendered all labor "dishonorable," leaving honest white men to bear an economic burden forced upon them by the rapacious newcomers. In

1877, one California state legislator echoed a charge leveled against African Americans in the North a few decades before, when he suggested that Chinese workers were forcing white men "from the field" of labor. Competition from the immigrants "drives [whites] to starvation. It is a competition that they cannot undertake."[28] The social equation was manifest: whites would suffer to the extent that the Chinese were able to find employment for themselves. No wonder then that California politicians of all stripes found the Chinese an easy scapegoat, and implored the federal government "to turn back this tide and to free the land from what is a monstrous evil and promises to be a lasting curse."[29] These charges inspired the formation of the California Workingmen's Party, a movement that enjoyed its greatest electoral successes at the state and local levels during the late 1870s.

In fact, most Chinese workers were "gap fillers," taking jobs that white men (and women) did not want, or were unavailable to do; and it was the railroad, bringing cheap goods from the East Coast, and not "degraded Chinese labor" that pushed manufacturing wages low and eventually killed off a number of fledgling local industries, including shoes and cigars. In the case of the San Francisco harness industry, the paltry pay accorded unskilled Chinese workers actually helped the industry to survive, providing jobs for skilled white workers. Virtually no Chinese men worked as bricklayers, carpenters, or carriage-makers, and yet when depression hit the state in the 1870s, whites in those crafts (and others) blamed their ill fortune on Chinese immigrants. Thus did Chinese entrepreneurs and wage workers serve as convenient targets for white men who expected to find their own "Gold Mountain" in California, but encountered instead a volatile and unpredictable economy – once again, one not so different from the one they had left behind in the East or the Midwest.

The California social division of labor also emerged out of a series of state and private actions designed specifically to curb the job opportunities of Chinese men and women. Congress denied Chinese immigrants the right to become naturalized citizens and in 1882 passed the Chinese Exclusion Act, which had the dual effect of drastically reducing the numbers of Chinese in the country, and stigmatizing those who remained. Chinese women were barred from entering the United States altogether unless they were the wives of wealthy merchants; the legislation however did not end the practice of smuggling young Chinese women (who were then forced into prostitution) into the country. Of all Chinese immigrants, these (representing 5 percent of about 100,000 Chinese in the 1880s), were the most vulnerable, and exploited by men of all groups. Besides suffering the health hazards attendant upon this kind of job, prostitutes like Chin Cook and Chin Wooey faced daily, and deadly, danger from men of their own group who attacked them physically (in the cases of these two San Francisco women, with knives and hatchets) if they refused to pay protection money.

Local municipalities imposed discriminatory taxes, licensing fees, and other restrictions on Chinese miners, peddlers, and laundry owners, and barred the Chinese from employment on public works projects altogether. Zoning laws confined vice districts to Chinese residental neighborhoods. A series of pogroms aimed at Chinese communities – in Los Angeles and San Francisco in 1871, for example – resulted in the murder of Chinese men and women, the wholesale destruction of their property, and, in some cases (in Humboldt County in 1885), the violent expulsion of all Chinese immigrants.

On the streets, "The peculiarity of the costume forms an excuse to provoke something of an animosity" as white men felt free to attack Chinese pedestrians.[30] Thus the Chinese as political targets became a uniting force for Republicans and Democrats, natives and European immigrants, and for workingmen's organizations throughout the state. No matter how promising the labor militance of Asian workers in general, the American Federation of Labor declared flatly that it would "under no circumstance accept membership of any Chinese or Japanese."

"Racial" hostility derived not from some innate, abstract prejudice on the part of whites against Asians in general, but more often than not reflected a particular group's perceived economic or political interest. In contrast to working-class white men, railroad barons and factory owners were effusive in their praise for the Chinese as reliable and conscientious workers, and throughout California, white housewives collectively resisted calls to join public expressions of racial hatred expressed by their husbands, and refrained from boycotting Chinese peddlers and laundries, and dismissing their own Chinese servants. For example, the white housewives of Chico, California (at least some of whom had been born in the antebellum South where they had enjoyed the services of black domestics), turned their backs on the efforts of the town's Anti-Chinese Association, which sponsored a steam laundry in order to displace Chinese hand launderers. The women complained that the machines did a poor job on the ornamentation that adorned their clothing and linens: "For fluting and manipulating ruffles, etc., the Chinaman stands without a rival."[31] At the same time, of course, this sense of equanimity stemmed not from principle but from the fact that these women relied on the services provided by Chinese workers and hoped to avoid performing those same services (free of charge) for their own households.

Because of the sex-ratio imbalance in mid-nineteenth century California, the Chinese managed to secure for themselves entrepreneurial niches by providing services to their compatriots and to the white community at large, especially in the laundry business. Again, these strategies were based on economic and not necessarily "cultural" factors; as Lee Chew, an immigrant, noted, "The Chinese laundryman does not learn his trade in China; there are no laundries in China. The women there do the washing in tubs and have no washboards or flat irons." Lew Chew himself had learned the laundry business from an American white woman.[32]

Single Chinese men formed partnerships in order to pursue these opportunities, as well as others in commercial agriculture. Clearly, demographic factors – the absence of family units – played a role in this form of labor organization. And as a community, the Chinese were aggressive in striking for higher wages and better working conditions, and in using the courts to challenge discriminatory legislation that threatened their livelihood. In response to the vicious attacks visited upon them in the 1870s and 1880s, whole neighborhoods scattered to find work where white people were scarce – on the railroads in Arizona, in the salmon canneries of the Northwest. In this latter job skilled Chinese butchers soon found themselves replaced by machines, in particular the so-called "iron chink" that deprived them of skilled jobs. By the early twentieth century, when the number of California Chinese were dwindling, the group began to enjoy a more favorable public image (conversely, the increasingly visible Japanese emerged as the new menace to the integrity of the "American" workingman and woman.) For example, Kan Tin Loy worked as a miner, farmer, translator, and grocer in Nevada County in the late nineteenth century. His hard work paid off in the form of the material success enjoyed by his children, John and Lily Tin Loy (her purchase of a "fine horse and buggy with which she intends to amuse herself and her numerous caucasian playmates" was deemed worthy of a mention in the local newspaper.)[33] Meanwhile, a succession of immigrants came to dominate California field labor during the period spanning the 1880s through the 1920s – the Chinese were succeeded by the Japanese, and in turn the Filipinos and Mexicans. Yet few African Americans or Chinese Americans would be able to afford the "fine horse and buggy" that served as a status symbol in late nineteeenth-century communities.

Despite the oppressiveness of racial ideologies and the political mechanisms that sustained those ideologies, some African Americans and Chinese emerged as leaders to challenge the mythos of servility that proved to be such a debilitating force. In the fall of 1890 William H. Holtzclaw entered Tuskegee Institute and studied the printer's trade. During his summers he taught at small rural schools in Georgia and Mississippi, noting that white planters "seemed to be afraid of the results of Negro education." In 1903, with the help of northern philanthropists and "a little band of Negro farmers," Holtzclaw founded the Utica Normal and Industrial Institute, located in Mississippi's Black Belt. Soon after, he ascended the national stage as a writer and speaker on behalf of black education and against school segregation (black children "must be educated, must be unfettered, set free"), providing sketches of his life for the *Saturday Evening Post* and *World's Work*, both popular magazines, and in 1915, publishing his autobiography, *The Black Man's Burden*.[34] In the process Holtzclaw contributed to a larger national debate about the meaning of work within a modernizing society, and for him and other leaders and educators like him, times were changing very quickly indeed.

FURTHER READING

Primary Sources

California Legislature. *Senate Special Committee on Chinese Immigration: Its Social, Moral, and Political Effects; Report to the California State Senate of the Special Committee on Chinese Immigration*. Sacramento, CA: State Printing Office, 1878.

DuBois, W. E. B. *The Philadelphia Negro: A Social Study*. New York: Schocken, 1967.

Fields, Mamie Garvin with Karen Fields. *Lemon Swamp and Other Places: A Carolina Memoir*. New York: Free Press, 1983.

Foner, Philip S. and Ronald L. Lewis, ed. *The Black Worker: A Documentary History from Colonial Times to the Present*. 4 vols. Philadelphia: Temple University Press, 1978.

Lerner, Gerda. *Black Women in White America: A Documentary History*. New York: Vintage, 1972.

Secondary Sources

Almaguer, Tomas. *Racial Fault Lines: The Historical Origins of White Supremacy in California*. California: University of California Press, 1994.

Arnesen, Eric. *Waterfront Workers of New Orleans: Race, Class, and Politics, 1863–1923*. New York: Oxford University Press, 1991.

Clark-Lewis, Elizabeth. *Living In, Living Out: African-American Domestics in Washington, D. C., 1910–1940*. Washington, DC: Smithsonian Institution Press, 1994.

Daniel, Pete. *The Shadow of Slavery: Peonage in the South, 1901–1969*. Urbana: University of Illinois Press, 1972.

Foner, Philip S. *Organized Labor and the Black Worker, 1619–1973.* New York: Praeger, 1974.

Hunter, Tera. *To Joy My Freedom: Southern Black Women's Lives and Labors After the Civil War.* Cambridge: Harvard University Press, 1997.

Jones, Jacqueline. *The Dispossessed: America's Underclasses from the Civil War to the Present.* New York: Basic Books, 1992.

Letwin, Daniel. *The Challenge of Interracial Unionism: Alabama Coal Miners, 1878–1921.* Chapel Hill: University of North Carolina Press, 1998.

Lewis, Ronald. *Black Coal Miners in America: Race, Class, and Community Conflict, 1780–1980.* Lexington: University Press of Kentucky, 1987.

Lichtenstein, Alex. *Twice the Work of Free Labor: The Political Economy of Convict Labor in the New South.* London: Verso: 1996.

McKiven, Henry M. *Iron and Steel: Class, Race, and Community in Birmingham, Alabama, 1875–1920.* Chapel Hill: University of North Carolina Press, 1995.

Saxton, Alexander. *The Indispensable Enemy: Labor and the Anti-Chinese Movement in California.* Berkeley: University of California Press, 1971.

6

The Laboring Classes in Turn-of-the-Century America

On the night of November 22, 1909, young women garment workers in New York City attended a mass meeting in the Great Hall of the People in Cooper Union. Over the last few months, a strike by shirtwaist workers of Local 25 had turned ugly, as women pickets were harrassed and beaten by city police and employers' private security guards. Sponsored by the International Ladies Garment Workers Union (ILGWU), the Cooper Union meeting featured some of the most prominent labor leaders of the city and the nation – Samuel Gompers, the cigarmaker who was now head of the American Federation of Labor (AFL); Leonora O'Reilly, an organizer for the Women's Trade Union League, an organization of middle-class supporters of women workers; and Jacob Panken of the Socialist Party. Speaker after speaker condemned the brutal working conditions characteristic of the garment industry on the Lower East Side – the long hours and meagre pay, the employers' disdain for basic health and safety measures. Finally a young worker, Clara Lemlich, called out from the floor, "I want to say a few words." A reporter in attendance recounted the scene that followed: "Cries came from all over the hall. 'Get up on the platform.' Willing hands lifted the frail little girl with the flashing black eyes to the stage and she said simply: 'I have listened to all the speakers. I would not have further patience for talk, as I am one of those who feels and suffers from the things pictured. I move that we go on a general strike.'" The crowd erupted into applause. The following day, 15,000 shirtwaist makers went out on strike, and thousands more followed over the next few weeks; the "Uprising of the Twenty Thousand" had begun with Clara Lemlich's call for action among the city's garment workers.[1]

Later, people would marvel that such a "frail little girl," such a "wisp of a girl," could generate so much excitement in Cooper Hall that evening.[2] Yet Clara Lemlich was no meek girl speaking out on the spur of the moment. By 1909 she had earned a reputation for herself as one of the most energetic and militant members of the ILGWU (she represented her local on the Executive Board of the union), she had been fired from several jobs for her attempts to organize her co-workers, and she was attending Socialist Party meetings on a regular basis. Her speech to the crowd represented not a beginning, or for that matter a culmination, of her devotion to the garment workers; rather, it was one among many opportunities she seized over the course of her lifetime to rally workers (paid and unpaid) to the cause of social justice.

Clara Lemlich was born in the Ukranian village of Gorodok in 1886. Her family fled to the United States in 1903, soon after pogroms devastated the Jewish community of nearby Kishinev. Like 2 million other Eastern European Jewish immigrants who came to the United States between 1881 and 1924, Lemlich and her family left behind a region in turmoil; the forces of industrialization were transforming the social landscape, dispossessing farmers and small tradesmen alike. Young Jewish men and women pushed off the land and into garment factories, along with their more privileged counterparts in the universities, debated the revolutionary theories of the day – Socialism, Zionism, Marxism, women's rights. Though her parents disapproved of her efforts to educate herself, Clara Lemlich persisted, and soon came to the conclusion that radical theories without the requisite political action would amount to little more than wishful thinking among the downtrodden.

The great strike of 1909 yielded mixed results. For months, young workers marched on the picket lines in the company of the well-to-do members of the Women's Trade Union League, and money poured in from all over the country to help sustain the strike. Yet in the end the ILGWU's male negotiators abandoned the issue of worker safety in favor of slight pay increases for some of their members. The consequences of this strategy were horrific. In 1911, the Triangle Shirtwaist Fire claimed the lives of 146 young women workers, most of whom died after jumping out of the flaming building onto the pavement below. The grim sight of their bodies piled deep on the blood-spattered sidewalk haunted labor activists like Lemlich for decades to come.

That night in November, 1909, Clara Lemlich had addressed the Cooper Union crowd in Yiddish, and we can only speculate about the effect the speech had on the Italian women who must have also crowded into the hall. Lemlich and other Jewish labor leaders came out of a culture suffused with radical ideas, and one that was committed to collective action on behalf of workers' rights. In contrast, the Italian community discouraged the kind of public speaking and public activity demanded of workers (especially women workers) caught up in the labor movement. The case of New York City garment workers reminds us that these workers constituted a myriad of overlapping, self-conscious groups – women, Jews, Italians, labor radicals, young people, shirtwaist or handkerchief workers (for example), residents of the Lower East Side. These various collective identities alternately fostered and inhibited coalitions among workers of all kinds.

Between the Civil War and World War I, first-generation immigrants and their children dominated the American industrial, mining, and construction working classes, and provided the muscle power that fueled an economic revolution. During those years, 25 million immigrants entered the United States, and, beginning in the 1880s, most of them hailed from Eastern and Southeastern Europe – Greeks, Poles, Russian Jews, Italians, Slavs, and Turks. Together with native-born workers, these groups formed a massive queue revealing the ethnic and demographic dimensions of the American work force: Protestant English-speakers found jobs in the new tertiary sector of the economy, working in office buildings and department stores; elite male artisans, some immigrant and some native-born, managed to retain their crafts in an era of technological innovation; ethnic entrepreneurs catered to the needs of their respective communities; and Italian, Polish, and Slavic men sought employment in construction and heavy industry. In 1890, 90 percent of New York's public works employees and 99 percent of Chicago's street workers were Italian immigrants. By the early twentieth century, more than 90 percent of Pennsylvania anthracite miners were foreign-born, most from Eastern and Southern Europe. In major cities like Chicago, Milwaukee, Detroit, New York, St Louis, Cleveland, and San Francisco, about eight out of ten workers were immigrants or the children of immigrants.

Modern industrial society is often associated with the image of men working machines, but in fact the turn-of-the-century work force was diverse in terms of workers' gender, age, and tasks. Women and children constituted a majority of garment and textile workers, and these groups of workers *qua* family members predominated in agriculture and in certain kinds of food processing. Moreover, as we have seen in the case of African-American laborers, whole groups of people continued to work in traditional ways, far removed from the factory workshop.

With the increased use of sophisticated technology and production processes, dangerous and unhealthful working conditions became one of the hallmarks of industrial labor; more and more, workers would evaluate their own situation not only according to how much money they made, but also according to the degree they might maintain their physical well-being in the course of a week, or a lifetime. In Chicago meatpacking plants, workers wielded huge cleavers in sub-freezing lockers; in Southern Piedmont textile mills, machine operatives breathed in a fine dust just as deadly as the soot that claimed the lives of coal miners; and workers all over the country lost their limbs and sometimes their lives as a result of speed-ups and industrial accidents. During the last decade of the nineteenth century, bakers worked more than 65 hours a week on average, and steelworkers exceeded that number, laboring 12-hour days, seven days a week, with one day off every two weeks, their crushing workload a direct consequence of the destruction of unionism at Andrew Carnegie's Homestead plant (near Pittsburgh) in 1892. Workers' wages hardly kept up with the spectacular growth of the American economy; indeed, most of the major strikes of this period resulted from employers' attempts to save on production costs by slashing wages.

If any product is representative of the vast changes affecting the American labor force during this period, it is the automobile. Cars rapidly became prized as status symbols as well as a means of transportation, but it was not until the 1920s that a substantial number of the people who made them could afford to buy one. Henry Ford's innovative assembly line made production more efficient and encouraged other manufacturers to experiment with labor-saving shop-floor routines and machines. In 1916, the Ford plant in Highland Park, Michigan, employed 33,000 workers, a striking innovation revealing of mass production in the service of high consumer demand. With the car came whole new job categories – auto mechanics and filling station attendants – and a boost to a variety of supporting industries, from glass and rubber to steel and oil; at the same time, workers in traditional crafts like blacksmithing and carriage-making gradually lost their jobs. Marketing and financing the purchase of cars required the services of bankers, local dealers, and advertising executives. From the worker who drilled the Pennsylvania oil that fueled the car, through the assembly-line workers who produced it and the Detroit executives who oversaw the selling of it, the auto industry encapsulated the major transformations in the American labor force.

Indeed, more generally, between the Civil War and World War I an economic revolution based upon the expansion of heavy industries like steel, oil, and railroads, provided the foundation for a consumer revolution that presented Americans with vast choices related to ready-made clothing; new household appliances such as refrigerators, electric stoves, and vacuum cleaners; and even canned and processed foods. These new products spawned new kinds of services provided by sales, insurance, and marketing agents; by bankers and financiers; and personnel managers. In the realm of office and clerical work, young native-born women found a ready-made place for themselves, for businesses were becoming increasingly conscious of the way they presented their products to the consumer. Hence, department stores favored attractive young white women (without the trace of an accent) as sales clerks, insurance corporations hired them as stenographers and office receptionists, and telephone companies favored applicants who could sound sweet and pleasing over the phone (and smile prettily in advertisements for phone company services).

Urban corporate and sales cultures were dominated by native-born Americans organized according to a gendered hierarchy – male managers, who were idealized as ambitious decision-makers, and their female assistants – secretaries, stenographers, typewriters, and file clerks – who were supposed to be personable, dependable, and efficient. A contemporary poet described office etiquette from the perspective of the female typist in "Ode to the Boss": "You think – and then I pound/When you are wrong and I am right/I never make a sound!"[3]

Depending on their ethnic status and level of formal education, white women found expanding job opportunities that reflected the development of a complex, modern society. As we have seen, the role of women in the Civil War accelerated the "feminization" of the "helping professions," especially in the fields of teaching and nursing. The social dislocations caused by foreign immigration, internal migration, and growing poverty contributed to the rise of a new group of reformers, including social settlement workers, missionaries, social workers, and local community activists; some of these workers received pay for their labors and others did not.

By the late nineteenth century, "Progressive" reformers promoted a vast array of activities designed to help specific groups "adjust" to the new realities of an industrial society. Academics; members of local voluntary associations and ladies' clubs; city and state employees; and directors of schools, prisons, and asylums sought to mediate between the restless, potentially "dangerous classes" (of which Clara Lemlich was presumably a prime example) on the one hand, and the arrogant, public-be-damned labor barons, men like Andrew Carnegie (steel) and George Pullman (railroad cars) on the other. Critics charged that such efforts simply encouraged employers to exploit their workforces with impunity, on the assumption that well-meaning reformers would ameliorate oppressive conditions by limiting the cases of actual homelessness or starvation, for example. An organizer for the AFL, Ida Van Etten told federation convention delegates in 1890 that "Charity has only succeeded in making it easier for the unscrupulous employers . . . to exploit [their workers] safely and respectably."[4]

The social agenda of black women as paid workers in the "helping professions" or as members of clubs affiliated with the National Association of Colored Women ([NACW] founded in 1896), differed in certain key respects from that of their white counterparts. For example, in the absence of aid from white-dominated charities and social settlements, local branches of the NACW sponsored orphanages, employment agencies, reading rooms, and working girls' homes; offered homemaking classes for poor women; and launched protests against the lynching of black men and women, a bloody tide that was sweeping the Southern states. Black women throughout the country worked actively to contribute to mutual aid and secret societies that helped them supplement their meagre pay in the paid labor force; these societies offered assistance to widows, the elderly, and the ill in times of need.

During this period (like any other period in history), women's unpaid work in the home served as the infrastructure of all kinds of endeavors outside the home. Housework presented challenges regardless of the class of women involved, and the work associated with domestic chores represented a wide spectrum, from lugging water into the house every day (among poor women) to supervising a small army of servants (among the wealthiest). Southern sharecroppers and Midwestern tenants, black and white, struggled to maintain some semblance of order within cabins that lacked closets, shelves, and storage compartments of all kinds – not to mention running water and electricity, even after those innovations had become commonplace in urban areas. Immigrant housewives waged a constant battle against the dirt and roaches that seemed ubiquitous in crowded tenement buildings. Some fulltime homemakers of necessity divided their time between caring for large families on the one hand and earning some money by making artificial flowers or taking in boarders on the other.

Middle-class women contended with problems of a different order; they eagerly invested in labor-saving devices like carpet sweepers (available in the 1880s), electric irons (1903), and electric vacuum cleaners (1907). In the process, however, they confronted a new and insidious standard of "the normal" in terms of household cleanliness, a standard that few ever felt they could live up to.

More often than not, of course, the work performed by any particular mother or daughter was directly related to the wage or salary work performed by a husband or father. It was a firmly established principle of labor economics around the turn of the century that a working-class family relied on the earning capacity of children and wives, for male manual laborers did not make a living wage (that is, enough money to sustain a family on the basis of their own pay alone).

Most immigrants to the United States settled in the vicinity of their compatriots and attempted to sustain distinctive ethnic family economies. In the late nineteenth century, some newcomers (especially Greeks and Italians) came as "birds of passage," single men who worked in this country from the spring through the fall, laying railroad tracks, digging canals and tunnels, and constructing bridges and roads. These men returned to their homeland for the winter; their priority was to earn good wages by working long hours. In contrast, many immigrants who came to stay (and this group included virtually all of the Jews brutally driven from the Pale of Settlement in Eastern Europe) attempted to accommodate their work lives to their family lives. Italian and Polish fathers disapproved of sending their daughters to work under the roof of another man (in a way that Scandinavian and Irish fathers did not). Most immigrant married women refrained from working outside the home for wages, though many engaged in home work or other forms of money-making within the confines of their own households.

Key to the long-range, intergenerational success of ethnic groups was their ability to locate entrepreneurial niches for themselves. It is possible to generalize about some of these niches – the Italians in barbering, landscape contracting, and the grocery business; Greeks in the restaurant business; Jews in peddling, garment-making, and retail; the Irish, who preceded Eastern Europeans to this country, in government employment, as operatives in the Democratic Party, and as contractors dependent on city patronage. Still, individual cities had their own ethnic job structures; for example, by 1907, 1,500 Greeks had settled in Tarpon Springs, Florida (near Tampa, on the Gulf of Mexico), and established themselves as divers for ocean sponges. In the same area, Cubans concentrated in the cigar industry.

As a means of economic security, and as avenues for upward mobility, ethnic niches served several functions. They channeled recent immigrants immediately into jobs, and they helped to create on-the-job solidarity among workers who were often members of extended kin groups. Niches offered internal ladders of mobility; the partisan-politics niche for the Irish, for example, held out the hope to a young man that he might ascend from the job of messenger boy (working for a local politician) to a powerful position on the city council someday. Niches allowed immigrants to accumulate cash and eventually move out of their own enclaves into better neighborhoods, where their children attended good schools, achieved higher levels of formal education, and eventually entered jobs outside their ethnic niches. On the other hand, the racial and ethnic exclusivity of niches inhibited working-class consciousness and contributed to inter-group rivalry. And some native-born employers used the notion of ethnic niches as a rationale for excluding immigrant workers from specific jobs – as when bosses considered the Italians "ill suited" for work in steel mills but enthusiastically accepted Polish applicants for those jobs. Black workers lacked niches of their own – in the North they had to compete with immigrants for service jobs like those of waiter and servant.[5]

Because production processes were in a constant state of flux – employers experimented with new machines as well as new ways of organizing their workers – the social composition of any particular labor force remained fluid and ever changing. In the cigar industry, the increased use of women accompanied the mechanization of the craft, and in the process displaced male workers who had long boasted of a proud, skilled tradition. Similarly, tailors were gradually replaced by semi-skilled cutters and sewing-machine operators. In the Midwest, where technology made dramatic inroads into the social division of labor, family farmers became a thing of the past, as "food factories" came to rely upon mechanical reapers and steam-powered threshers operated by transient laborers. In some cases these transformations provoked bitter resistance. For example, a contemporary conveyed a sense of wonder mixed with dread at the sight of a self-binding wheat reaper, "that perfection of farm machinery, that ghostly marvel of a thing, with the single sinister arm, tossing the finished sheaves from it in such a nervous, spiteful . . . style."[6] This particular machine required only one man to operate it, and virtually eliminated the need for hand reapers. In 1878, Ohio farm hands launched nighttime raids and destroyed the reapers, mowers, and threshers of their employers.

In heavy manufacturing, a procession of ethnic groups could change the face of a particular factory. In Chicago meatpacking plants around the turn of the century, for example, (in the words of a contemporary), "The Americans as wage-earners have been practically driven out of the stock yards and are being followed by the Irish and Germans. The older nationalities have already disappeared from the unskilled occupations, most of which are now entirely manned by Slovaks, Poles, and Lithuanians." Hiring practices at the Pennsylvania Steel Company at Steelton, Pennsylvania, reflected the order of arrival of the following groups: from 1870 to 1880: English, Irish, German, Welsh; from 1880 to 1890: German, Polish, Slovenian, Italian; from 1890 to 1900: German, Polish, Slovenian, Italian, Croatian; and after 1900: Slovenian, Italian, Croatian, Hungarian-German, Magyar, Serbian, Romanian, Macedonian.[7]

Predictably, the workers in individual industries developed certain shop-floor cultures that were contingent upon the demographic make-up of the workforce and the turnover rates of the employees themselves. Not all young women garment workers cast their lot with organized labor; some devoted their work days to gossiping about friends and dreaming about marriage; their evenings were spent not in union meetings but at dance halls and, increasingly, at moving picture shows, where they could meet men who would "treat" them – that is, pay for a good time.

Workers in a wide variety of industries, from meatpacking to auto and textile manufacturing, resisted the efforts of bosses to force them to establish a work pace that most of them would have a hard time maintaining. In Chicago, the International Harvester Corporation published a brochure to help Polish workers learn to speak and read English:

> I hear the whistle. I must hurry.
> I hear the five minute whistle.
> It is time to go into the shop.
> I take my check from the gate board and hang it on the department board
> I change my clothes and get ready to work.
> The starting whistle blows.
> I eat my lunch.
> It is forbidden to eat until then.[8]

That workers resented such regimentation is revealed by patterns of chronic absenteeism, by the "Blue Mondays" taken off to recover from the excesses of the weekend, and by the annual turnover rates (as high as 100 percent in some cases) that forced bosses into a never-ending cycle of hiring and training new employees.

Nevertheless, it would be a mistake to posit a stark dichotomy between the seasonal rhythms of agriculture and the

machine-based regimentation of various work-sites. Manufacturing establishments were vulnerable to periodic fluctua-
tions in the supply of raw materials and in consumer demand.
Moreover, the more elaborate or sohpisticated – or conversely,
the more primitive – the technology, the more likely operations would have to cease temporarily for repairs. In 1902, an
engineer described the convoluted process by which boilers
and steam engines (fueled by wood) supplied power to phosphate mining operations in Florida, and then concluded, "The
cost of repairs, which in itself, is a large item, is supplemented
by the money loss resulting from the shut-down of the plant
while repairs are being made. The effect of a shut-down has
also a demoralizing influence upon the workmen. It is estimated that at least two hours per day of twenty-four are lost
by shut-down."[9] The case of phosphate mining serves as a
reminder that employers usually considered labor to be their
most costly – as well as flexible – expense. This particular
type of extractive labor constituted a notoriously ill-paid, disagreeable, and hazardous occupation, and employers were
forced to deploy armed guards to keep workers on the job.

Technological innovation went hand-in-hand with the expansion of the unskilled labor force, an urban proletariat that
built the underground and above-ground transportation systems, water conduits, and large office buildings that were radically altering the urban landscape. Establishments like
meat-packing houses, iron and steel mills, and machine shops
included vast numbers of workers who had no specialized
skills. In 1899, Bethlehem Steel employed 600 shovelers in
their blast furnaces in a single plant. Frederick Winslow Taylor,
the scientific management expert, was hired by the company
to streamline their production processes; he managed to reduce the number of shovelers to 140.[10] At the same time, in
certain industries, the use of labor-saving technology was reducing the need for both skilled and unskilled labor; in the
steel industry, for example, the semi-skilled machine tender
represented the wave of the future, and in the Birmingham
District of Alabama, such changes provided an entrée for black
men into the industry; previously, the monopoly of skilled

white workers had barred blacks from jobs above menial labor.

Around the turn of the century, members of the American "chattering classes" – usually identified as intellectuals, policy makers, and reformers – engaged in a lively debate over the definition of the good society and the place of various groups within it. The wrenching effects of large-scale population movements, economic development, and urban growth captured the attention of observers who pressed any number of crusades, ranging from world peace to the conservation of natural resources, the disenfranchisement of poor and illiterate folk (black and white), women's right to vote, housing reform, workplace health and safety standards, and the abolition of the ward system of city government. The chattering classes hardly agreed among themselves on many issues (Theodore Roosevelt and Jane Addams both considered themselves "Progressives," a fact revealing of the slipperiness of the term), but they probably all would have acknowledged the centrality of the "labor question" to the new social order. For the most part, elite Americans alternately pitied the victims of the new technology, or vilified them as sources of social strife and disorder.

At the same time, workers of various stripes were doing a lot of "chattering" on their own, and more significantly, they were going beyond talking by organizing themselves and in this way thrusting labor issues to the forefront of a national debate about the social costs of industrialization. Workers communicated among themselves in the pages of union journals and newsletters; they spoke indirectly to a national audience through the muckraking exposés of investigative journalists; and they engaged in collective action, thereby reminding bosses and managers that actions often spoke louder than words.

During the early nineteenth century, craft guilds and fraternal orders had metamorphosed into craft unions; soon after the Civil War, labor groups began an active campaign to find common ground with each other. City trades assemblies, like those in Boston, New York, Chicago, Albany, Buffalo, Troy, Philadelphia, Cincinnati, Detroit, St Louis, Pittsburgh, and

San Francisco, raised money for the strike funds of their members, and also endorsed boycotts of offending employers – the "bannering" of "rat" employers.[11] Some of these trade assemblies published labor-reform journals, which served as forums for the discussion of issues related to workers' rights and the conditions of labor.

The history of national labor organizations begins in 1866, with the founding of the National Labor Union (NLU) in Baltimore. Over the next few years, the NLU came to represent a collection of unions including (for example) the National Typographical Union (founded in 1850), Sons of Vulcan (ironmakers, founded in 1862), Ship Carpenters' and Calkers' International Union (1864), Mule Spinners (1866), Knights of St Crispin (male shoemakers, 1867), Daughters of St Crispin (female shoemakers, 1869), Sons of Adam (cloth cutters, 1872), and Brotherhood of Locomotive Firemen (1873). (The names of some of these groups suggest their origins as fraternal orders.) The organization offered rhetorical support for the rights of white women and African-American workers, yet it failed to challenge the exclusive racial and gender policies of most of its member unions. Finding little common ground for workers concentrated in a wide range of specialized crafts and affected in disparate ways by new technology, the National Labor Union was defunct by the mid-1870s, but the elusive quest for workers' unity (too often defined by male trade unionists exclusively) was not.

The NLU and subsequent labor organizations were forced to contend with the deep hostility with which employers, conservative commentators, and government officials viewed unions of all kinds. For example, the October, 1877 issue of *Scribner's Monthly* devoted space to "The Great Strike" and condemned the violent work stoppages and demonstrations that had swept the country the previous summer. In July of that year, the Baltimore and Ohio Railroad had announced a third consecutive wage cut of 30 percent, prompting a strike of railroad workers in Martinsburg, West Virginia. That particular walk-out ended when President Rutherford B. Hayes sent federal troops to escort strikebreakers to work; but the contagion of resistance spread to other parts of the country like wild fire. In the Midwest, strikers tied up transportation lines. Bloody battles between workers on the one hand and scabs, private security forces, local police, and government troops on the other left people dead in Baltimore, Pittsburgh, Chicago, and Indianapolis. In St Louis and other cities, a variety of workers walked off the job to show their solidarity with railroad employees. An Executive Committee coordinating the general strike issued a proclamation that included the following resolution: "that, as every man willing to perform a use to society is entitled to a living, therefore, if our present system of production and distribution fails to provide for our wants, it then becomes the duty of the government to enact such laws as will ensure equal justice to all people of the nation."[12]

The *Scribner's* editorial writer expressed a widely held view among businessmen and government officials when he wrote,

> The day of the inauguration of trades unions and labor organizations in this country was a day the blackest and fullest menace to the popular prosperity and peace that ever dawned upon the nation. They have been an unmitigated curse to employers and employees alike. The nature and purpose of these organizations are simply outrageous. They have been despotic toward their own members, oppressive toward the class in whose interest they pretend to have been established, impertinent and intermeddling. They have assumed the right to control property and business in which they had no more right than if they lived on the moon.[13]

Still, the 1877 strike dramatized the widespread discontent among workers throughout the country in a wide range of industries; and events during that strife-torn July indicated that the battle lines had been drawn between labor organizers and their powerful opponents, representatives of both private industry and public order.

The Noble and Holy Order of the Knights of Labor, which began as a secret fraternal order in 1869 and developed into a national association in 1878, served as a transition group between traditional craft unions and a new industrial order encompassing a diversity of workers all over the country. (The Knights' motto declared, "An injury to one is an injury to all.") Led by a machinist, Terrence V. Powderly, the Knights welcomed into its ranks virtually everyone who worked for a living, with the exception of bankers, lawyers, liquor dealers, speculators, gamblers, and stock brokers. In certain Southern cities like Richmond the Knights enjoyed fleeting success as an umbrella group for a number of different unions (black members were relegated to segregated locals). By the late 1880s, bolstered by their part in the "great upheaval of 1884" in the coal fields of Pennsylvania and Ohio and in the railroad yards of Missouri and Illinois, the Knights claimed a national membership of 750,000. Yet this group too fell victim to the complex dynamics of an unwieldy national labor force composed of many different groups experiencing mechanization and displacement at different rates. Moreover, within the South, employers became adept at playing off black and white workers against each other. In Oxford, North Carolina, a white artisan noted that the biracial appeal of the local Knights assembly prompted this reaction among the general white population: "They pointed at us with scorn and kept crying 'Nigger! Nigger! until the two words 'nigger' and Knight became almost synonymous terms."[14]

These same dilemmas confronted the Populists, a political party that aspired to national prominence via coalitions of blacks and whites, farmers and industrial workers, Southerners and Midwesterners, city and rural folk. As heir to the Grange and the Farmers' Alliances (white and "Colored") the People's Party capitalized on the spreading unrest among small farmers in the Midwest and the South, where tenancy had engulfed the class of small landholders among the white population. (In 1900, nearly 50 percent of all Southern farms, and more than a quarter of all Midwestern farms, were operated by people who did not own the land they worked.)[15] At the grassroots level, the Populists tapped into a wellspring of discontent among workers who had lost the status of independent operators and now functioned more like a rural proletariat. Bankers and other creditors were their "employers," the railroads and grain-elevator operators their tormentors. In 1896 the decision of the Populists to cast their lot with the

Democratic candidate for president (William Jennings Bryan) spelled doom for the party as an independent movement, and soon after that, racial prejudice among whites tore the group apart in the South.

In the end, late nineteenth-century labor organizations that represented specific groups of workers were among those groups possessed of the most staying power. The rise of the American Federation of Labor (founded in 1886 by Samuel Gompers) signaled simultaneously the ascendency of skilled white men as leaders of organized labor and the vulnerablity of those men to larger forces of deskilling (Gompers's own craft, cigarmaking, was a case in point). The AFL shunned those very workers who were central to large-scale industrialization – the masses of unskilled shovelers and pickwielders, and the men, women, and children who tended machines. By limiting its membership to skilled workers, and by eschewing overarching theories of political change in favor of "bread and butter" issues like higher wages, shorter hours, and industrial safety, the AFL managed to survive – if not always prosper – during turbulent times.

A number of labor leaders spoke in terms more strident than those of the practical-minded Gompers, and a number of labor organizations offered an alternative and highly visible, if ultimately transitory, vision of labor-management relations compared to the AFL. The Industrial Workers of the World (IWW) was founded in 1905 and, by concentrating on workers shunned by the AFL, served as a forerunner of the Congress of Industrial Organizations. The IWW boasted the motto, "One Big Union," and organized "tramps" in the Northwest, timberworkers in the South, miners in the Southwest, and textile workers in the Northeast (especially in Lawrence, Massachusetts, in 1912). The Wobblies, as they called themselves, spoke and acted in such a militant manner that they of necessity became champions of free speech (or radical insurrection, depending upon one's point of view). During World War I, when the union called for strikes in war-related industries to protest against speed-ups and war-profiteering employers, the IWW found itself targeted by the Justice

Department, and it collapsed under the weight of dogged harrassment by government officials and brutal repression by private security forces.

Among western industrialized nations, the United States possessed a unique record of labor violence in the late nineteenth century, an indication of a tremendous amount of state power brought to bear against men and women desperate to claim a measure of dignity for themselves in the workplace. Some of the most bloody episodes of labor organizing resulted from attempts by organizations of miners and manufacturing workers to resist wage cuts and dangerous working conditions – for example, when the Molly Maguires (a secret inner circle of the Workingmen's Benevolent Association) struck against Pennsylvania coal mine operators in the mid-1870s (20 of their leaders were convicted and executed as a result) and when the Amalgamated Association of Iron and Steel Workers struck Carnegie's Homestead steel plant in Pittsburgh in 1892 (ten men were killed when the governor of Pennsylvania sent 8,000 militiamen to restore order in the town).

The American Railway Union (ARU), led by Eugene Debs, is an example of an early industrial union that transcended constitutive workers' groups – in this case the various Brotherhoods of railroad workers (though the ARU too barred blacks from membership). In 1894, the ARU conducted a strike against the Pullman Railway Car Company in Chicago in response to George Pullman's move to cut wages without reducing the cost of company housing. The Pullman Company eventually quelled the strike, but not before the federal government had committed 2,000 troops to suppress the workers, who had destroyed $340,000 worth of company property. The United Mine Workers too adopted militant tactics of protest, tactics commensurate with the hazards implicit in their jobs. A strike in 1902 claimed the energies of 50,000 miners, and resulted in a 10 percent wage increase and a shortened work day. Though the UMW failed to win recognition from mine owners in the anthracite coal mines of Pennsylvania, it did claim major victories in some of the bituminous fields of the Southern states, and it represented a significant wedge of both industrial unionism and interracialism within the AFL.

In seeking to resolve the 1902 strike, President Theodore Roosevelt had appointed a commission of experts to review the miners' wages and working conditions. Members of the commission included an army engineer, a mining engineer, a businessman familiar with the coal industry, a federal official, a judge, and a sociolgist. The composition of this group revealed the prevailing opinion among politicians and policymakers— that if the "labor question" was a central issue in modern American life, then it was one that could be answered by experts who compiled data and statistics and presented their findings to men and women who were neither laborers nor employers themselves, but rather interested in this issue from the perspective of consumers, humanitarians, civil libertarians, or social philosophers.

Through a variety of means, Americans examined the conditions under which the laboring classes toiled, and explored the larger ramifications of those conditions. Periodicals during the antebellum era had offered to their readers sentimental fiction, travellers' accounts, and ruminations on the two-party political system. After the Civil War, the casual reader perusing popular magazines regularly encountered editorials and articles dealing with "Topics of the Time," and often these topics included labor. Beginning in the 1880s, publications devoted to social issues, like *Charities and the Commons*, paid considerable attention to conditions of employment among various groups. For example, in the February 8, 1908, issue of that magazine, Frank Julian Warne (the compiler of information for a number of charitable organizations) discussed "The Unemployed in New York City." Rather than focusing on the alleged moral deficiencies of workers, Warne stressed the structural causes of unemployment and underemployment and pinpointed the lack of jobs, variable weather conditions, labor disputes, and workers' poor health and disabilities as principal factors that deprived men and women of the opportunity to make a living on a regular basis.

Some periodicals also tackled the the issue of racial

discrimination in the shaping of the modern industrial labor force. In an article published in the *Atlantic Monthly* in 1898, John Stephens Durham, who surveyed the racial division of labor throughout the country, pinpointed the exclusive membership policies of the skilled trades, policies that were at times backed up by "the muzzles of loaded rifles." Concluded Durham, "whenever the union develops effective strength the black workmen must put down the trowel and take up the tray."[16] The January–June 1906 issue of the *Annals of the American Academy of Political and Social Science* was devoted to articles by African-American scholars, including Professor Kelly Miller of Howard University and Professor R. R. Wright, Jr, a sociologist at the University of Pennsylvania. Their reports, focusing on "the economic handicap of the Negro in the North" and the dynamics of northward migration among Southern blacks, were buttressed by statistical information illuminating the exclusion of blacks from industrial workplaces all over the country, and in New York City in particular.

These articles were representative of a new kind of scholarship – the study of workers by highly trained researchers who relied on the extensive compilation of data, whether in the form of statistics, personal interviews, or first-hand observation. During the 1890s, and into the following decade, the scholar W. E. B. DuBois conducted a number of in-depth investigations of black workers in small Southern towns, on sharecropping plantations, and in Northern cities. Sensitive to the history that shaped a particular locale, DuBois explored black workers' thwarted struggles to find jobs commensurate with their abilities and ambitions. DuBois and others, like Mary White Ovington (in her book *Half a Man: The Status of the Negro in New York*, published in 1905) illuminated the ways that ill-paid, irregular work affected the integrity of black family and community life. Both DuBois and Ovington exemplified a larger principle of academic life during the early twentieth century – that distinguished scholars and researchers of all kinds saw no contradiction between "objective" gathering of data and "subjective" policy analysis.

Many researchers sought to let workers speak for themselves. The Russell Sage Foundation funded the Pittsburgh Survey, a six-volume study of industrial workers in the steel city that included personal interviews with laborers; an example is the study of a steel-mill town, "Homestead: The Households of a Mill Town," written by Margaret F. Byington and published in 1910. In some cases the end result of such surveys was a cacophony of voices revealing the barriers to collective action among workers between different industries as well as within specific industries. For *McClure's Magazine* in 1903, Ray Stannard Baker interviewed some of the Pennsylvania anthracite coal miners who refused to join in the 1902 strike. He titled his article "The Right to Work," and quoted extensively from interviews with men like Charles Monie, a Scottish immigrant living in Moosi, Pennsylvania, who declared, "Unionism is all right when it is kept within bounds. But when it says to any man, 'You can't work until we give you permission,' and when it plans to destroy property, I claim that the individual has a right to quit [the union]."[17]

While one hand of the state was using force to suppress strikes, another hand was employing researchers to investigate prevailing wage rates and working conditions. In keeping with the conventional wisdom of the day – that the compilation of raw data would lead to enlightened social policies – the United States government conducted studies of workers under the auspices of various departments and agencies – for example, tomato pickers, sharecroppers in the Mississippi Delta, and East-Coast truck farmers (Department of Agriculture reports); women in the canning and food processing industries (Women's Bureau); children in North Carolina tobacco fields (the Children's Bureau); coal miners in Western Pennsylvania (Department of Labor); and turpentine peons in the Florida swamps (Department of Justice).

Within state and local governments, the general condition of labor inspired not only study but also legislative activity. On the eve of World War I, 20 states had industrial departments for information gathering and oversight, and nearly all boasted bureaus of labor statistics. Still, legislative measures to protect the rights and well-being of workers were uneven during this period. For example, the hazards of coal mining attracted official scrutiny after several disasters within a two-year period (1907–9) claimed almost 1,000 lives; nevertheless, the flurry of state mine-safety legislation passed between 1905 and 1915 remained largely unenforced. In 1908, the Supreme Court upheld the constitutionality of laws designed to compensate workers for injuries suffered on the job, covering an estimated one-quarter of all industrial workers but leaving whole groups unaffected, including agricultural, casual, domestic, mercantile, clerical, and interstate railroad workers. Attempts to limit work hours met with some success – for example, in 1908 the Court upheld an Oregon law that limited the hours of working women. However, the Court's reasoning in this case suggested that legislation itself could serve to further divide workers by distinguishing certain groups from others; the majority of justices claimed they acted "in the firm belief that there was something in [a woman's] place and work in life which justified the legislature in forbidding her to contract for factory work beyond a limited time . . . The race needs her; her friends need her, in a way they do not need the other sex."[18] In the future, such assumptions – based on "musty paternalism" in the words of one historian[19] – would prove divisive among advocates of workers' rights who could not decide among themselves whether or not women workers deserved special consideration from the courts and from employers.

Many of the published studies were conducted by government agencies, private charities, or muckraking magazines with the express purpose of shaping legislation that would address the grim conditions under which these two groups labored. This was especially true in the cases of child laborers and convict workers. The United States Department of Labor Children's Bureau examined the children of Polish workers south of Baltimore who labored in the strawberry fields in the summer, and the young employees of canneries along the Mississippi Gulf coast.[20] The Bureau published exposés of rural child labor in states like Texas, where the public school system was "based upon the fact that the child will be at work until late in the fall and must leave school early in the spring."[21] In 1908, Justice Department investigators reported that, on Avery Island, off the coast of Louisiana, the children of Polish immigrant families who migrated southward seasonally from Baltimore toiled in the stench of unheated seafood packing sheds all winter, their bare feet bleeding from the oyster shells they stood on. The National Child Labor Committee enumerated the industries that relied on youngsters and published their findings in a special issue of the *Annals of the American Academy of Political and Social Science* in 1910.

Some of these studies found their way into (or were commissioned by) popular magazines. For example, in 1911, *The Survey* ran a story about Italian cranberry pickers in New Jersey. Titled "The Cost of the Cranberry Sauce," it was intended to prick the consciences of consumers. A. J. McKelway, an investigator for the Charity Organization Society, published a series of articles on child labor, including one in *The Charities* in 1909 detailing the long hours and grueling work of youthful spinners, doffers, and helpers, some as young as six years old, who toiled in the textile mills of North Carolina. Some of these children were illiterate, and some had worked for years only at night. Lewis Hine, the documentary photographer, wrote a story to accompany the pictures he took of child cotton pickers in the February 7, 1913 issue of *The Survey*: "The cotton picker's bag hanging about the neck of every child, bending his head with its weight and tripping him as he walks, is a symbol of the life his father leads and the life to which the child himself will come."[22] Nevertheless, employers remained unapologetic, citing the need for the children to learn the habits of industry and usefulness at an early age. Moreover, many working-class parents desperately needed the meagre wages of their children in order to keep their families together; these men and women considered the moral pronouncements of child-labor reformers to be misguided and ultimately threatening to the integrity of poor households.

Indeed, despite the potency of their studies and the implicit appeals for justice that accompanied them, advocates for children made little headway in securing the national legislation that would have affected the majority of young workers on the nation's farms and in Southern textile mills and coal mines. By the turn of the century, more than half of all states had passed laws limiting child labor, and in 1916, Congress enacted the Keating-Owen Child Labor Act regulating industries that engaged in interstate commerce. However, these measures affected only a small percentage of the country's nearly 2 million working children. Repeatedly, the Supreme Court interpreted the Consitution's commerce clause rigidly and declared child-labor laws unconstitutional (because such laws allegedly hindered the production of goods shipped between states), a legal argument buttressed by the political influence of manufacturers and by a persistent romanticization of sons and daughters working on the family farm.

In contrast, a number of investigative journalism pieces on peonage and convict labor had some impact in the courts and in state legislatures. Articles like the one by Richard Barry, "Slavery in the South ToDay," published in *Cosmopolitan Magazine* in March, 1907, included the sensational revelations "of appalling conditions in Florida and other states which make possible the actual enslavement of whites and blacks under trust domination." Noted Barry, "The monumental error made by the employers of Florida was in going beyond the black man with their slavery. Had they stuck to the racial division they might have escaped castigation." In Bailey *vs* Alabama (1911) the Supreme Court struck a blow at the practice of peonage that had become commonplace throughout the South. Alonzo Bailey was an African-American sharecropper who had agreed to work for an employer, but quit before his contract expired at the end of the year. He was arrested and charged with defrauding his employer (by accepting advances in the form of food and farm supplies). Bailey's lawyers (whose fees were partially paid by Booker T. Washington), successfully argued that quitting a job was not necessarily proof of a laborer's intent to defraud his employer. However, few workers forced to toil against their will possessed the knowledge or wherewithal that would have enabled them to challenge their captors, and peonage persisted, mostly hidden in forests and swamps throughout the South, well into the twentieth century.

That slavery was bad was about all that Americans could agree upon when it came to discussions of labor in the early twentieth century. Complicating the story was the fact that various groups of workers remained alienated from each other, unable to comprehend the larger forces of industrial change that were encompassing all of them, albeit in different ways. For employers, traditional prejudices – hostilities based upon religion, ethnicity, skin color, and gender – provided a fertile field in which the seeds of mistrust and suspicion could grow and yield the poisonous fruit of mutual antagonism among workers.

Still, this period in American history is notable for the cross-class alliances between middle-class and working-class activists that helped to thrust the everyday struggles of ordinary men and women into the mainstream of public consciousness. The Women's Trade Union League, an association of both prominent, well-to-do women and immigrant women laborers, served to advance the interests of groups like Lower East Side garment workers. Some middle-class women devoted their professional lives to the welfare of workers of all kinds. For example, Florence Kelley served as factory inspector for the state of Illinois from 1899 to 1932, and then as general secretary of the National Consumers League. This organization advocated limits on the working hours of women, and it also singled out fair, socially responsible employers and urged consumers to buy their products.

On the eve of World War I, Clara Lemlich found herself blacklisted by garment-industry employers, and shunned by the men in authority in the ILGWU as well; she had gained a reputation as a "troublemaker," and, as she recalled many years later, even male union organizers considered her a disruptive influence on the shopfloor: "They were afraid for the bosses. Such a radical . . . She'll turn things upside down!" In 1913, she wed Joe Shavelson, a printer and union activist. Making a new home in Brownsville (in Brooklyn), Lemlich Shavelson set about organizing housewives, both as supporters of their menfolk in unions and as community activists in their own right, under the assumption that women consumers could wield a great deal of power if they were determined to act together. In 1918, she helped found the Brownsville Tenants Union, which operated on the principles of a labor union – the idea that withholding one's rent (like withholding one's labor) was the only power that ordinary people could hope to wield against capitalists of all kinds. Still a fiery orator, and a veritable fixture on the radical-activist scene in Brooklyn, "Mother Shavelson" eventually transferred her allegiance away from the ILGWU and to the Communist Party. But even this most doctrinaire of organizations could not contain her. Neghbors would later recall sitting in her kitchen and listening to Lemlich Shavelson exhort her listeners, "You young ones don't understand. Women have to fight for what they want. You can't wait for the men to give it to you."[23]

Clara Lemlich Shavelson thus diverged from the paths of her friends, other women active in the Uprising of the Twenty Thousand, women like Fannia Cohn, who remained within the ILGWU as a life-long advocate for workers' education, and Rose Schneiderman and Pauline Newman, who saw in local New York City Democratic politics the means for insuring workers decent working conditions, a path that eventually took them to the White House and garnered them support from Franklin and Eleanor Roosevelt. Ironically, by that time, militant labor radicals, the ideological heirs of Lemlich Shavelson, had also decided to cast their lot with the federal government in order to secure for workers the right to bargain collectively with their employers, and the right to a certain measure of economic stability throughout their working lives, and beyond. Ultimately, this alliance between organized labor and the federal government produced a volatile partnership that would shape the everyday lives of working people for the rest of the twentieth century.

FURTHER READING

Primary Sources

Dublin, Thomas, ed. *Immigrant Voices: New Lives in America, 1773–1986*. Urbana: University of Illinois Press, 1993.

Foner, Philip, ed. *American Labor Songs of the Nineteenth Century*. Urbana: University of Illinois Press, 1975.

—— *Fellow Workers and Friends: IWW Free Speech Fights as Told by Participants*. Westport, CT: Greenwood, 1981.

—— *Women and the American Labor Movement*. New York: Free Press, 1979–80.

Schlissel, Lillian, ed. *Women's Diaries of the Westward Journey*. New York: Schocken, 1982.

Secondary Sources

Boris, Eileen. *Home to Work: Motherhood and the Politics of Industrial Homework in the United States*. Cambridge, MA: Cambridge University Press, 1994.

Cooper, Patricia. *Once a Cigar Maker: Men, Women, and Work Culture in American Cigar Factories, 1900–1919*. Urbana: University of Illinois Press, 1987.

Deutsch, Sarah. *No Separate Refuge: Culture, Class and Gender on an Anglo-Hispanic Frontier, 1890–1940*. New York: Oxford University Press, 1987.

Dubofsky, Melvyn. *We Shall Be All: A History of the Industrial Workers of the World*. Chicago: Quandrangle Books, 1969.

Fink, Leon. *Workingmen's Democracy: The Knights of Labor and American Politics*. Urbana: University of Illinois Press, 1983.

Janiewski, Dolores. *Sisterhood Denied: Race, Gender, and Class in a New South Community*. Philadelphia: Temple University Press, 1986.

Kleinberg, S. J. *In the Shadow of the Mills: Working-Class Families in Pittsburgh, 1870–1907*. Pittsburgh: University of Pittsburgh Press, 1989.

Licht, Walter. *Getting Work: Philadelphia, 1840–1950*. Cambridge, MA: Harvard University Press, 1992.

Nelson, Daniel. *Managers and Workers: Origins of the New Factory System in the United States, 1880–1920*. Madison: University of Wisconsin Press, 1975.

Orleck, Annelise. *Common Sense and a Little Fire: Women and Working-Class Politics in the United States, 1900–1965*. Chapel Hill: University of North Carolina Press, 1995.

Peiss, Kathy. *Cheap Amusements: Working Women and Leisure in New York City, 1880–1920*. Philadelphia: Temple University Press, 1986.

Sklar, Kathryn Kish. *Florence Kelley and the Nation's Work*. New Haven: Yale University Press, 1995.

7

The Rise of the State in Depression and War: The American Workforce, 1916–1945

Growing up in the coalfields of Pike County in eastern Kentucky during the 1940s, Jim Vernatter well understood the forces that had impelled workers and their families out of the region and into northern cities for the last quarter of a century. Vernatter's father and grandfather had toiled in the mines well before the federal government established health and safety regulations for the industry; after 36 years of digging coal, his father had died of black lung disease. The company store swallowed up everyone's check at the end of the week because it was only there that families could secure necessities – food, heating fuel for their homes, shoes for the children. As a result, "Some miners would go for years without drawing a nickel's worth of pay because the store took everything they made."[1] For the Vernatter family of eight boys and four girls, times were always hard.

Nevertheless, Jim Vernatter had warm memories of life in Pike County. Though bereft of bicycles and other store-bought playthings, he and his brothers and sisters made up games using an old rubber tire, and swam in the local swimming hole ("but girls weren't allowed because no one had a bathing suit"). The mining town constituted a community of workers, and in the absence of other commercialized forms of leisure, there was a lot of "socializing with your neighbors." Though poor, the Vernatter family was a loving one, and "when you have that in a home, the other things are second-ary."[2]

Mrs Vernatter, Jim's mother, left us nothing in the way of her own recollections, but she probably viewed the family's situation in a less sentimental way than her son did many years later. Six days a week her husband went off to work, and for the next ten hours she worried and waited, dreading the call (that came to so many other miners' wives) that the mine shaft had caved in, or that the dynamite used to blast the coal had ignited a seam of natural gas; coal mining was among the most dangerous of all jobs in the United States. At home fulltime (for there was virtually no wage work available to women of the coal towns), Mrs Vernatter did daily battle against the soot that covered every surface of the family's house. In the words of another resident of a Kentucky coal mining town, the dust "would seep through the windows, it was on everything. A woman would work from dawn till night and never keep it clean because you just couldn't get rid of all that dust."[3] Mrs Vernatter scrimped and saved to feed and clothe a family of 14 on the high-priced provisions from the company store. At night, her husband returned "with grease and grime all over him," so exhausted "he could barely get in the door" (in the words of Jim). The long hours and grueling conditions led many workers to drink or succumb to despair. Gradually, the mines did claim the life of her own husband, leaving her a widow dependent upon friends and family. Her son claimed that, compared to a family's love, "the other things are secondary," but Mrs Vernatter might well have ranked a safe job and a decent salary for her husband as additional things essential to a family's well-being.

When he got older, Jim Vernatter moved to Detroit, and while working for the Ford Motor Company, he drew upon the lessons he had learned from his father about the need for solidarity among workers. The older man had risked life and limb to join the United Mine Workers, and spent time in jail for walking a picket line. The younger Vernatter looked up to John L. Lewis, the United Mine Workers president who was instrumental in forming the Congress of Industrial Organizations (CIO) in 1937; Lewis had fought for better working conditions, a medical plan, and higher pay for all miners. Later in life, Jim Vernatter would work as a health and safety representative for the United Automobile Workers, insuring that the Ford Motor Company complied with standards established by the federal Occupational Safety and Health Administration. "I feel like I'm carrying on my father's fight," he said. "I saw the struggles [the miners] went through, and I am trying to fight for the workers like he did."[4]

The case of eastern Kentucky serves to illustrate key themes in the history of labor during the twentieth century – technological innovation at worksites of all kinds, the large-scale population movements caused by the displacement of workers, and the intervention of the federal government into the economy and the workplace. At the time of the Civil War, the Appalachian region was one of the few areas in the United States characterized by family subsistence farming. Then, in the 1880s, outsiders "discovered" not only the people of the hills but also the natural riches – coal and timber – embedded in those hills. The lumber camps and coal mining towns promised cash wages to families pushed off their farms, but these extractive industries were inherently unstable. The lumber barons "cut out and got out." Mine operators installed labor-saving devices, like the mechanical coal cutter, beginning in the 1920s, forcing large numbers of workers to migrate north, and eventually depleting whole counties in West Virginia and Kentucky through the 1950s and 1960s. Along with Northern black ghettoes, the hollows of Appalachia became symbols of persistent poverty and social distress. By the 1970s and 1980s, alternative sources of energy, coupled with increasing public and governmental concern about the pollution caused by coal-burning factories, depressed the demand for coal altogether, and the people who remained in the area became chambermaids and waiters in resorts and hotels that catered to tourists. By the end of the twentieth century, sophisticated methods of processing coal made its use cleaner and more cost-effective in the production of energy; but these new methods also allowed coal users to bypass Appalachia in favor of the vast, largely untapped coal fields of the western United States. The Appalachian coal towns had suffered the same fate as the lumber camps.

The period 1916 to 1945 was one of unprecedented industrial growth, coupled with active federal involvement in a whole host of issues related to workers. The rise of the semiskilled machine tender (and the consequent demise of both the skilled and unskilled worker) paved the way for the dramatic founding of the Congress of Industrial Organizations. Nevertheless, through the 1930s, traditional racial and gender divisions pertained; with the exception of black, immigrant, and very poor white women, few wives worked outside the home. Domestic service was still the largest category of employment for women. Children were an integral source of labor on farms, in coal mines, and in textile mills. Three-quarters of all female professionals were concentrated in the fields of teaching and nursing. The vast majority of black people in the South remained confined to the cotton fields and to the kitchens of white families, while Northern blacks worked as domestics and as manual laborers. In the United States, the process of modernization excluded black workers.

During the World War I era, the dynamics of modern labor relations (revealing an interplay among unions, employers, civil rights groups, and the federal government) came into focus. The Wilson administration sought to promote the efficiency and stability of labor by overseeing the employment policies of specific industries (for example, through the Fuel Administration, the Railway Administration, and the Shipbuilding Labor Administration Board) and by backing the principle of collective bargaining. The National War Labor Board consisted of both businessmen and leaders of the American Federation of Labor, and gave workers some reason to hope that the administration would advance "industrial democracy" by supporting workers' demands for an eight-hour day and the right to join a union.

In fact, however, the economic and demographic changes prompted by war-time conditions exceeded the grasp of any single federal agency. All over the country, workers seized upon new job opportunities to abandon their employer, whether a Southern landlord or Birmingham coal operator, and to seek out higher wages and better working conditions elsewhere. In its most dramatic form this quest assumed the dimensions of the Great Migration of black folk out of the South. Sharecroppers on cotton plantations devastated by the boll weevil, domestic servants locked in neoslavery, sons and fathers scrambling for wages in sawmills and turpentine camps, all voted with their feet in a mass, collective protest against the injustices of Jim Crow. Between 1916 and 1919 approximately half a million black men, women, and children heeded the call initially sounded by railroad labor agents at the beginning of the war – that the North offered plentiful work and decent wages in expanding defense industries – and echoed by kin who had preceded them and found jobs quickly. The nearly all-white labor force of the Chicago meatpacking industry was transformed overnight; in 1918, 20 percent of its 10,000 workers were black. Black men gained an entrée into this industry and others in their role as strikebreakers, causing some whites to look upon black co-workers as enemies allied with employers.

The wartime labor queue was systematic and predictable: In the North, black men found unskilled work in iron foundries and steel mills, in tanneries and in building construction.[5] White women took the places of blue-collar men who went off to fight in the war, while black women substituted for white women (and white boys) in certain kinds of factory work. In 1919, a researcher for the United States Forest Service reported on the emerging racial and gender division of labor in the Southern lumber industry. Over the previous three years, 5,000 women had entered this kind of work, prompted by the labor shortage. White women found jobs in planing mills because of their supposed "greater adaptability and quicker grasp of situations," and throughout the industry they were hired as timekeepers and checkers. In contrast, black women were relegated to the yards as members of clean-up gangs and to the forests as hostlers, teamsters, skidders, road-repairers, and wood-choppers ("where they handle an axe with great proficiency").[6]

The war also offered a variation on the traditional theme of displacement of one group by another working new kinds of machines. In Little Rock, Arkansas, commercial laundry operators introduced steam presses more generally, fired the "white girls," and employed black women at lower wages on the assumption that "it was too strenuous work for white girls and that the laundries should not allow white girls to handle that line of business."[7] Chicago meatpackers challenged the pride of craft among skilled white workers by mechanizing their operations and installing immigrants from Eastern Europe and black men from the South in their place.

During the World War I era, a number of African-American advocacy groups emerged and, though divergent in their ideologies, coalesced around the issue of employment opportunity. The National Association for the Advancement of Colored People (founded in 1909) attacked Jim Crow in the courts; the National Urban League (founded in 1911) sought to penetrate the barrier that limited clerical, retail, and skilled jobs to whites in Northern cities; and the Universal Negro Improvement Association (founded in 1914 by the Jamaican-born black nationalist Marcus Garvey) stressed the development of black-owned industries that would provide employment for black people from the level of department store clerk to lawyer and banker. Although the association collapsed in the mid-1920s, its short-lived Black Star Steamship Line, combined with a host of other UNIA-sponsored businesses, including a doll factory, printing plant, hotel, restaurants, grocery stores, and laundries, represented an explicit challenge to the discriminatory hiring policies that characterized virtually all forms of white-controlled employment.

Despite skyrocketing profits during the war, employers demonstrated their traditional hostility toward organized labor, reacting to the growth of unions with repression and violence. The head of the American Federation of Labor, Samuel Gompers, pledged that workers under his jurisdiction would refrain from striking until Germany was defeated, and AFL membership increased in the course of the conflict from 2.7 to 4 million members. However, beginning in 1918, a combination of several factors, including job competition from returning veterans and high inflation that caused food prices to double in the course of the war, prompted an unprecedented wave of strikes nationwide; during that year and the next, as many as 4 million workers (20 percent of the total labor force) walked off the job, including textile workers and actors, telephone operators and steelworkers, Arkansas laundresses and Boston police officers.

The Seattle General Strike of 1919 revealed that many workers had emerged radicalized from the crucible of war. In January of that year 35,000 shipyard workers, forming an alliance of craft unions, reacted to a federally mandated cap on their wages and went out on strike. They were quickly joined by 25,000 other Seattle workers representing 110 local unions. For five days a General Strike Committee ran the city, establishing economic cooperatives (like butcher shops) and maintaining civil order. Although the strikers won little in terms of wage concessions, they had demonstrated a high degree of working-class consciousness and working-class organization.

While the stresses of war produced new alliances among some groups of workers, those stresses also exacerbated racial prejudice. Increased militance among black workers, including war veterans who returned home only to find that they were once more expected to pay homage to Jim Crow, enraged whites throughout the country. In the South, between 1917 and 1919, lynch mobs murdered more than 150 black people, some of whom had recently donned the United States uniform to "make the world safe for democracy." In 1919 a wave of race riots swept the country, and claimed the lives of as many as 75 people in places ranging from Chicago to Washington, DC, Omaha, and rural Arkansas.

By this time, President Wilson had abandoned his wartime gestures supportive of industrial democracy, and now advocated a general crackdown of labor radicals. In this aim Wilson was aided and abetted by his Attorney General, A. Mitchell Palmer, working in tandem with the head of the General Intelligence Division (the precursor to the Federal Bureau of Investigation), J. Edgar Hoover. The Red Scare landed Eugene

V. Debs (still head of the American Railway Union, and now a leader of the Socialist Party) in jail for three years; it also led to the deportation of self-proclaimed anarchists like Emma Goldman, and inspired government raids on the offices of the Industrial Workers of the World all over the country. Whatever real or rhetorical support Wilson had accorded wartime organized labor vanished after 1919, ushering in an era of official hostility (among government officials and private employers) toward all unions and the principle of collective bargaining.

For ordinary working people, the decade of the twenties bore little resemblance to popularized images of the Jazz Age. In an apparent paradox, the diffusion of new forms of technology led to the proliferation of groups that labored in traditional, pre-industrial workplaces. For example, as the residents of the nation's largest cities became accustomed to finding fresh fruits and vegetables in their local grocery stores year-round, the demand for unskilled agricultural labor increased accordingly. By the 1920s in California, Filipino, Japanese, and Chinese field workers toiled stooped over in the fields owned not by family farmers but by large agribusiness corporations. Italians and Poles left the tenements of Philadelphia and Camden to work for the truck farmers of southern New Jersey during the summer and fall months. Landless whites and blacks from Georgia joined the emerging migrant-labor stream which stretched from the winter-bean fields of central Florida to the apple orchards of New York state. Refugees from the Mexican revolutions of the pre-World War I period crossed the border into Texas, where they worked in cotton fields. The fruit orchards of the Midwest relied on a growing, seasonal army of "tramps, Great Lakes sailors, agricultural students from the State university; chronic down-and-outers, and professional ex-soldiers." Some men embraced a life of transiency free from the encumbrances of family responsibilities; counseled one peach picker in the Upper Midwest, "Don't go back to an office, boy. Offices smell out loud, and the people in 'em. Walk the road, sleep in a ditch, stay by yourself away from the crowd. Trouble in the offices, in the crowd."[8]

Yet for the increasing numbers of whole families that had to hit the road in search of work, such exhortations held little meaning or appeal.

During the twenties, farm laborers in general suffered from stagnating wages, while the earnings of textile workers, unskilled railroad workers, and coal miners declined. Blue collar workers in New England and the Southern states especially felt the effects of demobilization after the war and the ensuing recession in the early part of the decade. Throughout the country, manufacturing, construction, and agricultural laborers faced chronic underemployment. For example, in 1924, almost one-third of Chicago workers lost up to six weeks' worth of wages due to layoffs or illness. The fact that these workers participated in the larger consumer economy testifies both to the proliferation of material goods and to the increasing vulnerability of families that relied on credit in order to pay the bills each month ("Buy now and pay later" became the salesman's mantra). If the twenties was a time of prosperity, that prosperity was limited primarily to white-collar workers – the real estate and advertising agents, factory supervisors, and banking and insurance officials who represented an increasingly significant sector of the American economy.

When the husband and wife research team of Helen and Robert Lynd subjected Muncie, Indiana, to scrutiny in the mid-1920s, they found that for most "Middletowners" – the bulk of the adult population earning a living – employment was strained through the bars of the dollar sign; that is, people worked in order to be able to buy things, rather than for the intrinsic satisfaction that productive labor might afford. The Lynds highlighted the place of the automobile in Middletown society; by the mid-twenties, fully two-thirds of all families in the town owned one (nationwide, the number of cars increased from 9 million in 1920 to 26.5 million in 1930). When a Sunday School teacher asked her class what temptations the youth of today faced that Jesus did not, one member of the class replied without hesitation, "Speed!"[9]

The Lynds concluded that, in this almost all-white Midwestern town, a great divide separated what they called the

Working Class (people who made their living with their hands) from the Business Class (people who sold things or managed money or other people). Despite the levelling effects of consumer culture, members of the two groups led separate lives. The 70 percent of the population in the working class spent more hours of the day on the job, rose earlier in the morning to go to work, suffered from periodic (and devastating) lay-offs, and barely managed to stay above the poverty line, in contrast to their business class counterparts. Between January and September, 1924, about 60 percent of working-class men surveyed had lost some time on the job (a third of those more than one month), increasing the stress on the budgets of families and fraying the nerves of husbands and wives alike. Members of the business class appeared decidedly unsympathetic to the plight of their less well-to-do neighbors. The wife of "a prominent business man" told the Lynds, "People come to the house a great deal and tell me they can't get work. . . . Of course, I don't really believe that. I believe that any one who really tries can get work of some kind." Even those middle-class people who understood the structural causes of under-employment believed there was little to be done about the problem: "[it] cannot possibly be helped. An employer cannot give employment to workmen if he cannot sell his goods."[10]

The installation of new kinds of factory machines contributed to the instability of the Muncie working class. The Lynds noted that, in many Muncie factories (primarily Ball Company glass-jar plants), "With the passing of apprenticeship the line between the skilled and unskilled worker has become so blurred as to be in some shops non-existent." One machine shop superintendent reported, "Seventy-five percent. of our force of 800 men can be taken from farm or high school and trained in a week's time."[11] This trend characterized workplaces in innumerable industries, beginning in the early twentieth century and continuing into the future. While business-class positions came increasingly to require a high-school diploma, more and more working-class jobs entailed less and less formal training, on-the-job or otherwise. Among the industries that underwent extensive mechanization in the

1920s were textiles, machine manufacturing, glass blowing, printing, cigar-making, and phosphate mining. The introduction of mechanical coal cutters in West Virginia during the 1930s and 1940s prompted the increase in numbers of machine operators, maintenance workers, and service personnel, simultaneously diminishing the demand for miners themselves.

As new machines were introduced at certain worksites, the new jobs that accompanied them were often labeled "white jobs"; thus black sharecroppers were barred from driving tractors in Georgia, and black draymen were denied the chance to drive delivery trucks in Chicago. As a young woman, Sara Brooks (born in 1911 in Alabama's Black Belt) followed a circuitous path that led her to a series of jobs, beginning (as a child) with unwaged labor on her family's farm, then to the arduous labor of a young housewife for five years, on to domestic service for a white family in the town of Bainbridge, and then as an employee in a barrel factory. She recalled, "I never did mind workin – I liked to work – but you'd have the heaviest and the hardest job all the time – coloreds. Cause we was handlin that wood and the white guy would be usin the electric saw that would be cuttin it." As an employee of a Mobile shipyard she found that no white women performed manual labor; "White women didn't work like that – they were workin in the office at the ship yard."[12]

Under these conditions, only hard work combined with good luck enabled African-American families to move up into the middle class. Hugh and Maggie Comer lived in East Chicago, Indiana, and although he worked as a custodian in a steel plant, he retained his job through the 1920s and 1930s; recalled Maggie Comer many years later, "The plant where Hugh worked kept only a few people working, and he was one of the few. He worked two or three days a week and was never off the payroll."[13] For her part, Maggie supplemented the family income by doing housework for whites, operating a small grocery store, taking in boarders, and working for a caterer. The money they made helped to buy a house and put their children through college and, in the case of their son James, medical school. Despite the pinched job opportunities it offered to blacks, for the Comers and others the North paved the way to their own American dream.

For many Americans, though, the Great Depression that began in 1929 came less as a shock than as a confirmation of their own precarious status in the workplace. The soft underbelly of the 1920s economy was revealed by the fact that consumer goods were being produced faster and more efficiently by people who were becoming less able to buy them. The stock market crash of October, 1929, set in motion a chain reaction that began in the corporate suites of Wall Street but quickly reverberated in the sharecropper's cabin and the factory worker's tenement. Between 1920 and 1930, 5,000 banks failed; during the four-year period beginning in 1929, that number doubled. The employers who lived on credit – small businessmen and Southern plantation owners – could not pay their workforces, and the families that lived on credit could not meet their financial obligations to local banks. Decreased consumer purchasing power led to plant closings and business failures. By 1933, fully one-third of the American workforce was unemployed, and those who retained their jobs were more likely to work part-time than full-time. Average household income had declined to $1500 in 1933 from $2300 four years earlier.

Despite these dramatic indicators of social distress, the Great Depression affected different groups of workers in different ways. Financial disaster fueled subeconomies (some of them characterized by illegal activities) that provided services and entertainment for people without hope for the future. In Hollywood, the director Busby Berkeley offered up distractions for millions of moviegoers, and temporary work for hundreds of aspiring actors and actresses and hundreds of filmcrew members, with his musical extravaganzas such as *Gold Diggers of 1933* and *42nd Street*. In most major cities, organized crime (now developed to the point where it resembled legitimate business with its use of modern communications and hierarchical "corporate" structures) employed people in a wide range of jobs, from messenger boy to bookmaker and pimp. In rural communities and in Northern enclaves of Southern migrants of both races, preachers and fortune tellers ministered to the faithful and the lovelorn.

For a while, at least, white women wage earners found themselves relatively insulated from mass unemployment; clustered in the sales, clerical, and social-service sector, they were more likely to keep their jobs after men who worked in factories had lost theirs. Nevertheless, women regardless of race found themselves subject to speed-ups in the home, as they scrambled to manage household expenses with shrinking resources, and as they (at times reluctantly) seized the initiative to compensate for their husband's loss of income – reaching out to friends and family for aid; applying for relief from a government agency or private charity; or taking a job themselves, despite a growing resentment over women in the workforce on the part of local public officials (like school boards). For "grass widows" (women deserted by their husbands but not formally divorced), the Great Depression entailed a dual family burden of caretaker and chief breadwinner.

Concern for their children's welfare might inspire some mothers to engage in what appeared to be radical activity – to work as a local Communist Party organizer in Harlem, participate in a rent strike, walk the picket line as a member of a women's auxiliary to a local union, or join one of the many Housewives' Leagues that staged militant demonstrations against price-gouging landlords and butcher-shop owners. Black women helped to support the "Don't Buy Where You Can't Work" boycotts against employers who hired only whites to work in neighborhood stores.

The desperation experienced by wage-earning mothers was given plaintive expression in a song called "Mill Mother's Lament," written by Ella May Wiggins, a single mother of nine (four of her children had died), and textile worker and union organizer, in Gastonia, North Carolina:

> We leave our home in the morning
> We kiss our children good-bye,
> While we slave for the bosses,
> Our children scream and cry.

And when we draw our money,
Our grocery bills to pay,
Not a cent to spend for clothing,
Not a cent to lay away.

And on that very evening
Our little son will say:
"I need some shoes, mother,
And so does sister May."

How it grieves the heart of a mother,
You every one must know;
But we can't buy for our children,
Our wages are too low.

It is for our little children,
That seem to us so dear,
But for us, nor them, dear workers,
The bosses do not care.

But understand, all workers,
Our union they do fear,
Let's stand together, workers,
And have a union here.[14]

Ella May Wiggins was killed by armed men during a strike by employees of the Loray mill in 1929. Her work as a union organizer illustrated in stark relief the connection between a mother's devotion to her children and her determination to take an active part in organized struggle.

Older workers of both sexes found themselves without the means to make a living. Interviewed in the late 1930s, one elderly Southerner, a farmer, explained his plight this way: "I guess I've lived too long." In cities, elderly workers were the first to be laid off; as many as two-thirds of all older Americans were poverty-stricken during the 1930s. Once again, the labor queue came into sharp relief, as workers were pushed down the ladder of job mobility, and some were expelled from the workforce altogether. A government researcher chronicled the life histories of a number of families that slipped from financial security into transiency – the Slades, whose father lost his job as a coalyard manager in Texas and moved his family to Denver, only to find he could not make a living there, either; Roy Harris, who lost his West Virginia coal-mining job of 30 years, and took his family with him to St Louis to be near his brother, but could not locate work. The stories of laid-off men were endless – brakemen on the Great Northern railroad, South Carolina textile workers, Chicago house painters, Kansas City carpenters.[15]

Consequently, almost overnight, white people vied for the "black jobs" they could previously afford to disdain. Black women were now forced to compete with white women for a smaller number of domestic-service jobs. For example, the number of available service jobs in Chicago dropped by 9,000 between 1929 and 1940; black women lost a total of 12,000 such jobs and white women gained 4,000 of them. A black migrant from Georgia, Grace K, was replaced by a white couple who worked together for only $7 a week, three dollars less than Grace herself had earned doing the same work.[16] The white men who found work in the nation's capital as custodians and gardeners also could have testified about the fluidity inherent in the nation's so-called racial division of labor. One Connecticut brass worker pointed out that in the 1920s, black workers were able to get the dirty jobs that whites shunned; but now, during the Depression: "jobs are so scarce that the white workers are doing the heavy jobs that the Negroes used to have."[17]

Without a doubt, the federal initiatives grouped under the heading the New Deal represented a watershed of major proportions in the history of American labor. However, rather than merely list programs and legislation that affected working people one way or another, it would be useful to approach the whole issue of the emerging welfare state in a more analytical way. The following discussion focuses on first, the lasting contributions of the New Deal to the rights and welfare of working people in the United States; second, the ambiguous effects of some of FDR's programs that pitted groups of workers against each other, or pitted groups of workers against overlapping groups such as consumers; third, the weaknesses of program initiatives based on racial and gender stereotypes; and finally, the long-term impact of the New Deal's ideological underpinnings, which did little to advance the interests of certain groups of workers and would-be workers.

Beginning in 1933, the federal government responded to growing unrest among working-class Americans and assumed an active role in ameliorating the baneful effects of a capitalist economy on the welfare of industrial workers. These effects included poverty among the elderly, loss of income suffered by victims of sporadic unemployment and job-related accidents, starvation-level wages, and the sufferings of women and children in households lacking a male breadwinner. Some policy initiatives had unintended consequences, and empowered marginalized workers to speak and agitate on their own behalf. The Agricultural Adjustment Act of 1933 inadvertently gave rise to the Southern Tenant Farmers' Union, an organization that challenged the political hegemony of white landlords all over the South. The Wagner Act (1935) guaranteed workers the right to organize and bargain collectively for the first time in American history, and spurred the growth of the American labor movement in the process. Other pieces of legislation established a minimum wage for workers, and provided for the unemployed to receive compensation for a stipulated number of weeks. Child labor in factories was prohibited in 1938. The Aid to Families with Dependent Children Program (AFDC) was created to provide temporary relief to households that had lost their breadwinner. Over the next few decades, the Social Security Act (1935) would decrease poverty rates among older people to a dramatic degree. Taken together, these guarantees of economic security and protection for unions brought the United States into line with other industrialized democracies of Western Europe, and held out the promise that working people as a group would be able to weather the periodic economic downturns that inevitably characterized a free-market economy.

The Roosevelt administration also implemented a number of public works programs, though the rationale behind such programs – that the best way to fight poverty was to put people to work on useful projects – was one that future presidents and congresses would abandon. Scattered around the country in 2,650 camps, soldiers in the Civilian Conservation Corps (CCC), FDR's "tree army," planted forests, constructed trails and irrigation systems, and built fire towers. During the nine years of its existence the CCC provided employment for a total of 2.5 million young men. The Civil Works Administration (1933) was a more ambitious project; within two months of its initiation, 4 million men were at work, eventually building a quarter of a million miles of roads, 40,000 schools, and 3,700 playgrounds. In 1938 the Works Progress Administration (WPA) employed 3.3 million people (and 8 million overall, from 1935 to 1941), and provided work for artists and actors as well as writers and oral historians (under the auspices of the Federal Writers Project).

It was during these years that federal officials tentatively advanced the notion that, in some sectors of the economy at least, project administrators should make special provisions to ensure that African-American workers received their fair share of jobs. (As a board member of the National Youth Administration, Mary McLeod Bethune encouraged that agency to eschew racial prejudice in approving job applications.) In general, black applicants for federal aid fared best in Northern cities, where by 1932 they had proved their loyalty to the Democratic Party and were deemed worthy of the benefits due a bona fide political constituency. The first government-sponsored program of affirmative-action hiring, in the Public Works Administration Housing Division, helped to distribute construction jobs between blacks and whites on a more equitable basis; a quota system for the hiring of blacks thus helped to circumvent the generations-old prejudice of the construction-trades unions.

The Federal Emergency Relief Administration distributed modest amounts of cash aid to needy families of both races, and AFDC administrators offered assistance to widows, single mothers, and their children. And finally, federal projects like the Tennessee Valley Authority (1935) transformed the everyday lives of ordinary working people, and helped to eliminate a considerable amount of drudge work performed by wives and mothers, by bringing electricity to rural communities in the South and Midwest.

Nevertheless, the New Deal represented not a consistent or principled approach to the problems of labor but a limited, highly politicized and ultimately contradictory hodgepodge of federal legislation. Efforts by the Agricultural Adjustment Administration to limit crop production had the desired effect of the raising of the prices of everything from soybeans to milk and cotton, but also placed added burdens on nonfarm-working folk who were trying to feed their families on shrinking budgets. Moreover, the crop reduction program hastened the eviction of hundreds of thousands of landless blacks and whites in the South: men, women, and children driven from the land by landlords who pocketed government subsidy checks (intended for tenants) and then used the money to invest in tractors, further decreasing the need for agricultural labor. In industries like North Carolina tobacco factories, the spread of workers' organizations inspired some employers to invest in labor-saving devices, leading to large-scale lay-offs and curtailing the power of fledlging unions.

The southern textile industry had always relied on the low-wage labor of family members; in 1930 nearly half of adult female mill employees were married and working. Yet the elimination of child workers from the industry drew even more women into the workforce – by 1940, almost three-quarters of the women employed were harried wives and mothers putting in long hours at two jobs, in the mill and in the home. Likewise, minimum wage legislation prompted some employers to fire their ill-paid black employees and replace them with whites, on the assumption that if they were going to have to pay a group of workers more than they were accustomed to, they might as well indulge their racist proclivities.

These examples suggest that the New Deal failed to live up to its name in the case of African Americans. Critics of FDR, then and since, have charged that he was held hostage by powerful southern congressmen – senior Democrats in control of key committees – and therefore acquiesced in overt and symbolic forms of racial discrimination (an example of the latter was the President's refusal to endorse an anti-lynching bill over the objections of Southern Democrats). It is true that in the South New-Deal Democrats often served as a guardians of a white-supremacist heritage. In October, 1937, members of the Workers Council of Colored People in Raleigh, North Carolina, wrote to Harry Hopkins, Director of the WPA, outlining the lengths to which local administrators had gone not only to deny local blacks their fair share of public jobs, but to humiliate and demean them. White officials sought to discourage black single mothers from applying for WPA jobs by offering them only work in tobacco fields, which required them to ride, standing, in open trucks for round-trips of 40 miles a day; the intention was to insure a suffcient supply of cheap laundresses and domestics for white women in Raleigh. In Florence, South Carolina, black people were not allowed to serve in any supervisory capacity whatever, and, according to one local black leader, "The Beautification Project appears to be 'For Negro Women Only.' . . . Women are worked in 'gangs' in connection with the City's dump pile, incinerator and ditch piles. Illnesses traced to such exposure as these women must face do not entitle them to medical aid at the expense of the WPA." In contrast, white women found work on WPA projects as seamstresses. In response to Harry Hopkins's bland pronouncement (in the summer of 1938) that all WPA workers should have the right to vote, blacks from all over the South wrote to inquire how they were to overcome the strictures of formal (constitutional) and informal disenfranchisement at the hands of Democratic registrars: "Sequoyan County, Oklahoma, have denied me the black W. P. A. boys from voting, they did it by not letting them register to vote. Please help us at once by sending us a man from Washington to register us for the general election."[18] As long as black men and women lacked basic citizenship rights in the South, they would remain the most exploited of workers.

At the same time, overtly discriminatory policies extended beyond the reach of Southern Congressmen and infected virtually all New Deal programs. CCC camps throughout the contry upheld Jim Crow principles of racial segregation.

National Recovery Administration wage standards permitted regional differentials for women and men, whites and blacks. The Federal Housing Authority placed its stamp of approval on the practice of red-lining by private banks – the denial of loans to residents of minority neighborhoods – and rejected black applicants who sought to buy homes in predominantly white areas.

Just as signficantly, by targeting industrial workers (and the employees of the largest corporations at that), New Deal programs relegated large numbers of already vulnerable workers to the further margins of the American economy. Excluded from the provisions of legislation implementing Social Security, unemployment compensation, and the minimum wage were domestic servants, farmers, migrant laborers, day workers, and of course, homemakers (taken together, at least 85 percent of all African-American workers). Without the advantage of these programs, countless black families were doomed to financial insecurity for the foreseeable future. Moreover, women of both races failed to advance beyond the status of welfare clients into full and equal citizenship; viewed as objects of charity rather than as productive members of society, single mothers in particular bore the stigma that accompanied their meagre AFDC payments.

Nevertheless, it is significant that Roosevelt's pro-union stance hastened the organization of all sorts of workers – including auto and steel workers, commercial cannery and laundry employees, and sharecroppers and tenant farmers – and the newly created National Labor Relations Board enabled certain unions to achieve significant victories. At the same time, these gestures toward the nation's working people failed to secure the cooperation of employers and public officials around the country who had a generations-long vested interest in preventing workers from joining unions or otherwise seeking a voice in the public arena. In the South, steel employers conflated the CIO, the Communist Party, and the NAACP, charging that any organization that brought blacks and whites together was inherently subversive to the "Southern way of life." Acknowledged Hosea Hudson, a Communist organizer in Birmingham, "That was something unusual, black and white together."[19]

Indeed, throughout the South, "mean things" were happening in the land as employers and public officials colluded to suppress bi-racial protests. On a winter day in Alabama in 1932, Ned Cobb, the black farmer, was wounded in a shoot-out with sheriff's deputies who were trying to repossess the belongings of another man; Cobb, as a member of the fledgling Sharecroppers Union, represented a threat not only to an economic order that depended on an unlimited supply of compliant agricultural labor, but also to a political order that allowed the white elite to lord over the poor of both races. Though jailed for 12 years, Cobb remained defiant for the rest of his life: "From my boy days comin along, ever since I been in God's world, I've never had no rights, no voice in nothin that the white man didn't want me to have – even been cut out of education, book learnin, been deprived of that. How could I favor such rulins as have been the past?"[20]

In the textile mills of North Carolina's Piedmont region, and in the vast steel mills of Chicago, efforts of workers to strike – or even gather peacefully on a Sunday afternoon – met with stiff resistance from bosses, local police forces, and hired security guards. In Chicago on Memorial Day, 1937, an outing of steel workers and their families turned into a rout, as private security guards and Chicago police fired into the crowd, killing ten people (most of them shot in the back). In contrast to United States Steel employers, who by 1937 had grudgingly agreed to recognize the Steel Workers' Organizing Committee (SWOC), employers for smaller steel companies ("Little Steel") remained firm in their opposition to the new industrial union (similar to the Ford Motor Company's resistance to the United Automobile Workers after all other car manufacturers had recognized the group; Ford did not agree to bargain with the UAW until 1941). "Little Steel" businessmen claimed that workers' demands for higher wages and for safer working conditions would undermine profit margins within the highly competitive economy. The twin imperatives of profit and principle, then, help to explain the bloody clashes between labor and management in the 1930s.

Viewed from the perspective of the pre-1930s period, the Congress of Industrial Organizations' "culture of unity" represented a significant breakthrough in the history of the American labor movement; long fractured by racial, ethnic, and skill-based animosities, segments of the American working classes began to cohere and recognize that, whatever the differences among them, their collective interests often diverged from those of employers as a group. Within a year of its founding, the CIO claimed 4 million members. Throughout the country, black and white workers came together (in many cases for the first time) to press their grievances and march shoulder-to-shoulder on picket lines – the women of New York commercial laundries; the auto workers of Flint, Michigan; the steel workers of Birmingham, Alabama; employees of Chicago packing houses and Winston-Salem tobacco factories; cannery workers and fruit and vegetable pickers in California; and coal miners in Harlan County, Kentucky. Union membership brought tangible advantages to workers like Anna Novak, an employee of the Armour Meatpacking Company in Chicago, who, after being elected union steward of her department, lost no time in challenging company policy on such varied issues as mandatory gift-giving ("We used to have to buy the foremen presents"), lay-off policy ("when it comes to getting work [the boss is] God Almighty as far as Armour's is concerned") and racist job-assignments (black women "hardly ever get a chance at anything but the dirtiest, wettest jobs, that even the white men can't stand or just wouldn't take").[21]

The CIO offered a dramatic challenge to the conservative American Federation of Labor not only in terms of the workers it organized but also in terms of the collective-action strategies it employed. In particular, the sit-down strike represented a new and creative tactic by automobile workers in Michigan. By refusing to leave the factory, these workers prevented employers from hiring strikebreakers and maintaining production during labor unrest. Sit-downs also helped to mobilize the local communities of strikers' families in general. For example, on December 31, 1936, workers in the Flint, Michigan, Fisher Body Plant no. 1 (owned by General Motors) conducted a sit-down strike over the issues of long hours, low wages, the killing speed of the assembly line, the absence of a seniority system, and recognition of the UAW. The Women's Emergency Brigade, an auxiliary of the UAW, threw up picket lines around the plant, sponsored rallies on the workers' behalf, and provided food and other support services for the men inside. The women also helped to coordinate a sit-down strike at Chevrolet plant no. 4, a tactic that effectively shut down General Motors production in the city and paved the way for the car company to cede to the strikers' demands (on February 3, 1937).

Though the militance of the CIO (and a variety of other workers' organizations, like Communist-backed Unemployed Councils) is often juxtaposed to the more cautious tendencies of New Deal bureaucrats, in fact the labor movement in general did little to transform the essential outlines of the racial and gender division of labor. The successes scored by the United Automobile Workers and the SWOC in the late 1930s transformed industries that had long relied upon the quiescence of workforces that included a minority of black workers.

Still, viewed from a long-term perspective, these successes were limited in the sense that their leaders did not address the fundamental issues that would continue to shape the American labor force over the next half century – the privileged position accorded white workers by the seniority system, the displacement of workers by labor-saving technology, and the persistently desperate plight of the majority of American workers who were not under the umbrella of the organized labor movement.

Because Congress defeated a Wagner-Act amendment that would have offered a federal challenge to racist unions, representatives of about 200 African-American organizations met in Chicago in 1936 to form the National Negro Congress (NNC) and to press for a civil rights agenda that included equality in the workplace. A. Philip Randolph, the first president of the NNC, was not able to expand its base, and by 1940 the organization, by this time an adjunct to the Communist Party, was defunct for all intents and purposes. Still, the activism inspired by the NNC served as the foundation for increased black militancy that emerged during World War II.

By the 1940s and 1950s it had become abundantly clear that the gains achieved for workers as a group during the Great Depression were limited to a favored few. Even those groups who were brought into the labor movement for the first time in the 1930s, like black men and women and white women, maintained only a second-class, and ultimately tenuous, status within the relatively well-paid blue-collar labor force in terms of job opportunities and union leadership positions. African Americans were excluded from the payrolls of the largest corporations which, beginning in the 1930s, served as the engines of American working-class welfare. By the 1940s, giant companies like the auto makers had made a pact with their employees; workers would receive decent wages, paid vacations, medical insurance, and old-age pensions to supplement Social Security payments in return for industrial peace and an increasingly conservative labor-union movement. By linking basic welfare services to a certain kind of employment (that is, a job with a large corporation), this arrangement catapulted some industrial workers into the middle class, leaving behind those who suffered the cumulative effects of ill health and poor wages.

Interviewed in the early 1970s in New Jersey, one African-American woman recounted the story of her family when they were living in Georgia, a story revealing of the long-term effects of a vicious cycle:

> See, now, my oldest son, he left on account of the back-breaking work tobacco was. And his back hurt. He left then and went to get him a job into the Coca-Cola plant, capping bottles. And he stayed there about a year or so, and then he came back to where we were and got a job at the Model Clay Company. And that's where he stayed there, five years, until it make his health bad. See, the dust, he inhale that stuff until he got to the place where all he could do was sleep. And a lot of it was because the father was sick right along at the time. Got sick, and my son would try to work extra hours to make a living, 'cause he had to pay out money for his father's doctor's bills. Then we

had to travel back and forth, didn't have no convenience, paying people to take you back and forth to the doctor.[22]

For many poor families, unhealthful working conditions, combined with a lack of employer-sponsored medical benefits, mandated "early retirement" – and poverty. Benefits packages offered by large companies would continue to inhibit relatively well-to-do workers from supporting national health insurance proposals in the future. Increasingly, all workers judged their employment status not only according to the money they made, the hours they worked, and the job security they enjoyed, but also according to the benefits they did or did not receive.

The limits of the New Deal were suggested by the fact that the United States shook off the Great Depression only when the country began to mobilize for war. In 1940, the onset of armed conflict in Europe began to stoke the American economy, and in 1941, the United States unemployment rate fell below 14.3 percent for the first time in 11 years (and even that relatively high figure was buttressed by public works programs like the WPA, which had employed nearly four out of ten unemployed Americans by the time it was dismantled in 1941). The conversion of peacetime plants to wartime industries proved to be an uneven process, even as government policies that subsidized equipment purchases and new plant construction held out the promise of high wages and full employment for workers all over the country. The production of war planes intensified over the four-year period of the conflict (from 6,000 in 1940 to 86,000 three years later and 100,000 by the end of the war), and relied upon a succession of workers drawn into the labor force: white men followed by white women during the first two years of the conflict, and black men and then black women by 1943. Black employment opportunity flowed not only from intense labor demand, but also from pressure exerted by civil rights leaders like the NNC leader A. Philip Randolph (also head of the Brotherhood of Sleeping Car Porters), who threatened to sponsor a March on Washington of 150,000 people to demand that government defense contractors open their doors to African-American applicants.

In response to the March on Washington movement, Roosevelt created the Fair Employment Practices Committee (FEPC) to oversee hiring practices among private employers. Once again, however, government agencies worked at cross purposes; for example, the United States Employment Service actively promoted racial discrimination, barring blacks from job training programs and channeling them into traditional service jobs instead of hghly paid defense work. In 1945, reporting on the place of black women in the wartime labor force, the Women's Bureau quoted approvingly the president of a large West-Coast aircraft company: "*We think every worker we can place in a laundry is worth three new workers in our plants.*"[23] According to this approach, then, black women in canneries, laundries, and restaurants would continue to serve as support workers for white women now in factories. The FEPC managed to crack the all-white job barrier in several urban transit systems; but the agency did little to address the unequal status of black women, interpreting their problems as "gender" and not "racial" (and thus outside its purview). At the national level, racist employment policies were most glaring in the Armed Services; the Army maintained segregated units, some of which relegated black servicemen to fatigue work only; the Navy confined black sailors to service jobs; and the Marines barred them altogether.

Challenges to traditional social divisions of labor lifted millions of families out of poverty, as older and married and middle-class white women found jobs in factories for the first time, and as black men and women too finally broke through the barrier of conventional wisdom that held they could not operate complicated machinery. At the same time, it was apparent to the most prescient contemporary observers that these gains were likely to be short-lived. Women who a few months ago were urged to yield their places in the workforce to men were now urged to join Uncle Sam's domestic army and forego the "indulgent" pleasures of staying home full-time with their children. Government propaganda films suggested that working a lathe and using a riveting gun were tasks not unlike those used in sewing clothing – cutting out and stitching together pieces of cloth – and in the process employers felt no compunction about redefining certain kinds of skilled jobs as semi-skilled (and so now paid less than when men did them). Federal and state governments stubbornly refused to support day care policies that would have enabled women to cope with the double day – work for wages and housework for their families – which remained intact throughout the war. Although the leaders of some unions (most notably the United Automobile Workers) appreciated the daunting responsibilities faced by women workers, shop floors remained sites of tension, as men adjusted only grudgingly to the demise of the (all-white) assembly-line fraternity.

The imposition of long hours and overtime, the pressures of using new kinds of technology to make new kinds of matériel, and organized labor's "no strike" pledge during the war brought the issue of "worker control" to the fore in many industries. In recently racially integrated businesses, managers varied in the degree to which they facilitated the smooth incorporation of black workers into lunchrooms and locker areas. In Portland, Oregon, the Commercial Iron Works established segregated eating facilities for its black employees out of deference to the prejudices of white employees. In that same city, white members of the International Longshoremen's and Warehousemen's Union, Local 8, justified their exclusion of a black man, Harry Mills, by claiming, "We are not opposed to Harry Mills. We are fighting the Negro race! We cannot open our doors to the Negro people after having kept them closed all this time."[24] In some industries, white workers violently protested the racial integration of their workplaces by conducting "hate strikes."

Employers who tolerated this kind of behavior often claimed that businesses were not social-welfare institutions responsible for changing the prejudices of their employees. In response to an FEPC investigation of their hiring policies, railroad owners dismissed evidence that black men had been denied good jobs, and that violence perpetrated by whites against blacks was endemic to the industry: "The railroads cannot undertake to push the solution of these problems beyond

that reached by civilization as a whole. Railroads do not operate in a vacuum, or in a theoretical utopia. They have to
operate in and serve the civilization in which they find themselves and must adopt their operations and employment practices to the social solution of racial questions as worked out by
the prevailing mores and legal system of the states they serve."[25]

Predictably, then, the convergence of a variety of groups
into centers of war production exacerbated social animosities
even as it heightened (at times blandly rhetorical) expressions
of national unity. In the South, poor folk abandoned the farms
and settled on the fringes of wartime boom towns, though
construction projects were often temporary and the men and
women who built them lacked the skills to find permanent
jobs in them. The out-migration of Southerners of both races
into the upper Midwest and out to the West Coast contributed to overcrowded conditions in the working-class
neighborhoods of cities like Detroit and Oakland. In 1943,
Polish-Americans in Detroit gave violent expression to their
determination that no black families should be allowed to live
in apartments in a new public housing project (named after
the slave-abolitionist Sojourner Truth); 35 blacks and nine
whites were killed as a result.

For black workers, the legacy left by wartime was mixed.
With victory over Japan and the Axis powers, black and white
women were unceremoniously ushered out of the industrial
labor force, their departure hastened by returning GIs seeking
work, and by union leaders bent on adhering to the seniority
rules that governed lay-offs. While black men managed to gain
a foothold in the semi-skilled manufacturing sector as a result
of the war, black women had few alternatives but to seek jobs
as office custodians and as food service workers. In 1950,
more than three-quarters of all black women workers were in
private or institutional service jobs (up from 60 percent ten
years earlier). In cities throughout the country, the expansion
of the black voter base yielded public jobs like those of bus
driver and police officer. In New Orleans, Carlton Picot, a
war veteran and college graduate, ranked near the top of police applicants who took the civil service exam, but he was

rejected by the city police department. Only after the local NAACP chapter applied pressure, and a new superintendent of police approved his candidacy, did Picot take his place on the police force (in 1950).[26]

Middle-class and married white women too hoped to continue to earn wages, but they followed a path into the fastest growing sectors of (white) female employment – into office suites, as secretaries and receptionists, and into beauty parlors and department-store work. For many white women, the war had offered the promise of good jobs and good wages – a promise that the postwar era could not fulfill, but one that would eventually inspire the modern women's movement of the 1960s.

In some respects, the early 1950s represented the high-water mark in the history of the organization of the American industrial working classes. Soon after the end of the war, some major industries (like shipbuilding) virtually disappeared altogether, and others (like auto manufacture) embarked on an ambitious program of automation that would profoundly transform not only the conditions under which blue-collar workers labored, but also the numbers of people employed in the industry altogether. If the war and the succeeding decade or so represented the apex of organized labor, it also represented the beginning of the end of smokestack America.

Hired as a 23-year old by the Ford Motor Company in the mid-1960s, Jim Vernatter (recently transplanted to Michigan from Kentucky) had first-hand experience with the conditions that were demoralizing workers all over the industry. Pressed to meet the high demand for new cars, the company (and other auto makers) instituted assembly-line speed-ups and treated their employees like machines capable of repeating the same motions hundreds of times a day. ("We were working 12 hours a day; there was no limit on overtime then.")[27] In some plants, workers retaliated with imaginative forms of industrial sabotage – a tuna sandwich welded into a side door panel (emitting a smell that would never go away), a broom handle strategically wedged between the fuel tank and the trunk (causing a knock-knock-knock that would cost a considerable amount of time and trouble to eliminate).

Complaints about dangers posed by conditions in the spray-paint shop, or the back problems suffered by workers lifting 85-pound tires or 90-pound rear springs routinely, went unheeded by managers desperate to keep production levels high. By this time the money was good – UAW members were able to buy their own homes and look forward to sending their children to college. Some were able to buy two cars, or motorboats, or summer cottages on Lake Michigan. Yet the emotional and physical strain of the job dampened their hopes for a well-earned rest in the form of retirement; "If you're dead from cancer or crippled from being injured, you can't very well enjoy it. And no matter how much money you make, if you leave there in bad health, it's useless."[28]

In the coming years, the case of the United States auto industry would illustrate in dramatic terms the impermanence of the labor-relations principles that were forged during depression and war – the conviction that America's manufacturing sector would contine to grow and provide the highest standard of living for blue-collar workers anywhere in the world. Subject to political pressure, the belief that New Deal entitlement programs and social-welfare legislation would rescue the neediest workers from poverty and deprivation also proved to be an artifact of a particular time and economy. The global assembly line carried forth its own logic, and during the first half of the twentieth century neither union officials nor politicians expended much time or energy preparing for the devastation that the new world economy would wreak on the future of American workers who lacked increasingly specialized "credentials."

FURTHER READING

Primary Sources

Banks, Ann, ed. *First-Person America*. New York: Vintage Books, 1980.
Denby, Charles. *Indignant Heart: Testimony of a Black American Worker*. London: Pluto Press, 1979.
Lynd, Alice and Staughton Lynd, eds. *Rank and File: Personal Histories by Working-Class Organizers*. Princeton: Princeton University Press, 1981.
Painter, Nell Irvin. *Narrative of Hosea Hudson: His Life as a Negro Communist in the South*. Cambridge, MA: Harvard University Press, 1979.
Shackelford, Laurel and Bill Weinberg, eds. *Our Appalachia: An Oral History*. New York: Hill and Wang, 1977.
Terkel, Studs. *Hard Times: An Oral History of the Great Depression*. New York: Avon Books, 1970.
These Are Our Lives: As Told by the People and Written by Members of the Federal Writers Project . . . New York: W. W. Norton, 1967.

Secondary Sources

Cohen, Lizabeth. *Making a New Deal: Industrial Workers in Chicago, 1919–1939*. New York: Cambridge University Press, 1990.
Fraser, Steve. *Labor Will Rule: Sidney Hillman and the Rise of American Labor*. New York: Free Press, 1991.
Freeman, Joshua. *In Transit: The Transport Workers Union in New York City, 1933–1966*. New York: Oxford University Press, 1989.
Gerstle, Gary. *Working-Class Americanism: The Politics of Labor in a Textile City, 1914–1960*. Cambridge: Cambridge University Press, 1989.
Greenwald, Maurine Weiner. *Women, War, and Work: The Impact of World War I on Women Workers in the United States*. Westport, CT: Greenwood Press, 1980.
Griffler, Keith P. *What Price Alliance: Black Radicals Confront White Labor, 1918–1938* (New York: Garland, 1995).
Hall, Jacquelyn Dowd, James Leloudis, Robert Korstad, Mary Murphy, Lou Ann Jones, and Christopher Daly. *Like a Family: The Making of a Southern Cotton Mill World*. Chapel Hill: University of North Carolina Press, 1987.
Kelley, Robin D. G. *Race Rebels: Culture, Politics, and the Black Working Class*. New York: Free Press, 1994.
Lemke-Santangelo, Gretchen. *Abiding Courage: African American Migrant Women and the East Bay Community*. Chapel Hill: University of North Carolina Press, 1996.
Ruiz, Vicki. *Cannery Women, Cannery Lives: Mexican Women, Unionization,*

and the California Food Processing Industry, 1930–1950. Albuquerque: University of New Mexico Press, 1987.

Trotter, Joe William. *Black Milwaukee: The Making of an Industrial Proletariat, 1915–1945*. Urbana: University of Illinois Press, 1985.

8

American Workers and the New World Order in the Second Half of the Twentieth Century

Viewed from the grand sweep of the history of American labor history, Hattie Canty represented an unlikely leader of the nation's fastest growing private-sector union local in the mid-1990s. An African American born in rural Alabama, 62 years old, a widow, the mother of ten children, and a maid at the Maxim Casino and Hotel in Las Vegas, Canty served as president of the 40,000-strong Culinary Workers Union Local 226 (a member of the expanding Hotel and Restaurant Employees International Union, affiliated with the AFL-CIO). Though composed primarily of women, the local had long been led by men workers from the "front of the house" in hotels – bellhops, doormen, and waiters. In fact, Hattie Canty's election was revealing of a larger transformation in the structure of the American workforce, and a new direction for the labor movement, in the late twentieth century. In Las Vegas in the mid–1990s, union maids earned an hourly wage of $9.25 (more than double the miniumum wage), and received health care benefits and a retirement pension. In an interview with *New Yorker* writer Sara Mosle, Canty noted, "My house is paid for. I bought cars while I was a maid. I bought furniture, I bought the things I needed for my family while I was a maid. And the way I did it was through organized labor."[1]

Over the generations, the site of labor organizing had shifted, from the textile mills of Lowell and the shoe factories of

Lawrence in the mid-nineteenth century, to the steel mills of Gary and Pittsburgh and the auto plants of Detroit during the period 1880 to 1975 and finally to the nursing homes, restaurants, and hotel rooms of "post-industrial" America. By the 1990s, moreover, diverse groups of workers fought on a number of fronts, some novel and surprising; wealthy major-league baseball players struck for the right to earn as much as the marketplace would pay them; teaching assistants at Yale University demanded they be considered waged employees rather than priviliged apprentices so that they might claim the right to organize and bargain collectively with their employer; workers for the United Parcel Service union, full-time and part-time alike, joined forces to protest the proliferation of part-time jobs.

Throughout most of American history, service jobs had remained outside the purview of organized labor; characterized by high rates of turnover, dominated by women and minorities, these positions seemed to have little in common with those in the heavy-manufacturing sector. Nevertheless, in the 1990s, places like Las Vegas offered a growing number of jobs for workers who lacked formal education and skills; in that sense, these workplaces were the equivalent of the Lower East Side in the early twentieth century – sites of opportunity, and sites of labor militance as well.

During the last two decades of the twentieth century, "Fourth Wave" immigrants helped to change the face of American labor. Hispanic immigrants now took up leadership roles in the Service Employees International Union; Justice for Janitors; the United Needletrades, Industrial and Textile Employees Union; and the Hotel and Restaurant Employees International Union. These organizations infused life into a labor movment in danger of becoming moribund in the Rust Belt and the Northeast. Said one Las Vegas labor organizer, "Some cities haven't had a strike in forty years, but we've always had a history of fighting for the union in this town. We've had strikes all along."

With their emphasis on worker efficiency and high standards of customer satisfaction, hotel managers of the 1990s had standardized the responsibilities of chambermaid so that an individual woman might be expected to clean as many as 16 rooms within an eight-hour period (Las Vegas had 90,000 hotel rooms, and was adding more every year). Berenice Thomas recalled that when she started working as a maid in the town, "I had a bucket with soap, and I had this big old brush, and I had to rub and scrub. Nowadays, they got everything so it's spray and wipe – they got the soap in the bottle and you spray it on and you rinse it off." Union members accommodated themselves to the routinization of cleaning; at the same time, they challenged certain eternal verities of the hotel-management business – specifically, the gender division of labor that decreed that only men could work as bar-tenders and room-service waiters. Said Peggy Pierce, who worked in the latter job, "The only women in this country who are absolutely guaranteed to make the same amount of money as the men standing next to them doing the same work are women in unions. If you're not in a union and you're a woman and you work, you're getting screwed."[2]

Las Vegas blended commercial entertainment and big business as part of a multi-billion dollar industry. Yet throughout the United States, other cities exhibited similar configurations of glass-paneled skyscrapers cleaned and tended by an army of service workers consisting of new immigrants and African Americans. Within just four decades, then, the locus of union militancy had moved from the sprawling factories of the Midwest to high-rise hotels and corporate offices, with public white-collar employees and service workers taking up the labor standard. This dramatic shift reflected not only changes in the domestic political economy, but developments on the international stage as well. Now American workers were part of a global assembly line, one that relied as much upon the labor of the cleaning woman as it did upon the high-tech skills of the computer programmer.

To some extent, the size and structure of the American labor force had always reflected what was happening in other parts of the world – when war and revolution sent refugees to American shores, when military conflict elsewhere provoked

American involvement and defense mobilization. Yet in the post-World War II period, the onset of the Cold War shaped domestic labor politics in new and striking ways. During the war, organized labor had abided by a "no strike" pledge, and workers had grudgingly endured speed-ups in order to meet higher production quotas. In 1946, 4.5 million workers struck to reverse the wage losses they had suffered since 1941. Yet President Harry Truman was quick to label collective action as intrinsically harmful to the national interest; he managed to supress a strike of miners in 1946 by alternately threatening to send military troops to restore order in the mine fields, and appealing to the men's patriotic impulses – to "keep America warm" during the ensuing winter. A year later, Congress passsed the Labor-Management Relations Act of 1947 (the Taft-Hartley Act), a direct attempt to weaken the Wagner Act and roll back labor's gains of the 1930s. The Taft-Hartley Act severely curtailed the real and potential power of organized labor by outlawing the closed shop (workplaces where all employees were automatically members of a union), and by mandating a "cooling off period" in order to delay strikes.

The memory of labor's bloody battles just a decade earlier fresh in their minds, leaders of the country's largest labor unions seemed to have good reason to want to consolidate their gains in terms of higher wages and better working conditions, to demonstrate their loyalty to America by distancing themselves from radicalism in any form, and to concentrate on insuring job security for their members. Men who had risked their lives on picket lines and in sit-down strikes a few years before now dined with the President of the United States and members of Congress. In 1956, when the AFL merged with the CIO, the president of the giant union, George Meany, could point with satisfaction to the 4 percent rate of unemployment, rapid economic growth, stable prices, and low inflation that seemed to serve the interests of everyone, managers and workers alike.

Union members (whites at least) now joined with other Americans in an exodus out of the cities and into the suburbs, where their children attended brand-new public schools (built for the post-war baby boom generation) and where they could partake more fully of the blessings of 1950s prosperity. It was during this period that some large manufacturers began to construct new plants in the farmland surrounding cities in order to take advantage of cheap land; at the same time these employers aimed to bring the worksite closer to the white laboring population and to decentralize the industry so that it would be less vulnerable during an enemy air attack. For example, in the 1950s, Ex-Cell-O, a large Detroit machinery manufacturer, constructed six new plants in the virtually all-white hinterland regions of Ohio and Indiana, and simulanteously reduced its Detroit employees through attrition and the introduction of new forms of machinery. This process of industrial relocation would eventually drain American cities of their multi-class vitality, leaving behind the poorest people of color in tenements and the wealthiest whites in penthouse condominiums.

Composed of both white-collar and blue-collar workers, new suburban housing tracts served an overt political purpose during the Cold War era by glorifying the nuclear famly, which was now apparently safely ensconced in its own little paradise stocked with the latest in appliances. The full-time wife and mother played an integral part in this brave new suburban world; she was supposed to view homemaking as a profession, a career. Women's magazines provided hints on turning last night's leftovers into tonight's gourmet meal, while chauffeuring the children – to scouts and music lessons, ball games and birthday parties – became an ever more prominent part of the housewife's responsibilities.

The "feminine mystique" of the 1950s represented a rhetorical turn not unlike the "Cult of True Womanhood" of the antebellum period, with a couple of crucial differences. First, the 1950s version lacked the earlier stress on religious piety inspired by evangelical Protestantism – now, a peculiarly American brand of consumption constituted the country's secular religion. Second, an emergent group of psychologists, primarily popularizers of the theories of Sigmund Freud, warned that housewives were in danger of becoming obsessive about their own importance in the home, and that single-minded devotion to their children would ultimately smother and stunt them, yielding effeminate sons and neurotic daughers.

The popular television show *Leave it to Beaver* represented an idealized image of the 1950s American waged and unwaged workforces. The father, Ward, left the house each morning in his gray flannel suit to go off to a job that was never identified, but there was no doubt that he sat at a desk, used the telephone, and earned a good living. His wife, June, vacuumed the house and made dinner decked out in a dress and a string of pearls. The Cleavers' gleaming kitchen – with a five-and-a-half-foot-high white refrigerator as its centerpiece – symbolized the superiority of American capitalism compared to Soviet communism in the famous "kitchen debate" between Vice President Richard Nixon and Soviet Premier Nikita Khrushchev in Moscow in 1959.

Under the bland veneer of TV-land lay a much more complicated reality, as American workers became an ever more diverse, and ultimately divided, lot. No doubt stocked in the Cleaver's refrigerator and lining their kitchen shelves were the fruits of the labor of several groups of migrant workers – the African Americans, and, increasingly, off-shore migrants from Puerto Rico and the Bahamas, who went "on the season" up the coast from Florida to the vegetable fields of Maryland, Delaware, and New Jersey; the Mexican Americans who travelled to the North Central and Mountain states working the sugar-beet and wheat harvests; the native-born whites, who began their trek in Oklahoma, Arkansas, and Western Tennessee, and picked fruits and vegetables; and the multi-ethnic, multi-racial workforces that harvested a variety of crops in the California valleys. On both coasts, American agribusiness employers welcomed with open arms refugees from Latin America and Southeast Asia. A report issued by the President's Commission on Migratory Labor in 1951 noted, "We depend on misfortune to build up our force of migratory workers and, when our supply is low because there is not enough misfortune at home, we rely on misfortune abroad to replenish the supply."

Left out of the New Deal system of worker protection, migrant workers continued to toil without the benefit of a minimum wage, social security, health insurance, or unemployment compensation. In the 1950s, journalists initiated a cycle that would repeat itself for at least the next half century – a hard-hitting exposé would reveal migrants' deplorable working conditions, the public would express indignation, lawmakers would debate and then defeat proposed reform legislation, and the issue would recede for another few years. In 1953, one New York reporter described the way migrants were transported out of Florida and into the Northern truck-farm fields "packed like animals on the way to market. . . . Crowded in trucks equipped with crude benches or orange crates for seats, men, women, and children roll through the Carolinas and Virginia, sharing their common misery and exhaustion. Sometimes they stop for a hamburger and a Coke. Mostly they just keep rolling along." Concluded the reporter, "The Federal goverment has established rules for the shipment of cattle. . . . Migrant workers have no such protection."[3]

Rural Southerners in general faced hard times during the "affluent decade" of the 1950s. In Mississippi, Alabama, and Georgia, the mechanical cotton picker displaced thousands of African-American sharecroppers. In their trek north, they joined white families fleeing the depressed coal industry of Appalachia. Although both groups left home with little in the way of formal education or work experience in modern factories, their paths diverged signficantly once they reached the Midwest. By and large, black men remained confined to day labor and unskilled factory jobs; their white counterparts however more often secured the semi-skilled factory jobs that represented the bottom rung of internal ladders of labor mobility. In the Miami Valley of Ohio, whole communities of transplanted mountain folk followed a classic "chain migration" pattern and dominated the workforces of individual factories, where personnel officials tended to favor the kin of the workers they already had.

Whether in the Uptown section of Chicago, or the Lower Price Hill community of Cincinnati, inner-city enclaves of

Southern white migrants underwent a continuous process of fragmentation, as more settled workers gradually gained stable jobs and managed to move their families to better neighborhoods – a working-class section on the fringes of town, or even a middle-class suburb. In their freedom to go as far as their paychecks would take them – to find better jobs for themselves and better schools for their children – Appalachian migrants possessed a distinct advantage over blacks, who remained confined to poor and increasingly all-black neighborhoods. These black ghettoes were political entities shaped by racist neighborhood "improvement associations" and real estate agents, by the discriminatory loan policies of bankers, and by the mandates of city councils and zoning boards.

In the 1950s, then, the distinct liabilities of Northern blacks' relative residential immobility became abundantly clear; in many cases they faced long commutes to work, as factories receded further and further from the inner-city core. Left behind were service jobs that paid only a fraction of blue-collar manufacturing positions. The reluctance of local white-dominated school boards to continue to invest in increasingly segregated inner-city schools meant that the children of black workers would remain at a disadvantage compared to their white counterparts, now that more and more jobs came to require formal education.

In suburbs around the country, the local, brand-new public schools served as community centers that not only provided excellent education, but also sponsored athletic programs and offered instruction in art and music. These institutions depended on the labor, both paid and unpaid, of women. School-teaching, especially at the lower grades, became the almost exclusive domain of women, though the positions of principal and superintendent more likely than not went to men. Cafeteria workers tended to be mostly female; in certain rural counties, the public school served as the largest source of jobs for unskilled women in the area. Just as significant as these employees, however, were the mothers who devoted a considerable portion of their waking hours to school-related activities, coordinating bake sales to raise money for new playground equipment; serving as teachers' aides and as chaperones for field trips; sewing cheerleaders' uniforms and painting scenery for the school play.

Prominent among the ranks of those dedicated to their local parent-teacher organization however were increasing numbers of women who worked fulltime outside the home, apparently in defiance of the standards set by the Cleaver family and extolled in women's magazines. During the 1950s and 1960s, the "pink collar ghetto" expanded, swollen with middle-class married women who worked as beauty parlor attendants, office receptionists, medical technicians, sales clerks, and social workers so that their families could afford to buy a second car, put an addition on the house, or send the kids to college. Women's work paid less than men's, and few "pink collar jobs" held much promise of promotion or professional advancement; these were jobs that offered no "tomorrow." In government office buildings, some clerical employees engaged in time-honored forms of resistance to mind-numbing work and arrogant supervisors; they "messed up" on their typing, left work early, called in sick, and went out of their way to ridicule their male bosses.[4]

The compartmentalization of American workers – the racial and gender segregation of the work force – carried within it the seeds of change in the 1950s. The southern system of Jim Crow had long rested upon the economic subordination of black men, women, and children confined to the most menial kinds of work the region had to offer. It was no coincidence then that the first concerted, grass-roots challenge to Jim Crow, the Montgomery bus boycott of 1955–6, depended on the commitment and staying power of a generations-old fixture of southern labor – African-American women domestics. Over the next decade, a variety of black workers would come to the fore, workers with their own set of grievances against white employers, yet united in a common cause. Sharecropppers like Mississippi's Fannie Lou Hamer dared to challenge exploitative rural labor practices and the lily-white Democratic Party that sustained them throughout the South.

The schoolteachers of Selma offered a new kind of civics lesson for their pupils when they marched and sang in defiance of Jim-Crow voter registrars and policemen. Lawyers working for the National Association for the Advancement of Colored People put their skills to work on a critical battlefield – the federal courtroom.

In the South, traditionally stolid Chambers of Commerce provided some unexpected support for black protesters. Well aware of the riches awaiting businesses that could tap into the so-called military industrial complex (federally subsidized private companies that fueled America's Cold-War machine at home and abroad), these white men became increasingly conscious of, and self-conscious about, the disturbing image of the South that was coming into focus on the television screen each evening. German shepherds attacking school children, firemen pulling the corpses of black girls out of bombed churches, public officials from sheriffs to governors vowing to resist segregation today, tomorrow, forever – these sights and sounds were bad for business. As long as shocking images dominated the evening news, Northern industrialists would resist moving their plants to the South, cheap labor or no, and federal authorities would withhold contracts from Southern corporations. This realization helped to pave the way for the Sunbelt South of the 1970s.

In the early 1960s, in a development reminiscent of the antebellum period, when women's rights advocates derived inspiration from the abolitionist cause, women from all walks of life began to challenge the dictum that biology is destiny, and to take their case to the public via print and electronic media. The women's movement, which assumed institutional form with the founding of the National Organization for Women (1966), was a creature of 1950s suburbia. In her ground-breaking book, *The Feminine Mystique* (1963), Betty Friedan provided a first-hand critique of women ensconced in comfortable, well-appointed homes, women suffering from the "problem that has no name." She thereby identified a particular group of women – college graduates with husbands who were professionals or white-collar workers. According to Friedan, the malaise that accompanied full-time homemaking – what she identified as the boredom, the seemingly endless round of chores and ultimately meaningless volunteer activities – could only be banished with a well-paying job. In her call to action, she underestimated the difficulties faced by women who tried to re-enter the work force after the hiatus of their child-rearing years, and she overestimated the redemptive power of paid employment for women of all kinds. Indeed, many African-American women yearned for the day when they could quit the white woman's kitchen and attend to their own children, and many white women lacked the educational background that would help them secure well-paying, challenging jobs.

During the 1960s, homemaking came under scrutiny as a highly political and politicized activity. Some feminists conflated the scrubbing of floors with the tending of children, and suggested that all manner of duties carried out within the home were by definition damaging to a woman's sense of herself as an independent human being. These critics scorned the notion that women served to "contain" all sorts of threats – the spread of godless communism, with its denigration of American values like family life, and the contagion of unbridled sexuality represented by decadent European movie actresses. It was time, feminists claimed, that women climb out of the bomb shelter and assume their rightful place in the workforce – making a good salary in the office suites long dominated by men.

Founded in 1963, the National Welfare Rights Organization (NWRO) offered a strikingly different perspective on the issue of family and work compared to that of the emerging (middle-class) women's movement. In communities hit hard by deindustrialization and long-term structural employment – rural Appalachia and inner city black ghettoes prominent among them – the Aid to Families with Dependent Children program had evolved from a stop-gap welfare program into the economic mainstay of a growing number of families. In the words of Johnnie Tillmon, the first Chairwoman of the NWRO, "Welfare is a women's issue," and entangled in the morass of bureaucratic red tape were certain fundamental assumptions about poor women – the notion that an AFDC recipient must sever the relationship with the father of her children ("the man in the house rule" forbade a husband or father to live with a family receiving aid), that she must abide by her case worker's strictures about "what to buy, what not to buy, where to buy it, and how much things [should] cost." Middle-class women were exhorted to stay home full-time with their children, but poor women who stayed at home with their children were perceived as lazy and immoral. Well-to-do Americans thus rendered "womanhood" in explicitly class terms; for, according to Tillmon, the poor woman "learns that a 'real woman' spends her time worrying about how her bathroom bowl smells; that being important means being middle class, having two cars, a house in the suburbs, and a minidress under your maxicoat. In other words, an A. F. D. C. mother learns that being a 'real woman' means having all the things she isn't and having all the things she can't have."[5] The stigma attached to "welfare" revealed that child-care and homemaking did not qualify as productive labor as long as that kind of work was performed by poverty-stricken women, whether or not they worked for wages.

The NWRO represented a novel form of labor organization, shaped as it was by poor, mostly African-American urban women whose work on behalf of their own children earned them little but the contempt of "affluent America." At the same time, other minority workers began to transform the face of the American labor movement. In the lush fields of California's central valleys, Chicano workers led by Cesar Chavez launched a campaign for worker organization, and gained national attention (in 1969) by calling for a boycott of table grapes as long as growers refused to bargain collectively with their workers. Eventually, in California, the United Farm Workers won passage of a state act that guaranteed them and certain other agricultural laborers the protections that the National Labor Relations Act had afforded industrial workers for more than 35 years. Chavez inspired a whole generation of activists, young people like Maria Elena Lucas, a

Mexican-American born in Brownsville, Texas. Lucas approached field workers with the question, "Have you ever heard of Cesar Chavez? He is like Moses in the Bible. He took into his hands a whole nation of farm workers and has tried to lead us out into a better land."[6]

In Detroit auto assembly plants, young African-American men blended the rhetoric of black nationalism with resistance to the assembly-line speed-ups; the League of Revolutionary Black Workers (including plant-based organizations like the Eldon Avenue Revolutionary Union Movement (ELRUM), a group of Chrylser employees) launched a multi-pronged attack on supervisors who instituted speed-ups while disregarding basic safety precautions. In 1970, Gary Johnson, a 22-year-old Vietnam War veteran and Eldon employee, died when the defective motorized cart he was riding turned over and crushed him. A report by a UAW safety director confirmed official negligence as the cause of Johnson's death: "I examined the equipment and found the emergency brake to be broken; as a matter of fact, it was never connected. The shifter lever to the transmission was loose and sloppy. The equipment generally was sadly in need of maintenance, having a loose steering wheel in addition to other general needs."[7] As workers at the lowest echelon of the plant hierarchy, blacks were most vulnerable to the lay-offs, compulsory overtime, and frenetic pace that were now the hallmark of auto work. Detroit blues singer Joe L. Carter put their grievances to music: "Please, Mr. Foreman, slow down your assembly line./ Please, Mr. Foreman, slow down your assembly line./ No, I don't mind workin,' but I do mind dying.'"[8]

Despite their focus on racism in the workplace, ELRUM and other black-nationalist workers' organizations represented but a variation on the theme of an emerging blue-collar critique of industrial labor. Auto workers like Gary Bryner, president of the UAW local at the General Motors plant in Lordstown, Ohio ("the most automated, fastest line in the world"), condemned the bosses' prevailing philosophy: "production first, people second."[9] To make workers "more efficient, more productive, like a robot,"[10] the auto companies broke down every task into ever more discrete parts; if every worker saved a second every minute of every day, the company could save a million dollars every year (or so the thinking went). For individual men (and, increasingly, women), the key was to dissociate one's mind from one's body: "A guy could be there eight hours and there was some other body doing the same job over and over, all day long, all week long, all year long. Years. If you thought about it, you'd go stir [crazy]."[11] What supervisors did not anticipate was the turnover among workers who sought to take advantage of the high demand for labor and in their "quit" and absentee rates made the assembly line considerably less efficient than it would have been otherwise.

If technology was the key factor in shaping the tasks performed within the industrial workplace, then politics was the key factor in shaping the gender and racial composition of the workforce. In response to the Southern-based civil rights movement of the 1950s and 1960s, Congress passed the 1964 Civil Rights Act, and as a result of Title VII of the act, the legal basis of all-white and all-male workforces collapsed. For the first time in American history, it was unlawful for employers to discriminate against prospective employees on the basis of race, gender, religion, or national origin; or to institute unequal pay scales for whites and blacks, men and women. This seemingly straight-forward piece of legislation (and its administrative apparatus, the Equal Employment Opportunity Commission) yielded some unintended and unanticipated consequences.

The immediate beneficiaries of Title VII included well-educated white women and blacks on the one hand, and white women and black men and women in regions with a high demand for unskilled labor on the other. Racial and gender discrimination had pervaded the highest echelons of the workforce (no group was agitating for the right to work as garbage collectors, day-care attendants, or migrant laborers). Women college graduates pressed for entrée into jobs reserved for men within the sectors of education, clerical work, and sales – as school principals and superintendents, as office managers and supervisors, as commission and "big ticket" salespeople. Because of Title VII, the black middle class began to expand dramatically, now that college-educated men and women could aspire to positions commensurate with their talents and training. The outlawing of restrictive residential covenants opened the way to the suburbs, but only for blacks who could afford to move there; in the process they secured for their children the quality public education that was a defining characteristic of suburbia.

Yet progress remained uneven, and some black workers who aspired to jobs at previously all-white worksites found their way blocked as much by their potential white co-workers as by employers. In the mid-1960s, some unions affiliated with the AFL-CIO (like the United Papermakers and Paperworkers; the Pulp, Sulphite and Paper Mill Workers; the Brotherhood of Railway Clerks; Tobacco Workers International; and the American Federation of Musicians) still insisted on racially segregated locals. Throughout the country, unions served as gatekeepers, limiting the number of (or excluding altogether) black applicants for apprenticeships and skilled jobs. For example, in 1960, only 67 out of 11,125 skilled General Motors workers were black, and only 2,005 of 86,966 apprentices nationwide were black (and virtually none were women). Despite Title VII, many unions continued to use antiquated application and seniority procedures to circumvent the law's intent.

In the South, Title VII had a noticeable effect on the textile mill workforce; in this case, employers had real incentives to overcome the shop-floor resistance on the part of white workers opposed to racial integration. Long a bastion of all-white labor, the textile industry was under growing pressure from a flood of cheap foreign imports. African-American men, who had worked as sweepers and haulers in the mills, pressed for the job of machine operative, and black women filled out application forms with more hope than ever before. Although some employers refused to hire any black people, others proceeded to integrate their workforces relatively smoothly. White men and women were abandoning the mills in favor of lighter, cleaner work elsewhere, and the "blackening" of the work force allowed the industry to maintain its supply of cheap labor and survive, for at least another decade or so.

All over the South, struggles of black workers brought labor organizing and the principles of the civil rights movement together. Public employees were especially prominent in this effort, and the American Federation of State, County, and Municipal Employees (AFSCME) managed to double its membership nationwide during a seven-year period (to 350,000 in 1967). Affiliated with AFSCME, sanitation workers in Memphis, Tennessee, went out on strike in 1968, demanding dignity as well as decent wages, benefits and job security; their motto was "I AM A MAN." The appearance in Memphis of the Rev. Martin Luther King, Jr, and his assassination in that city in April, 1968, highlighted the enduring connection between economic well-being and civil rights. A year later, women hospital workers in Charleston, South Carolina, organized into Local 1199B (affiliated with a New York City hospital workers' union), and went out on strike. The issue was the unequal pay and treatment that differentiated white from black workers. In their solidarity, the strikers derived strength from their common religious devotion; they were "church sisters" with a collectively raised consciousness. Ernestine Bryant, one of the strikers, revealed that the full import of Title VII served as an inspiration at the grass-roots level, and that money was not the only issue at stake, observing "When you're working around people who discriminate against you you really feel like – you know – fighting all the time because – you know – 'hey girl,' and they have these nicknames, they call you like 'dooflotchie' and 'monkey grunt' and all this carrying on and I think all of us are due respect regardless of age, race, or creed."[12] Beaten and jailed, the strikers hung on for 116 days, and their cause (a "civil rights union") received national media attention, though they themselves gained little in the way of tangible concessions from the hospitals.

Simultaneously, a similar struggle was being waged in the chicken-processing plants of the Deep South, where mostly minority women workers gutted and dressed up to 90,000 birds in a single day in a single plant. Mississippi poultry workers challenged the "plantation conditions" that had become standard in the industry – "pay just over the minimum wage, no regular hours, unsafe conditions, no seniority or regular vacations or pension plan, and above all, a denial of human dignity."[13] Faced with the intransigence of employers, workers in Forest, Mississippi, forged a coalition of black freedom movement activists, workers' organizations, community groups, and churches in an effort to win better wages and more job security; but employers' heavy-handed tactics of intimidation blocked their efforts.

It was during the early 1970s that the booming economy bolstered by American involvement in the war in Southeast Asia enabled young people to attend college in unprecedented numbers. For some who believed that the war in Vietnam was immoral, and that United States corporations were by definition immoral institutions, wage labor held few charms; any kind of employment in "the system" signalled complicity in the death machine otherwise known as the American economy. Nevertheless, student radicals like the founders of the Students for a Democratic Society (founded in 1962) advanced the idea (at once so traditional and so revolutionary) that work should be fulfilling and self-affirming; theirs was a countercultural critique of the place of labor within an advanced capitalist state. In any case, the wartime economy meant that jobs in the white-collar sector were college students' for the picking.

These flush times were about to end, however, as the world economy (shaped by the expansion of trade no less than military conflict) began to penetrate into different kinds and growing numbers of American workplaces. For example, the 1974 oil embargo sponsored by the Arab states immediately affected all of the industries associated with auto-making – not only the Big Three car producers of Chrysler, General Motors, and Ford, but glass, steel, and rubber companies as well. Rapidly repacing the big, Detroit-made, unpredictable gas guzzlers sitting in American driveways were more compact, efficient models imported from Japan and Germany.

By this time, an emerging environmental movement, combined with competition from abroad in a whole host of industries, prompted the reconfiguration of American businesses, and also encouraged those businesses to build plants wherever they could find the cheapest source of labor. In some cases that meant relocating from the Upper Midwest or New England to the Southern states (where labor unions had traditionally encountered stiff resistance from public officials, and many workers as well), in other cases that meant relocating to Malaysia or South Korea. Consequently, the mid-1970s represented the high-water point for American workers in such industries as steel and apparel. Within the next two decades, their jobs would rapidly disappear, the work taken over by robots and computers (in new mini-mill steel plants) or by cheap labor in Southeast Asia (in garment work and textiles).

Meanwhile, the American workforce was becoming more diverse as relaxed immigration laws opened the way for refugees from Latin America and Southeast Asia. Many of these "Fourth Wave" immigrants competed with African Americans for jobs in the service sector; indeed, employers came to favor the newcomers, for they seemed relatively compliant, willing to work for low wages and to endure unpleasant working conditions without complaining or talking back to their supervisors. (Black workers were gaining a reputation as "difficult" employees, quick to challenge a racist boss, reluctant to abide by rules and regulations they believed to be unfair or discriminatory.) Not all immigrants arrived with the same skills and personal resources; at one extreme were the refugees from civil war and revolution in Central America and Cambodia – men, women, and children, who just barely managed to escape with the clothes on their back, and their lives. At the other extreme were the well-educated Koreans who arrived with some measure of personal savings, a nest egg that enabled them to open small businesses and parlay those businesses into a middle-class way of life. Many Arab and West-Indian immigrants also showed entrepreneurial proclivities.

The Reagan Revolution of the 1980s actually constituted a devolution, a dismantling of both the welfare state and the machinery of federal economic regulation. Reagan made no secret of his hostility to labor unions; in 1981 he fired 11,000 striking air traffic controllers and in the process inspired private employers around the country to engage in an aggressive anti-union campaign. Moreover, the President's relentless attack on "big government" found a receptive audience among many Americans who believed the Washington, DC bureaucracy existed in order to coddle "welfare queens" and other alleged freeloaders. (On the other hand, Reagan embraced the side of "big government" that continued to fuel the arms race and, in the process, it was hoped, provoke civil unrest among residents of the Eastern Bloc who resented the proliferation of nuclear weapons and chronic shortages of food and consumer goods.) Reagan's plan, to cut taxes and devolve social-welfare responsibilties to individual states, had an immediate impact upon the ranks of government employees (blacks a disproportionate number of them), and, more generally, signalled the concerted attack upon the poor that was soon to come.

Thus workers in the 1980s were squeezed by a growing international economy that sent dispossessed workers to the United States to compete with their native-born counterparts, and at the same time facilitated the mobility of American capital that paid foreign workers to produce goods that had previously relied on the skill and expertise of Americans. In his efforts to harrass members of labor unions, to pare down worker-protection policies and programs like the Occupational Safety and Health Administration, and to discourage economic regulation of all kind, Reagan lent his tacit support to the growing gap between rich and poor. Between the late 1970s and the early 1990s, this trend became abundantly clear; the real wages of low-skilled workers fell dramatically in absolute terms and in comparison with the wages of high-skilled workers. During the 1980s, the richest 5 percent of Americans enjoyed a 29.1 percent rise in their incomes, while middle-class families saw their wages cut by 4.6 percent. In fact, the broad middle class that had prospered from 1947 to 1973 now consisted of two distinct groups – an elite stratum of well-educated "information managers" on the one hand, and a much larger group of unskilled and semi-skilled workers who could barely make ends meet each month on the other. (In terms of purchasing power, the minimum wage in 1995 was 25 percent less than the minimum wage in 1967.) Contributing to their distress was the precipitous decline in union strength (by the early 1990s down to about 15 percent of the work force) and increased foreign immigration which flooded the labor market with cheap (that is desperate) workers. Sensational newspaper headlines alerted (generally complacent) readers to the fact that sweatshop labor – and even debt peonage – constituted a cornerstone of the late twentieth-century high-tech economy; in the garment industry for example, smuggled Chinese workers were held in a state of near bondage in New York City, while on the West Coast Thai immigrants were virtually enslaved. Over the next few years, the gap between rich and poor would continue to grow, until by the end of the century, the wealth of a single man – Bill Gates, the head of the Microsoft computer company – equaled the total assets of the bottom 40 percent of the American population (about 125 million people).

In the 1980s, the forces of corporate consolidation and technological innovation that for three decades had gradually eroded the employment security of lower-level blue-collar workers finally burst into national headlines, now that white-collar employees were finding themselves dismissed at a moment's notice. Bank tellers, newspaper print compositors, and secretaries found themselves replaced by computers and the new, ill-paid part-time and contract workers who operated them. Indeed, the structure of the American workforce underwent a seismic shift; replacing the mid-twentieth-century broad middle class, composed of both relatively well-paid blue-collar union members as well as white-collar workers, was the late twentieth-century bifurcated workforce, composed of a relatively small group of highly educated workers working full-time and receiving generous job-related benefits, and a growing army of service and technical workers working part-time and receiving no benefits at all (and in some cases laboring for no pay in prisons). Still, the rather boring work associated with computer programming helped to account for a shortage of workers willing to sit at their work stations and hack away at their computers all day long; as a result, policy makers began to debate ways to lure overeducated and unemployed PhDs away from English literature and into the cubicles of high-tech companies.

Behind these general trends lay diverse stories of hardship that affected working families all over the United States. The proliferation of multi-racial, multi-ethnic distressed communities in the North and South, on the East Coast and West Coast, in urban and rural areas, challenged conventional wisdom about the nature of employment opportunity and the shape of the American workforce. In the new world economy, the historical trajectory of a particular kind of job overshadowed personal ambition as a determining factor in the life of an individudal worker. And traditional assumptions about black–white differences in the workplace gave way to a more complex reality, where certain white workers understood that the processes of deindustrialization and corporate consolidation were essentially color-blind, rendering them as vulnerable as African Americans and other minorities.

In the decaying textile mill towns of the Southern Piedmont, and in the vicinity of shuttered steel plants in the Midwest, displaced manufacturing workers faced cruel choices – to sever ties of mutual support with neighbors and kin and move in search of new jobs, or to remain rooted in their communities and commute long distances to work in shopping malls or all-night drugstores, or to apply for food stamps and "welfare." Like Waterloo, Iowa, where a farm machinery factory and a meatpacking plant closed their doors in the 1970s, rural communities of all kinds became "stranded," stripped of their economic bases. As a result, the texture of family and community life changed dramatically; gone was the daily rhythm shaped by the factory whistle, a rhythm that allowed families to eat dinner together, and bowling leagues and church prayer groups to meet in the early evening. In its place was a fractured day and night, during which workers of all ages (and increasingly younger ones as well) scattered to jobs that paid low wages but demanded long hours, like those in fast-food restaurants and nursing homes.

From the backroad by-ways of New England to the hills and hollows of Appalachia and the exclusive ski resorts of the Rocky Mountains, workers who made their living in the tourist economy pieced together a livelihood through hunting, fishing, and relying on their neighbors. Increasingly, gift-shop clerks, chambermaids, and waitresses found it difficult to live near their jobs, so high were real-estate prices in popular vacation spots; they therefore faced the prospect of spending their hourly wages on long commutes from cheaper areas in the housing market.

The migrant workers in Belle Glade, Florida, who suffered from high rates of AIDS, drug addiction and tuberculosis; the Sioux Indians on Pine Ridge Reservation in South Dakota, who by any measure of poverty were among the poorest people in the United States; the Cambodian immigrant community of Lowell, Massachusetts; Chinese sweatshop workers in New York City, outside the reach of even minimal provisions of worker protection laws; the Dolomite, Alabama coke workers, who for years had endured 130-degree heat in return for $14–$17 hourly wages and now found themselves thrown out of work, their jobs the casualties of Environmental Production Agency standards as well as more efficient sources of fuel – all these workers paid the price for the new world economic order as it affected the United States. In addition, by the early 1990s, the collapse of communism in the Soviet Union and Eastern Europe had produced the "peace dividend" distressed community, where a closed army base or defense plant propelled the best-educated workers out of town in search of new jobs, while the region's infrastructure (composed of dry-cleaning establishments and restaurants, schools and shopping centers) began to decay slowly.

These processes of economic and political transformation accelerated in the course of the decade. In 1993, Congress approved the North American Free Trade Agreement (NAFTA), which facilitated the movement of goods and capital (but not workers) throughout the Western hemisphere.

Manufacturers extolled the virtues of a worldwide free market that provided them with compliant workers abroad and high demand for their products at home. Between 1990 and 1995, the Dallas-based Haggar shirt company eliminated 1,534 jobs in Texas and created 1,561 jobs in the Dominican Republic. The company's president attributed the move to purely altruistic motives: "We cannot sit on this globe, in America, with a population of 230 million, compared with the world population of 4.5 billion, with a great disproportionate share of the world's wealth, and not help our fellow nations."[14] He neglected to mention the appeal of setting up shop in a country where human rights abuses of workers were routine and wages pitifully low. Within five years of the passage of NAFTA, an estimated 150,000 Americans had lost their jobs as a result; meanwhile, in 1998, Mexican workers were making on average one-half the amount they had earned nearly two decades earlier. Moreover, the shape of Asian financial and labor markets reverberated in American workplaces, when Japanese bank failures threatened to tighten credit and when Vietnamese workers in American-built shoe factories proved to be highly productive and vulnerable to barbaric forms of physical abuse from their bosses.

At the end of the twentieth century, technological progress produced poverty as well as prosperity. Although the United States Census Bureau estimated the poverty rate at 14 percent, in all likelihood at least twice that number of American families lived precariously, month to month, just a health-care crisis away from complete and utter disaster. Indeed, if we calculate poverty not according to an arbitrary figure (by official calculations, $14,000 a year for a family of four), but rather according to what percentage of households could just barely make ends meet in terms of paying for necessities like food, rent, and clothing, then the "robust economy" of the 1990s appeared uneven, to say the least.

Compounding the contradictions inherent in prosperity was the role of restrictive federal monetary policy in bolstering stock market prices and at the same time contributing to the loss of jobs (in 1995 alone, an estimated 750,000). The

Federal Reserve Board dreaded full employment (hence the dip in the stock market everytime unemployment rates fell), since a tight labor market meant that workers were in a position to demand higher wages, a move that prompted employers to raise prices, thus setting off an inflationary spiral (and necessitating tighter credit). However, higher interest rates served to attract speculative capital from abroad, boosting the value of the dollar and making American goods more expensive (less competitive) on the world market.

In 1996, 14.5 percent of American workers (16.3 million people) belonged to a union (down from 33 percent in the early 1950s). Nevertheless, the election of John Sweeney as president of the AFL-CIO in 1995 signalled a turning point in labor organizing. Sweeney declared the need for a renewed commitment to grass-roots organizing and militant demonstrations. Stepping into the breach left by the slow demise of the heavy-industry unions were groups like the American Federation of State, County, and Municipal Employees (more than a third of all public employees were unionized in contrast to only 17.2 percent of all workers in manufacturing). Nevertheless, Sweeney and other labor leaders understood that one of their greatest challenges was to contend with the increasing significance of contract, temporary, and part-time labor. In the "high-tech" sector these positions were concentrated in accounting and computer consulting. Increasingly, professionals relied on temporary legal secretaries and dental assistants; clerical workers found jobs by the day, week, and month as typists and word processors; and manual labor pools drew upon unskilled men, some of them homeless and suffering from alcohol and drug abuse.

Larger social tensions were refracted through debates over work in its various forms. In 1992, President Bill Clinton gave his blessing to the Family and Medical Leave Act. This measure, supported by a well-organized group of women professionals and lobbyists on Capitol Hill, allowed employees of large businesses to take time off after the birth of a child, or to care for an ill or elderly family member, without fear of losing their jobs. Washington thus put its official stamp of approval on a law that acknowledged the importance of family life in general, and the role of women workers in sustaining that family life in particular. Yet within three years, several pieces of legislation under the rubric "welfare reform" revealed the hypocrisy of legislators, who now proceeded to shred the New Deal "safety net" for women and children, by eliminating a federal guarantee of aid for the poor, without providing for the decent jobs and good wages that would enable mothers to become truly self-sufficient. A gender-based double standard was evident in the legislators' single-minded focus on women, who already bore the dual burdens of poverty and motherhood, in contrast to their official neglect of fathers, for whom decent employment opportunities would have in all probablity eliminated the need for welfare for their children and the mothers of their children.

The cross-currents of social and class tensions were also apparent in debates over immigration policy during the decade. With their large immigrant populations, New York, Florida, Texas, and California possessed cheap work forces that allowed agribusinesses, garment and textile manufacturers, and industrial machinery employers to remain competitive within a global economy. Yet native-born voters and tax payers perceived the newcomers primarily as a drain on the public coffers, their children crowding public school classrooms, their elderly relatives applying for aid and social services.

In addition, the convergence of "affirmative action" policies with the downsizing of many American workplaces heightened tensions between whites and African Americans. For generations, regardless of their qualifications for a particular job, white workers had moved to the head of the employment queue, leaving black workers to suffer disproportionately the brunt of underemployment and seasonal downturns in the economy. Now that some whites found themselves at the back of the queue, they were quick to call "Foul!" and to indulge in racist stereotypes, simultaneously condemning black people as lazy and unwilling to work (*qua* welfare recipients) and at the same time as aggressive in their quest for the best jobs for themselves and educational opportunities for their children (*qua* recipients of affirmative-action policies). Despite the attention accorded this issue in the national news media and in the courts, the fact of the matter was that affirmative-action gains for African-American workers were not universal or uniform, but rather concentrated in public-sector jobs like school teaching, firefighting, law enforcement, and the postal service – positions that required formal job training or a college education. Moreover, even many black professionals worked in jobs that were vulnerable to budget cuts and downsizing; in corporate offices, black men and women were often relegated to human resources or personnel offices, and in public and state employment, blacks vied with whites for a shrinking number of jobs in government. Although decisions made in the boardrooms of multinational corporations were more likely to affect a white worker's job status than the application form filled out by a black man or woman, political leaders of both races often persisted in discussing labor in purely black and white terms. In the end, the heated, bitter debate over affirmative-action policies only served as a distraction from larger forces of economic change.

And finally, the fact that seven out of every ten mothers with children under 17 worked for wages underscored the profound effects of the brave new economy on the quality of American family life. Deb Escala, working a rotating seven-day shift on a California assembly line, and putting in five extra hours in overtime each week, nevertheless expressed a preference for her job at the factory over her job at home: "I thought about staying home with the kids, but they drove me nuts. Maybe it's just my kids, but they are a wild bunch . . . I think I'd rather be working. . . . If work's what you have to do to get away [from home], so be it. Plus, I'm getting paid for it." One researcher who studied Deb Escala and 800 of her co-workers concluded, "Nowadays, men and women both may leave unwashed dishes, unresolved quarrels, crying tots, testy teenagers, and unresponsive mates behind to arrive at work early and call out, 'Hi fellas, I'm here.'"[15]

At the end of the twentieth century, groups of American workers judged their relative status according to a matrix of factors – whether or not they worked at a job that paid a living wage (enough to support themselves and their families), a job that guaranteed them health and safety protection, a job that allowed them a role in decision-making and self-direction, a job that had a future or one that might lead to a better job. In 1996, the "Massachusetts Miracle" produced 90,000 new jobs; but in that same year, 65,000 fewer of the state's residents were covered by health insurance compared to the year before. By this time, an employee's loyalty to a particular kind of job or a particular company seemed hopelessly naive and short-sighted, for employers proved almost principled in their refusal to reciprocate. Reluctant to confront head-on the realities of the postindustrial, high-tech, service-driven economy, politicians and policymakers as well mocked the notion that Americans had the right to a job, any kind of job. Indeed, although the American electorate showed little tolerance for law-based inequality between the sexes and among the races in education, housing, and employment, they remained remarkably tolerant of concrete, dramatic forms of inequality – between rich and poor school systems, rich and poor neighborhoods, good jobs and bad jobs.

"I am blessed to live and work in Las Vegas," Hattie Canty told an interviewer in 1996. (In 1995, blue-collar union workers took home wages that were 63.2 percent higher, and received health benefits that were 148.9 percent higher, and pension benefits that were 322.6 percent higher, than their nonunionized counterparts.) Yet less than 100 miles away from Las Vegas, in the town of Laughlin, Nevada, hotel and casino employees continued to labor under pre-union conditions. Workers remained subject to surveillance cameras and to routine intimidation from bosses. Rebecca Amoto, a waitress able to balance a serving tray laden with 25 drinks at a time, observed that the arbitrary firing of workers was "a power thing" with managers; "It doesn't matter how loyal you are to the company. If someone decides that you did something wrong or they don't like you or you didn't smile at them in the right way or their cousin's brother's uncle needs a job, then *you don't have a job*."[16]

In the late twentieth century, many American wage-earners
– those who did not belong to a union or did not have tenure
at a college or university – shared Rebecca Amoto's appre-
hension that each new day might bring a dismissal notice.
(On the other hand, most married women realized that there
was little chance they would find relief from the rigors of
unwaged work at home.) The glorification of the marketplace
reduced men and women trying to support their families to a
fungible expense in the production of cars, clothing, or late-
night entertainment, Las Vegas style. Policy-makers and politicians proved adept at deflecting voter attention away from
the sources of economic insecurity and instability and instead
contributed to the scapegoating of the poor and most vulnerable members of society. In late twentieth-century America,
the issues of welfare, affirmative action, and foreign immigration provoked passionate debate; and yet Americans lacked
the collective will to press for a new kind of national community, one where everyone was guaranteed the right to a good
job. Only inspired political leadership, combined with a
strengthened labor movement, would hold out the promise,
the hope, of such a radical departure from four centuries of
American labor history.

FURTHER READING

Primary Sources

Cose, Ellis. *The Rage of a Privileged Class*. New York: Harper Collins, 1993.
Feldman, Richard and Michael Betzold, eds. *End of the Line: Autoworkers and the American Dream*. New York: Weidenfeld and Nicolson, 1988.
Moore, Marat. *Women in the Mines: Stories of Life and Work*. New York: Twayne Publishers, 1996.
Terkel, Studs. *Working*. New York: Avon Books, 1975.

Secondary Sources

Cumbler, John T. *A Social History of Economic Decline: Business, Politics, and Work in Trenton*. New Brunswick, NJ: Rutgers University Press, 1989.

Dudley, Kathryn Marie. *The End of the Line: Lost Jobs, New Lives in Postindustrial America*. Chicago: University of Chicago Press, 1994.

Fink, Leon and Brian Greenberg. *Upheaval in the Quiet Zone: A History of Hospital Workers' Union, Local 1199*. Urbana: University of Illinois Press, 1989.

Friedman, Sara Ann. *Work Matters: Women Talk About Their Jobs and Their Lives*. New York: Viking, 1996.

Geschwender, James A. *Class, Race, and Worker Insurgency: The League of Revolutionary Black Workers*. Cambridge, MA: Cambridge University Press, 1977.

Gordon, David M. *Fat and Mean: The Corporate Squeeze of Working Americans and the Myth of Managerial 'Downsizing'*. New York: Martin Kessler Books, 1996.

Honey, Michael K. *Southern Labor and Black Civil Rights: Organizing Memphis Workers*. Urbana: University of Illinois Press, 1993.

Jones, Jacqueline. *American Work: Four Centuries of Black and White Labor*. New York: W. W. Norton, 1998.

Massey, Douglas S. and Nancy A. Denton. *American Apartheid: Segregation and the Making of the Underclass*. Cambridge, MA: Harvard University Press, 1993.

Rank, Mark Robert. *Living on the Edge: The Realities of Welfare in America*. New York: Columbia University Press, 1994.

Schor, Juliet. *The Overworked American: The Unexpected Decline of Leisure*. New York: Basic Books, 1991.

Sugrue, Thomas J. *The Origins of the Urban Crisis: A History of Inequality in Detroit, 1940–1967*. Princeton: Princeton University Press, 1996.

Waldinger, Roger. *Still the Promised City? African-Americans and the New Immigrants in Postindustrial New York*. Cambridge, MA: Harvard University Press, 1996.

Wilson, William Julius. *When Work Disappears: The World of the New Urban Poor*. New York: Knopf, 1996.

Notes

Notes to chapter 1

1   This case is taken from J. Hall Pleasants, ed., *Archives of Maryland*, vol. 54, Proceedings of the County Courts of Kent, 1648–1676, Talbot, 1662–1674, and Somerset, 1665–1674 (Baltimore: Maryland Historical Society, 1937), pp. 167–9, 178–80, 213, 224–5, 234. It is reprinted in Nancy F. Cott, et al., eds, *Root of Bitterness: Documents of the Social History of American Women*, 2nd edn (Boston: Northeastern University Press, Boston, 1996), pp. 24–8.

2   Peter Force, *Tracts and Other Papers Relating Principally to the Origins, Settlement, and Progress of the Colonies in North America*, vol. I (New York: Peter Smith, 1947), pp. 7–8.

3   Steven R. Potter, "Early English Effects on Virginia Algonquian Exchange and Tribute in the Tidewater Potomac," in Peter Wood, et al., eds, *Powhatan's Mantle: Indians in the Colonial Southeast* (Lincoln: University of Nebraska Press, 1989), p. 154.

4   Quoted in Jean Marie O'Brien, "Community Dynamics in the Indian-English Town of Natick, Massachusetts, 1650–1790," Unpub. PhD diss., University of Chicago, 1990, p. 49.

5   *Winthrop Papers*, vol. IV (Boston: Massachusetts Historical Society), pp. 68–9.

6   Alden T. Vaughan, ed., *William Wood's New England's Prospect* (Amherst, MA: University of Massachusetts Press, 1977), p. 71.

7   Alice Morse Earle, *Home Life in Colonial Days* (Stockbridge, MA; Berkshire Traveller Press, 1974; orig. pub. 1898), p. 235.

8   James Axtell, ed. "The Vengeful Women of Marblehead: Robert Roules's Deposition of 1677," *William and Mary Quarterly* 3rd series 31 (Oct. 1974): 647–52.

9   Francis Higginson, "New-Englands Plantation," [1630] in Perry Miller and Thomas H. Johnson, eds, *The Puritans* (New York: American Book Company, 1938), p. 125.

10 David R. Ransome, "Wives for Virginia, 1621," *William and Mary Quarterly* 3rd series 48 (Jan. 1991): 15.

11 Warren M. Billings, ed., *The Old Dominion in the Seventeenth Century: A Documentary History of Virginia, 1606–1687* (Chapel Hill: University of North Carolina Press, 1975), p. 135.

12 Susie M. Ames, *County Court Records of Accomack-Northampton, Virginia, 1632–1640* (Washington, DC: American Historical Association, 1954), p. 61.

13 *Archives of Maryland*, vol. 41, *Proceedings of the Provincial Court, 1658–1662*, p. 316.

14 T. H. Breen, James H. Lewis, and Keith Schlesinger, "Motive for Murder: A Servant's Life in Virginia, 1678," *William and Mary Quarterly*, 3rd series, 40 (Jan. 1983): 106–20.

15 H. R. McIlwaine, ed., *Executive Journals of the Council of Colonial Virginia*, vol. I (June 11, 1680–June 22, 1699) (Richmond: Davis Bratton, 1925), p. 149.

16 "Poor Children to be Sent to Virginia," *Virginia Magazine of History and Biography* 6 (Jan. 1899): 232.

17 John Hammond, "Leah and Rachel," in Clayton Colman Hall, ed., *Narratives of Early Maryland* (New York: Barnes and Noble, 1946), p. 284.

Notes to chapter 2

1 Louis P. Masur, ed., *The Autobiography of Benjamin Franklin*, (Boston: Bedford Books, 1993), p. 100.

2 Ibid., p. 122–3.

3 Quoted in Alice Morse Earle, *Home Life in Colonial Days* (Stockbridge, MA: Berkshire Traveller Press, 1974; orig. pub. 1898), pp. 292–3.

4 Janet Schaw, *Journal of a Lady of Quality: Being the Narrative of a Journey from Scotland to the West Indies, North Carolina, and Portugal, in the years 1774 to 1776* (New Haven: Yale University Press, 1934), p. 155.

5 Quoted in Bernard Bailyn, *Voyagers to the West: A Passage in the Peopling of America on the Eve of the Revolution* (New York: Knopf, 1986), p. 172.

6 Quoted in Jonathan Prude, "Runway Ads and the Appearance of Unfree Laborers in America, 1750–1800," *Journal of American History* 78 (June 1991): 124.

7 Billy G. Smith, "The Precarious Freedom of Blacks in the Mid-Atlantic Region: Excerpts from the *Pennsylvania Gazette*, 1728–1776," *Pennsylvania Magazine of History and Biography* 103 (April 1989): 244.

8 Fred Shelley, ed., "The Journal of Ebenezer Hazard in Virginia, 1777," *Virginia Magazine of History and Biography* 62 (Oct. 1954): 406.

9   Marshall J. Becker, "Hannah Freeman: An Eighteenth-Century Lenape Living and Working Among Colonial Farmers," *Pennsylvania Magazine of History and Biography* 194 (April 1990): 252.
10 Quoted in Kenneth Wiggins Porter, "Negroes on the Southern Frontier, 1670–1763," *Journal of Negro History* 33 (Jan. 1948): 62.
11 [Benjamin West] in Willie Lee Rose, ed., *Documentary History of Slavery in North America* (New York: Oxford, 1976) pp. 55–6.
12 Quoted in Aaron M. Shatzman, *Servants Into Planters: The Origin of an American Image: Land Acquisition and Status Mobility in Eighteenth-Century South Carolina* (New York: Garland, 1989), p. 21.
13 Washington quoted in Gerald Mullin, *Flight and Rebellion: Slave Resistance in Eighteenth-Century Virginia* (New York: Oxford University Press, 1972), p. 55.
14 Philip Curtin, ed., *Africa Remembered: Narratives by West Africans from the Era of the Slave Trade* (Madison: University of Wisconsin Press, 1967), p. 41.
15 Thomas N. Ingersoll, "'Releese us out of this Cruell Bondegg': An Appeal from Virginia in 1723," *William and Mary Quarterly* 51 3rd series (Oct. 1994): 781.
16 *The Journal of Nicholas Cresswell, 1774–1777* (New York: Dial Press, 1924), pp. 18–19.
17 [July 12, 1736] Marion Tinling, ed., *The Correspondence of the Three William Byrds of Westover, Virginia, 1684–1776* (Charlottesville: University Press of Virginia, 1977), p. 488.
18 Samuel Sewall, "The Selling of Joseph," *Proceedings of the Massachusetts Historical Society*, series 1, vol. 7 (Oct. 1863): 162.
19 Samuel Abbott Green, "Slavery at Groton, Massachusetts, in Provincial Times" (Cambridge: John Wilson and Son, 1909), p. 9.
20 George Sheldon, "Negro Slavery in Old Deerfield," *New England Magazine* (March 1893): 55.
21 James Phinney Baxter, *Documentary History of the State of Maine*, vol. IX (Portland, ME: Maine Historical Society, 1907), pp. 100–1.
22 Quoted in Billy G. Smith, *The 'Lower Sort': Philadelphia's Laboring People, 1750–1800* (Ithaca: Cornell University Press, 1990), p. 170.
23 Daniel E. Williams, *Pillars of Salt: An Anthology of Early American Criminal Narratives* (Madison, WI: Madison House, 1993), p. 164.
24 Quoted in Philip D. Morgan, "Black Life in Eighteenth-Century Charleston," *Perspectives in American History*, new series, I (1984): 213.
25 Silvia Dubois, in Bert James Loewenberg and Ruth Bogin, eds, *Black Women in Nineteenth-Century American Life: Their Words, Their Thoughts, Their Feelings* (University Park: Pennsylvania State University Press, 1976), p. 47.
26 David John Jeremy, *Henry Wansey and His American Journal* (Philadelphia: American Philosphical Society, 1970), p. 83.

27   Quotations from Paul W. Conner, *Poor Richard's Politicks: Benjamin Franklin and His New American Order* (New York; Oxford, 1965), pp. 76, 78; and Verner W. Crane, *Benjamin Franklin's Letters to the Press, 1758–1775* (Chapel Hill: University of North Carolina Press, 1950), p. 189.

28   Quoted in "A conversation between an Englishman, a Scotchman, and an American, on the Subject of Slavery," in Crane, ed. *Benjamin Franklin's Letters to the Press 1758–1775*, pp. 190–1.

Notes to chapter 3

1   Frederick Douglass, *Narrative of the Life of Frederick Douglass, An American Slave* (ed. by Houston A. Baker, Jr) (New York: Penguin Books, 1982; orig. pub. 1845), p. 51.

2   Ibid., p. 115.

3   Ibid., p. 69.

4   Ibid., p. 105.

5   Ibid., p. 83.

6   Ibid., p. 140.

7   James Henry Hammond, "Letter to an English Abolitionist," in Drew Gilpin Faust, ed., *The Ideology of Slavery: Proslavery Thought in the Antebellum South, 1830–1860* (Baton Rouge: Louisiana State University Press, 1981), p. 187.

8   J. B. DeBow, *DeBow's Review* (New Orleans), vol. XXI (1861): 347–61.

9   Frederick Law Olmsted, *A Journey in the Back Country, 1853–54* (New York: 1860), p. 219.

10   Kenneth Stampp, ed., Records of Southern Antebellum Plantations from the Revolution through the Civil War (Microfilm Collection), Series A, Pt. 1, Reel 14 (Miscellaneous Plantation Books, 1840–1857) (Frederick, MD: University Publications of America, 1985).

11   Quoted in Mark S. Schantz, "'A very Serious Business': Managerial Relationships on the Ball Plantations, 1800–1835," *South Carolina Historical Magazine* 88 (Jan. 1987):4.

12   Meta Morris quoted in Anne Firor Scott, *The Southern Lady from Pedestal to Politics, 1830–1930* (Chicago: University of Chicago Press, 1970), p. 32.

13   George Rawaick, ed. *The American Slave: A Collective Autobiography*, vol. 7, Miss. Narrs. (Greenwood, CT: Westport Press, 1977), p. 114.

14   Rawick, ed., Ala. Narrs., vol. 6, pt 1, p. 174.

15   Roderick A. McDonald, *The Economic and Material Culture of Slaves: Goods and Chattels on the Sugar Plantations of Jamaica and Louisiana* (Baton Rouge: Louisiana State University Press, 1993).

16 James Hugo Johnston, "The Participation of White Men in Virginia Negro Insurrections," *Journal of Negro History* 16 (April 1931): 162.

17 Quoted in J. William Harris, *Plain Folk and Gentry in a Slave Society: White Liberty and Black Slavery in Augusta's Hinterlands* (Middletown, CT: Wesleyan University Press, 1985), p. 60.

18 Stephanie McCurry, *Masters of Small Worlds: Yeomen Households, Gender Relations, and the Political Culture of the Antebellum South Carolina Low Country* (New York Oxford Uiversity Press, 1995), p. 50.

19 Frederick Law Olmsted, *The Cotton Kingdom* (New York: Knopf, 1953), p. 527.

20 Sir Charles Lyell, *A Second Visit to the United States of North America* (London: J. Murray, 1849), vol. I, p. 217.

21 John Edmund Stealey III, "Slavery and the Western Virginia Salt Industry," *Journal of Negro History* 49 (April 1974): 116.

22 Quoted in Richard W. Griffin, "The Origins of the Industrial Revolution in Georgia: Cotton Textiles, 1810–1865," *Georgia Historical Quarterly* 42 (Dec. 1958): 361.

23 H. A. Kellar, ed., *Solon Robinson, Pioneer and Agriculturist, Selected Writings* (New York: Da Capo Press, 1968), p. 216.

24 Quoted in Christopher Silver, "A New Look at Old South Urbanization: The Irish Worker in Charleston, South Carolina," *South Atlantic Urban Studies*, vol. 3 (Charleston: University of South Carolina Press, 1979), p. 156.

25 "Memorial of the Citizens of Charleston to the Senate and House of Representatives of the State of South Carolina," in U. B. Phillips, ed., *Plantation and Frontier, 1649–1863*, vol. II of John R. Commons, ed., *A Documentary History of American Industrial Society* (Cleveland: Arthur H. Clark Co., 1910), pp. 103–16.

26 Quoted in Marianne Buroff Sheldon, "Black-White Relations in Richmond, Virginia, 1782–1820," *Journal of Southern History* 45 (Feb. 1979): 35.

27 Documents in Phillips, ed., *Plantation and Frontier, 1649–1863*, pp. 360, 367.

28 *Narrative*, p. 132.

Notes to chapter 4

1 Louisa May Alcott, *Work* (New York: Penguin Books, 1994; orig. pub. 1873), pp. 9, 13.

2 Ibid., pp. 11–12, 16, 23, 168, 41, 63, 68, 110–11, 117, 277, 325, 344.

3 Charles Mackay, *Life and Liberty in America; Or, Sketches of a Tour in the United States and Canada* (London: Smith, Elder and Co., 1859), p. 47.

4 Richard B. Lyman, Jr, "'What is Done in My Absence?' Levi Lincoln's Oakham, Massachusetts, Farm workers, 1807–20," and Jack Larkin, "'Labor is the Great Thing in Farming': The Farm Laborers of the Ward Family of Shrewsbury, Massachusetts, 1787–1860," *Proceedings of the American Antiquarian Society*, 1989, pp. 151–226.

5 Quoted in Lillian Schlissel, *Women's Diaries of the Westward Journey* (New York: Schocken Books, 1982), p. 35.

6 Thomas Dublin, ed., *Immigrant Voices: New Lives in America, 1773–1986* (Urbana: University of Illinois Press, 1993), pp. 97–109.

7 Quoted in Schlissel, *Women's Diaries of the Westward Journey* p. 61.

8 Bert James Loewenberg and Ruth Bogin, eds, *Black Women in Nineteenth-Century American Life: Their Words, Their Thoughts, Their Feelings* (University Park: Pennsylvania State University Press, 1976), p. 87.

9 *Douglass' Monthly* (July 1859), p. 109.

10 Monica Roberts, "Pathway to Freedom: The Historical Development of the African-American Lawyer," Brandeis University McNair Scholars Program, July, 1997, pp. 17–18 (paper in author's possession).

11 Quoted in Christine Stansell, *City of Women: Sex and Class in New York, 1789–1860* (Urbana: University of Illinois Press, 1986), p. 71.

12 Alcott, *Work*, p. 25.

13 Edward S. Abdy, *Journal of a Residence and Tour in the United States of North America*, vol. 3 (London: John Murray, 1835), pp. 246–7.

14 Martin Robison Delany, *The Condition, Elevation, Emigration, and Destiny of the Colored People of the United States, Politically Considered* (New York: Arno Press, 1968; orig. pub. 1852), p. 43.

15 Quoted in Jacqueline Jones, *Soldiers of Light and Love: Northern Teachers and Georgia Blacks, 1865–1873* (Chapel Hill: University of North Carolina Press, 1980), p. 40.

16 Quoted in De Anne Blanton, "Women Soldiers of the Civil War," *Prologue* 25 (Spring 1993): 27–33.

17 Louisa May Alcott, "Hospital Sketches," in *Louisa May Alcott: An Intimate Anthology* (New York: Bantam Doubleday Dell, 1987), pp. 47, 97, 117. This work is a fictionalized account of Alcott's own work in a Union hospital.

Notes to chapter 5

1 William H. Holtzclaw, *The Black Man's Burden* (New York: Neale Publishing Co., 1915), pp. 17–31.

2 Theodore Rosengarten, *All God's Dangers: The Life of Nate Shaw*, (New York: Vintage, 1974), p. 321.

3 *Anthropological Review* quoted in Stuart Creighton Miller, *The Unwelcome Immigrant: The American Image of the Chinese, 1785–1882* (Berkeley: University of California, 1969), p. 145.

4   John Stephens Durham, "The Labor Unions and the Negro," *Atlantic Monthly* 81 (Feb. 1898): 222.

5   Ira Berlin, Steven Hahn, Steven F. Miller, Joseph P. Reidy, and Leslie S. Rowland, eds, "The Terrain of Freedom: The Struggle Over the Meaning of Free Labor in the U.S. South," *History Workshop* 22 (Autumn 1986): 122.

6   Quoted in Jacqueline Jones, *The Dispossessed: America's Underclasses from the Civil War to the Present* (New York: Basic Books, 1992), p. 4.

7   Charles Nordhoff, *The Cotton States in the Spring and Summer of 1875* (New York: D. Appleton, 1975), p. 72.

8   W. E. B. DuBois, "The Negroes of Farmville, Virginia: A Social Study," in Dan S. Green and Edwin D. Driver, eds, *W. E. B. DuBois on Sociology and the Black Community* (Chicago: University of Chicago Press, 1978).

9   Rosser H. Taylor, ed., "Post-Bellum Southern Rental Contracts," *Agricultural History* 17 (1943): 123.

10 Alfred Holt Stone, "Italian Cotton-Growers in Arkansas," *American Monthly Review of Books* 35 (Feb. 1907):209–13.

11 United States Department of Justice Classified Subject Files Correspondence, Box no. 10803, case no. 50–277, Record Group 60, National Archives, Washington, DC.

12 Ibid., Box no. 10804, case no. 50–310.

13 Mary Ellen Curtin, "The 'Human World' of Black Women in Alabama Prisons, 1870–1900," in Virginia Bernhard, Betty Brandon, Elizabeth Fox-Genovese, Theda Purdue, and Elizabeth Hayes Turner, eds, *Hidden Histories of Women in the New South* (Columbia: University of Missouri Press, 1994), p. 20.

14 Charles B. Spahr, "America's Working People," *The Outlook* 62 (May 6, 1899), p. 33.

15 *United States Industrial Commission Report*, vol. 4 (Washington: Government Printing Office, 1900–1), p. 267.

16 Henry M. McKiven, Jr, *Iron and Steel: Class, Race and Community in Birmingham, Alabama, 1875–1920* (University of North Carolina Press, 1995).

17 Mamie Garvin Fields with Karen Fields, *Lemon Swamp and Other Places: A Carolina Memoir* (New York: Free Press, 1983), p. xiv.

18 DuBois, *Philadelphia Negro*, p. 123.

19 Quoted in Joe William Trotter, Jr, *Black Milwaukee: The Making of An Industrial Proletariat, 1915–1945* (Urban: University of Illinois Press, 1985), p. 53.

20 "Negro Women in Industry," United States Department of Labor Women's Bureau, Bulletin no. 20 (1922), p. 34.

21 Alma Herbst, *The Negro in the Slaughtering and Meat-Packing Industry in Chicago* (Boston: Houghton-Mifflin, 1932), p. 77.

22 DuBois, *Philadelphia Negro*, p. 130.

23   John W. Blassingame and John R. McKivigan, eds, *The Frederick Douglass Papers, Series One: Speeches, Debates, and Interviews,* vol. 4: 1864–1880 (New London: Yale University Press, 1991), pp. 232–3.

24   California Legislature, *Senate Special Committee on Chinese Immigration: Its Social, Moral, and Political Effects; Report to the California State Senate of the Special Committee on Chinese Immigration* (Sacramento, CA: State Printing Office, 1878), p. 41.

25   John W. Blassingame and John R. McKivigan, eds, *The Frederick Douglass Papers: Series One: Speeches, Debates, and Interviews,* vol. 4:1864–80 (New Haven: Yale University Press, 1991), pp. 250–1.

26   California Legislature, *Senate Special Committee on Chinese Immigration,* p. 62.

27   Ibid., p. 25.

28   *Report of the Special Joint Committee to Investigate Chinese Immigration.* 44th congress, 2nd Sess., Senate Report no. 689 (Washington: Government Printing Office, 1877), p. 19.

29   California Legislature, *Senate Special Committee on Chinese Immigration,* p. 4.

30   United States Congress, *Report of the Joint Special Commttee to Investigate Chinese Immigration,* 44th Cong., 2nd sess., report no. 689 (Washington, DC: Government Printing Office, 1877), p. 821.

31   Quoted in Michele Shover, "Chico Women: Nemesis of a Rural Town's Anti-Chinese Campaigns, 1876–1888," *California History* 67 (Dec. 1988): 236.

32   "The Life Story of a Chinaman," in Hamilton Holt, ed. *The Life Stories of Undistinguished Americans as Told by Themselves* (New York: James Pott and Co., 1906), p. 289.

33   David Beesley, "From Chinese to Chinese American: Chinese Women and Families in a Sierra Nevada County," *California History* 67 (Sept. 1988): 177.

34   Holtzclaw, *Black Man's Burden,* pp. 226, 231.

Notes to chapter 6

1   Quoted in Anneliese Orleck, *Common Sense and a Little Fire: Women and Working-Class Politics in the United States, 1900–1965* (Chapel Hill: University of North Carolina Press, 1995), p. 60.

2   Ibid.

3   Quoted in Angel Kwolek-Folland, *Engendering Business: Men and Women in the Corporate Office, 1870–1930* (Baltimore: Johns Hopkins University Press, 1994), p. 71.

4 Ida Van Etten, "The Sweating System, Charity, and Organization," in Nancy F. Cott, ed., *The Root of Bitterness: Documents of the Social History of American Women* (New York: E. P. Dutton, 1972), p. 331.

5 Suzanne Model, "The Ethnic Niche and the Structure of Opportunity: Immigrants and Minorities in New York City," in Michael B. Katz. ed., *The 'Underclass Debate': Views from History* (Princeton: Princeton University Press, 1993), pp. 161–93.

6 Quoted in Peter H. Argersinger and Jo Ann E. Argersinger, "The Machine Breakers: Farmworkers and Social Change in the Rural Midwest of the 1870s," *Agricultural History* 58 (July 1984):399.

7 Daniel Nelson, *Managers and Workers: Origins of the New Factory System in the United States, 1880–1920* (Madison: University of Wisconsin Press, 1975), pp. 84–85.

8 Quoted in James Kirby Martin, Randy Roberts, Steve Mintz, Linda O. McMurry, and James H. Jones, *America and Its People*, vol. II: from 1865 (New York: Harper Collins, second edn., 1993), p. 606.

9 Quoted in Arch Blakey, *The Florida Phosphate Industry: A History of the Development and Use of a Vital Mineral* (Cambridge: Harvard University Press, 1973), p. 50.

10 Andrea Graziosi, "Common Laborers, Unskilled Workers: 1880–1915," *Labor History* 22 (Fall 1981): 512–44.

11 David Montgomery, *Beyond Equality: Labor and the Radical Republicans, 1862–1872* (New York: Knopf, 1967), p. 161.

12 Quoted in David R. Roediger, "America's First General Strike: The St. Louis 'Commune' of 1877," *Midwest Quarterly* 21 (Winter 1980): 200.

13 "The Great Strike," *Scribner's Monthly* 14 (Oct. 1877): 853.

14 Quoted in Leon Fink, *Workingmen's Democracy: The Knights of Labor and American Politics* (Urbana: University of Illinois Press, 1983), p. 163.

15 Jeremy Atack, "Tenants and Yeoman in the Nineteenth Century," *Agricultural History* 62 (1988): 9.

16 Durham, "The Labor Unions and the Negro," *Atlantic Monthly* 81 (Feb. 1898): 226.

17 Ellen Fitzpatrick, *Muckraking: Three Landmark Articles* (Boston: Bedford Books, 1994), p. 84.

18 Quoted in Morton Keller, *Regulating a New Society: Public Policy and Social Change in America, 1900–1933* (Cambridge, MA: Harvard University Press, 1994), p. 204.

19 Ibid.

20 See for example, Edward F. Brown, "The Neglected Human Resources of the Gulf Coast States," *Child Labor Bulletin* 2 (May 1913).

21 John M. Gillette, "Rural Child Labor," *Child Labor Bulletin* 1 (June 1912): 156.

22 Lewis W. Hine, "Children or Cotton?" *Survey* 31 (Feb. 7, 1914): 592.

23 Orleck, *Common Sense*, pp. 215–29; quote on p. 227.

Notes to chapter 7

1 Interview with Jim Vernatter, *End of the Line: Autoworkers and the American Dream*, ed. by Richard Feldman and Michael Betzold (New York: Weidenfeld and Nicolson, 1988), p. 178.

2 Ibid., pp. 176–7.

3 Marvin Gullett quoted in Laurel Shackelford and Bill Weinberg, eds, *Our Appalachia: An Oral History* (New York: Hill and Wang, 1977), p. 220.

4 Ibid., pp. 176–7, 169.

5 Joe William Trotter, Jr, *Black Milwaukee: The Making of an Industrial Proletariat, 1915–1945* (Urbana: University of Illinois Press, 1985), p. 53.

6 Edw. N. Munns, "Women in Southern Lumbering Operations," *Journal of Forestry* 17 (Feb. 1919): 144–7.

7 Quoted in Elizabeth Haiken, "'The Lord Helps Those Who Help Themselves': Black Laundresses in Little Rock, Arkansas, 1917–1921," *Arkansas Historical Quarterly* 49 (Spring 1990): 31.

8 Quoted in Charles Sampson, "Peach Harvest," *American Mercury* 15 (Oct. 1928): 224.

9 Robert S. Lynd and Helen Merrill Lynd, *Middletown: A Study in American Culture* (New York: Harcourt, Brace, and World, 1929), p. 258.

10 Ibid., p. 59.

11 Ibid., p. 74.

12 Thordis Simonsen, ed., *You May Plow Here: The Narrative of Sara Brooks* (New York: Simon and Schuster, 1986), p. 182.

13 Maggie Comer and James Comer, *Maggie's American Dream* (New York: New American Library, 1988), p. 60.

14 Rosalyn Baxandall, Linda Gordon, and Susan Reverby, eds, *America's Working Women* (New York: Vintage Books, 1976), pp. 263–4.

15 John N. Webb and Malcolm Brown, "Migrant Families" (Washington: Government Printing Office, 1938), pp. 21–3.

16 Lois Rita Helmbold, "Downward Occupational Mobility During the Great Depression: Urban Black and White Working Women," *Labor History* 29 (Spring 1988): 163–4.

17 Quoted in P. K. Russo, "The Negro in Bridgeport," in Robert Hall, ed., *Making a Living: The Work Experience of African Americans in New England* (Boston: New England Foundation for the Humanities, 1995). pp. 544–5.

18 Alfred Edgar Smith, "Negro Project Workers: An Annual Report . . ." (Federal Works Progress Administration, Jan. 1939, p. 39, Record Group 69, National Archives, Washington, DC.

19 Nell Irvin Painter, *The Narrative of Hosea Hudson: His Life as a Negro Communist in the South* (Cambridge: Harvard University Press, 1979), p. 253.

20 Theodore Rosengarten, *All God's Dangers: The Life of Nate Shaw* (New York: Vintage Books, 1974), p. 314.
21 Ann Banks, ed., *First-Person America* (New York: Vintage Books, 1980), pp. 63–4.
22 Audrey O. Faulkner, ed. *When I was Comin' Up: An Oral History of Aged Blacks* (New York: Archon Books, 1982), p. 135.
23 "Negro Women War Workers," Women's Bureau Bulletin No. 205 (1945): 8.
24 Quoted in Quintard Taylor, "The Great Migration: The Afro-American Communities of Seattle and Portland During the 1940s," *Arizona and the West* 23 (Summer 1981): 121.
25 Quoted in Alexa B. Henderson, "FEPC and the Southern Railway Case: An Investigation into the Discriminatory Practices of Railroads During World War II," *Journal of Negro History* 61 (April 1976): 184.
26 Vanessa Brown, "A Historical Overview of the Emergence of African American Police Officers in the United States," p. 12, Brandeis University McNair Scholars Program, July, 1997, (paper in author's possession).
27 *End of the Line*, p. 178.
28 Ibid., p. 169.

Notes to chapter 8

1 Sara Mosle, "Letter from Las Vegas: How the Maids Fought Back," *New Yorker* (Feb. 26/March 4, 1996): 148, 151.
2 Ibid., pp. 151, 148, 155.
3 Quoted in Herbert Hill, "No Harvest for the Reaper: The Story of the Migratory Agricultural Worker in the United States" (New York: NAACP, c. 1958), p. 8.
4 Interview with Diane Wilson, process clerk, in Studs Terkel, *Working: People Talk About What They Do All Day and How They Feel About What They Do* (New York: Pantheon, 1974), pp. 457–62.
5 Rosalyn Baxandall, Linda Gordon and Susan Reverby, eds, *America's Working Women* (New York: Vintage Books, 1976), pp. 356–8.
6 Quoted in Christine I. DeLeon, "An Overview of Hispanic Labor in the United States: 1845 to the Present," p. 15, Brandeis University, McNair Scholars Program, July, 1997, (paper in author's possession).
7 Quoted in Dan Georgakas and Marvin Surkin, *Detroit: I Do Mind Dying: A Study in Urban Revolution* (New York: St. Martin's Press, 1975), p. 103.
8 Ibid.
9 Studs Terkel, *Working*, pp. 256–7.
10 Ibid., p. 261.

11 Ibid., p. 259.
12 Baxandall, et al., eds, *America's Working Women*, p. 360.
13 Ken Lawrence and Anne Braden, "The Long Struggle," *Southern Exposure* 11 (Nov./Dec., 1983): 88.
14 Ed Haggar, Sr, quoted in Eric Bates, "Losing Our Shirts," *Southern Exposure* 22 (Spring 1994): 35.
15 Arlie Hochschild, "The Time Bind," in *Working USA* (July–August 1997): 22, 25.
16 Mosle, "How the Maids Fought Back," p. 155.

Index